Blood, Sweat and Tears

DAVID CLAYTON-THOMAS

Blood, Sweat and Tears

VIKING
CANADA

VIKING CANADA

Published by the Penguin Group

Penguin Group (Canada), 90 Eglinton Avenue East, Suite 700, Toronto, Ontario,
Canada M4P 2Y3 (a division of Pearson Canada Inc.)

Penguin Group (USA) Inc., 375 Hudson Street, New York, New York 10014, U.S.A.
Penguin Books Ltd, 80 Strand, London WC2R 0RL, England
Penguin Ireland, 25 St Stephen's Green, Dublin 2, Ireland (a division of Penguin Books Ltd)
Penguin Group (Australia), 250 Camberwell Road, Camberwell, Victoria 3124, Australia
(a division of Pearson Australia Group Pty Ltd)
Penguin Books India Pvt Ltd, 11 Community Centre, Panchsheel Park, New Delhi – 110 017, India
Penguin Group (NZ), 67 Apollo Drive, Rosedale, North Shore 0632, New Zealand
(a division of Pearson New Zealand Ltd)
Penguin Books (South Africa) (Pty) Ltd, 24 Sturdee Avenue, Rosebank, Johannesburg 2196, South Africa

Penguin Books Ltd, Registered Offices: 80 Strand, London WC2R 0RL, England

First published 2010

1 2 3 4 5 6 7 8 9 10 (RRD)

Copyright © Antoinette Music Prod Inc., 2010

Author representation: Westwood Creative Artists
94 Harbord Street, Toronto, Ontario M5S 1G6

"Lucretia MacEvil"
Words and Music by David Clayton Thomas
© 1970 (Renewed 1998) EMI BLACKWOOD MUSIC INC. and BAY MUSIC LTD.
All Rights Controlled and Administered by EMI BLACKWOOD MUSIC INC.
All Rights Reserved   International Copyright Secured   Used by Permission
Reprinted by permission of Hal Leonard Corporation

"Go Down Gamblin'"
Words and Music by David Clayton Thomas and Fred Lipsius
© 1971 (Renewed 1999) EMI BLACKWOOD MUSIC INC. and MINNESINGERS
PUBLISHING LTD.
All Rights Controlled and Administered by EMI BLACKWOOD MUSIC INC.
All Rights Reserved   International Copyright Secured   Used by Permission
Reprinted by permission of Hal Leonard Corporation

"Redemption"
Words and Music by David Clayton Thomas, Richard Halligan and Steven Katz
© 1971 (Renewed 1999) EMI BLACKWOOD MUSIC INC.
All Rights Reserved   International Copyright Secured   Used by Permission
Reprinted by permission of Hal Leonard Corporation

"Spinning Wheel"
Words and Music by David Clayton Thomas
© 1968 (Renewed 1996) EMI BLACKWOOD MUSIC INC. and BAY MUSIC LTD.
All Rights Controlled and Administered by EMI BLACKWOOD MUSIC INC.
All Rights Reserved   International Copyright Secured   Used by Permission
Reprinted by permission of Hal Leonard Corporation

LIBRARY AND ARCHIVES CANADA CATALOGUING IN PUBLICATION

Clayton-Thomas, David, 1941–
Blood, Sweat and Tears / David Clayton-Thomas.

Includes index.
ISBN 978-0-670-06469-4

1. Clayton-Thomas, David, 1941–. 2. Singers—Canada—Biography.
3. Blood, Sweat & Tears (Musical group). I. Title.

ML420.C622A3 2010   782.42164092   C2010-904487-8

Visit the Penguin Group (Canada) website at **www.penguin.ca**

Special and corporate bulk purchase rates available; please see **www.penguin.ca/corporatesales**
or call 1-800-810-3104, ext. 2477 or 2474

Dedicated to the memory of Doug Riley, 1945–2007

Contents

Introduction

It's ironic that I should have joined a band called Blood Sweat & Tears. It's a phrase that has followed me through life, beginning with Winston Churchill's famous speech during the war that brought me into this world and later as the name of the band that catapulted me to international fame. Those three words say so much about my journey.

Blood means passion and sacrifice. You must be willing to put your life on the line for what you want. It's been said that my story is courageous. I don't see it that way. Courage is selfless sacrifice—this is just a story of raw survival. When you come from less than nothing, you'll do almost anything to be somebody. Blood was shed in prison, where I learned to fight for respect. Blood means practicing until your fingers bleed. Blood gave me the gift of music, which I inherited from my mother. Blood is life and what a life it has been.

Sweat represents the work it takes—swinging a ten-pound hammer on a prison work gang, working eight-hour shifts in a factory so you can afford to play music for free, playing on street corners for spare change, grinding out five shows a night in funky bars, driving through the night with no sleep to make a gig. Sweat means giving every ounce of yourself to a performance even when no one shows up. Sweat means hard work and nothing happens without it.

Tears signify not only my darkest moments but the pain I brought to those who loved me—tears cried by those who were caught up in my obsessive drive to succeed, tears shed in moments of triumph and at times of tragedy. There are tears of joy and tears of grief in this story, tears of rage and tears of absolute despair. Tears mean you care, that you can feel. Tears mean you're alive.

Blood Sweat & Tears, a rock band born of power politics and massive egos. A band that rocketed to the very top of the music world then imploded just as spectacularly. Blood, sweat and tears—the basic elements of life. It's the story of my life and there could be no better title for this book.

Putting your story down on paper brings new perspective to your life. It's a difficult exercise, one that requires absolute honesty and painful self-examination. In order to survive we compartmentalize our failures and unpleasant episodes and push them to the furthest recesses of our minds. It's the only way we could possibly move beyond the calamities and foolish decisions that must inevitably come to us all. In writing your autobiography you must first make a decision: are you going to sugar-coat the story, make yourself the hero and blame everyone else for your mistakes, or are you ready to dredge those dark corners of your life and tell it like it was? There's no in between ... it's all or nothing.

My friends and family already know the truth and they wouldn't be happy with a self-serving story. They'd expect me to get it right. Everything is connected in the play that is your life. So what I am writing is as nakedly honest as I can possibly make it.

There are no good guys or bad guys in this story. I'm sure that the recollections of some of the people I write about will differ from mine and that's just how it is. I've learned that very few of us are one thing or another. We are all heroes and villains in the play of our lives—it all depends on which act we are watching and who is writing the script. This is my story.

Blood,
Sweat
and
Tears

Blackberry Wine

Linda came from Willowdale
The sun shone out of her face
At the time she was my world
My world was such a simpler place
And the legend lives on, and the truth somehow fades
That's the way it's always been, that's the way it is today
If I could just go back in time, I'd be with Linda in the meadow
With a beatin' heart and blackberry wine

What a time it was for us
We would live forever it seemed
If we knew what we know now
The way we turned out, who woulda dreamed
And the mystery's gone, and the memory fades
That's the way it's aways been, that's the way it is today
If I could just go back in time, I'd be with Linda in the meadow
With a beatin' heart and blackberry wine

1

WILLOWDALE

Freda May Smith was just seventeen when she met Fred Thomsett in war-torn England in 1940. She was a pretty, petite music student, an only child from a loving British family. Her father made his living working at the local waterworks in Surrey. By night he was a music-hall entertainer, a song-and-dance man who performed popular songs of the day like "Knees Up Mother Brown" and "I've Got a Lovely Bunch of Coconuts." He was a gentle, caring man who ran a hand-puppet show for the kids in local hospitals and doted on his daughter, Freda. His wife was a typical British mum, a housewife and mother who kept their little cottage in Walton-on-Thames tidy and had a traditional British rockery—a garden of coloured stones, seashells and flowers—in their tiny backyard.

Freda was studying the piano when the war broke out and, following the family tradition of community service, she began playing for the troops in a London hospital. There she met a genuine Canadian war hero. His name was Fred Thomsett and he was one the most highly decorated soldiers of World War II. He had taken a shrapnel wound in North Africa and had been sent to England for medical care. She instantly fell in love with the handsome young Canadian, and when Fred was released from the hospital for rehabilitation they began dating. In the urgency of the war years their relationship progressed rapidly. Before Fred shipped out to return to the front they were married, and in this chaotic time I was conceived.

Freda continued to live with her parents in Walton-on-Thames, in Surrey, carrying her baby while the battle of Britain raged around them. Bombs rained down on the English country-side. When her due date arrived Freda was taken down to the underground hospital. Three times that night, traumatized by the constant shelling and unable to give birth, she was returned to the house. The last time she was carried up from the bomb shelter the house was gone, as was most of the block. It had taken a direct hit by a V-2 rocket. Freda was taken back to the shelter and thirty-six hours later, in the midst of earth-shaking bomb blasts, I arrived. David Henry Thomsett was born.

Fred, a motorcycle dispatch rider with the Royal Canadian Signal Corps, was again in the thick of the fighting with Montgomery in North Africa. It was a dangerous job with a high mortality rate—three out of five dispatch riders were killed. Riding through enemy lines on a motorcycle with a dispatch pouch and a Sten gun, dispatch riders often found themselves in hand-to-hand combat. He was wounded again, this time taking a machine-gun bullet in his hip, and was returned to England, where his young son had just been born. He spent a few short months with his new family and again returned to the front. This time he was slogging through the mud of Italy, participating in some of the most brutal battles of the war—Sicily, Monte Cassino. When I was three years old my mother and I left England and immigrated to Canada to live with Fred's family in Willowdale, Ontario, and waited for the war to end.

Willowdale in the 1950s was a small rural town north of Toronto, consisting of a few service stations, small family-owned businesses and farms, with a scattering of postwar subdivisions. Divided right down the middle by the northern stretches of Yonge Street, it was mostly blue-collar. Italian and British to the east and predominately Jewish to the west—a mixture of homegrown Canucks and immigrants who came to Canada following World War II. It was still mostly farm country in the fifties, with rolling cornfields and dairy farms. There were large wooded areas for a youngster to play in and creeks and ponds for swimming. Facing north from the city limits of Toronto in those days you looked out over miles of rolling farmland, the skyline of Willowdale dominated by the two-storey Dempsey's hardware store.

My mother and her parents raised me until I was three, when we sailed for Canada, after which we lived with Fred's sister for nearly a year. Then my father came home. A big, rough man, six feet tall, 200 pounds, with a vicious temper hardened by the horrors of war, he was the complete opposite of my gentle grandfather with his funny songs and his puppet shows, and he terrified me. This enraged Fred. After all, he had given everything for his country, endured unspeakable hardships, and now he couldn't understand why his young son recoiled from him. The problem was that the boy's mother and maternal grandfather had been too soft on him. The army had taught Fred that discipline was the answer to everything. He'd toughen the youngster up. And the beatings began. In later years I realized how traumatized and psychologically damaged my father was by the war. The horrors he saw changed him forever and he never truly recovered. He became as brutal as the war that he relived for the rest of his life.

The war was not the only contributing factor to Fred's violent nature. He was a brutal and controlling tyrant from a long line of tyrants. His father had raised his family by the old-world code that "children are to be seen, not heard," and his children lived in absolute terror of him. A word spoken out of turn by a child at Grandpa's dinner table sent that child, spitting blood and teeth, flying across the room from a deadly accurate backhand. Tyrannical patriarchs like the Thomsetts were a throwback to another age.

My mother was helpless in the face of Fred's temper. A gentle, artistic girl barely out of her teens and a long way from home, she had her own way of dealing with my father's rages. She would never confront him directly. His temper would flare and then soon burn out. He'd become contrite and then she would get her way. She loved Fred unconditionally and always believed he would mellow as time passed.

In 1947 Freda gave birth to their second child, my brother, John. Now there were two boys who were the targets of their father's uncontrollable temper. My earliest memories were of the beatings. They came in many forms, from a razor strop across the buttocks in the basement to sudden vicious attacks with boots and fists for the slightest infraction of Fred Thomsett's rules. The two boys reacted differently to the beatings. My brother, John, would curl up in a ball on the floor and cry, "I love you, Dad, I'll never do it again, I'm sorry, I'm sorry …" My brother wasn't a bad guy—he was a victim too. He learned early on how to con his way out of the beatings, and that was his way of dealing with things his whole life. John became a hustler, always just a few days away from his next big score. He was constantly in and out of jail. He was never a big-time criminal—he just always seemed to be in the wrong place at the wrong time with the wrong people. He died a hopeless alcoholic, a broken man. But the damage had been done years before. He was broken as a child by our father, and he went to his grave early, still desperately seeking the old man's approval. I never really got to know John. When I left home at fifteen he was still a kid, and over the years I had almost no contact with him. He was either in jail or kissing up to the old man, and I wanted no part of either of them. John and I were very different. He was slim and blond-haired, a good-looking boy who could charm his way out of anything. I was stocky and dark-haired with a bad attitude. I'd defy Fred at every opportunity. Even as a youngster I wouldn't take the beatings lying down. I refused to drop my pants and bend over obediently for a whipping. Fred would have to drag me to the basement for punishment, biting, kicking and screaming.

My father was a big man and tough as nails, a rugged outdoorsman with years of military training. A ten-year-old didn't stand a chance against him. I took the worst of the beatings. I was six years older than John. Unlike John I wouldn't submit passively and plead, "I love you, Dad, don't hit me." That got John off easy. He'd take a few licks and it was over. Besides, he was still just a kid and I was getting old enough to challenge the old man. The ultimate sin in Fred's world was to challenge his authority. "So you think you're a man, eh! You think you're big enough to take me?" BAM!

He'd knock me clear across the room for some breach of his rules, and I would come up off the floor and charge at him, flailing away with my little fists and taking bloody beatings. My mother would plead with me, "Don't fight him, you'll only make it worse." I hated this man with a passion and would often cry myself to sleep at night wishing he were dead. I took my suppressed rage out at school. I was a big strong kid and met the slightest perceived insult with flying fists. I didn't realize it at the time, but I was becoming just like the father I hated.

Fred worked as a constable on the Willowdale police force for a while, but that didn't last long. Rumour had it that he couldn't control his temper and was let go for beating prisoners. He bounced from job to job until he settled on a lifetime career with North York Hydro as a lineman. He hated the job. Standing on his spurs on a hydro pole in a sub-zero blizzard repairing downed power lines was not what he expected from life. He stayed there for forty years, just for the retirement benefits. He was a bitter, angry man who felt the world had betrayed him. After coming back from seven years of war, twice wounded and a highly decorated veteran, he thought he would return home a national hero, but when wars are over heroes are forgotten, and he was relegated to blue-collar jobs commensurate with his grade-school education. He worked long, hard hours for his money and he let us know it at every opportunity. We weren't poor—he made decent money at Hydro and my mother worked full-time as a secretary at the township offices—but Fred was born of the Great Depression, and it had left him almost pathologically frugal. He sent his boys to school in bargain-basement clothes and hand-me-downs … not exactly the way to build self-esteem in the peer-oriented world of young people.

Fred would count candies, fruit, cookies and the contents of the fridge before he went to work in the morning. When he came home, if anything was missing, it was down to the basement, where John and I would be alternately whipped until one of us confessed to the unspeakable crime of stealing a slice of pie. Fred and Freda both worked until 5:00 p.m., so John and I would be home alone for a few hours after school every day. Leaving two boys alone in the house with cookies and candies was just too much temptation for a kid. So we would take turns confessing— "I took the whipping yesterday, it's your turn today." We were never allowed to feel that it was our home and that it was okay to have a piece of pie after school. It was Fred Thomsett's house— everything in it belonged to him and nothing happened without his permission. Fred ruled his world like a master sergeant, barking orders enforced by slaps and insults—never a word of approval, never a hint of affection. Fred Thomsett's word was law and God help anyone who didn't snap to and obey him instantly. That may have worked in the army but it's not what a kid needs from his father. I hated every minute I was forced to spend with him.

Fred was a hunter and kept a large kennel of dogs in the backyard—blueticks, redbones, black and tans, a big, rugged hunting pack. Fred's dogs were his pride and joy. I inherited from him a lifelong love of dogs but I didn't share his love of hunting. Lying in wait in the bush, shivering in the cold morning air under the always critical eye of my father, waiting for the dogs to drive a beautiful animal up the ravine so you could kill it was not my idea of a good time.

My best friend in those days was Bill Pugliese. He lived a few doors away on McKee Avenue, and from grade six on we had a special friendship. Bill's dad ran a two-chair barbershop in Willowdale and was well liked by everyone. Sam Pugliese was a kindly Italian immigrant with a thick accent. He and his wife were always good to me. Bill and I walked to school together every day and we hit it off right away. When something funny happened in class and no one else seemed to notice, I knew if I caught Bill's eye there would be a twinkle that said "I get it." We shared the same sense of humour and we loved the same kind of music. In our early teens we would sit up in his room late at night listening to the R&B stations from Buffalo on his portable radio. Little Richard, Fats Domino and Bo Diddley—the best R&B was played on a late-night Buffalo station by a DJ called the Hound: "Round sounds from the Hound, awooooo … The Hound's around." Country music was king in Canada but Bill and I only listened to "black music."

The Pugliese home became a refuge for me. When the beatings and abuse became too much at my house I could always escape to the warmth and kindness of Bill's place. My habit of running to Bill's house when I had problems would last for the rest of my life. In later years, when he had become a very wealthy man, there was always a room at Bill's place that the family laughingly referred to as "David's room." Whenever I needed help—for marital problems, business concerns—or when I just needed to get away for a few days, I could call Bill and, without question, my room was made ready.

Marlon Brando was our hero from the first time we saw *The Wild One*. We wanted to be rebel bikers just like Brando and had to have motorcycles to impress the local girls. As soon as we were old enough Bill and I had Harleys, cast-off cop bikes with a three-speed shifter on the tank and a suicide clutch, which we bought cheap at police auctions and stripped down for the street. We wore black leather jackets with chrome studs, greasy blue jeans and motorcycle boots, our hair slicked back with Brylcreem. We'd roar around Willowdale on our straight-piped Harleys and cruise the local drive-in for chicks.

I began running away from home at an early age. I remember once when I was no more than twelve I hitchhiked to Niagara Falls and tried to cross the border into the States. The border guards took one look at this kid with no luggage, no identification, and detained me until I told them where I lived. My father drove down to the border and took me home, bitching and complaining all the way that he had to lose time from work to come down and pick up his useless no-good son. It never occurred to him to wonder why a twelve-year-old was so terrified of going home that he was trying to jump the border to get away. This was all just an embarrassing inconvenience to him and I knew when he got me home I was really going to get it.

Over the next three years things got worse at home. I found out in later years that Fred had developed a serious drinking problem around that time. His temper was out of control and his rebellious son wasn't helping matters. Of course the fact that he was drinking didn't really register with a young teenager. All I knew was that home was not a pleasant place to be and I tried to run away several more times. Each time, the cops picked me up and brought me back for yet another beating. Now I was getting big enough to be a physical challenge to my father. Our battles got more violent. When we clashed it was serious. Furniture got broken. My mother was afraid one of us was going to kill the other. Finally, there was an incident that brought the hostilities to an explosion.

When I was about fifteen I had an adolescent crush on a girl named Diane. She came from a nice middle-class neighbourhood. Her dad was an accountant. They were a kind and loving family and made me feel welcome in their home. Diane, for some reason, really liked this scruffy working-class kid and one evening she invited me to have dinner with her family. I was painfully aware of my shabby clothes and tattered, smelly old sneakers so I took a chance. I decided to "borrow" a pair of my father's shoes, hoping I could bring them back before he discovered they were missing. They were three sizes too big, but at least I would have neat, clean shoes for my dinner with Diane's family. Halfway through dinner there was a commotion at the front door. It was my father in a rage because his shoes were missing. He stormed into the house and dragged me by the scruff of the neck into their backyard, where he beat the hell out of me. Fists and boots, karate chops—the works. Fred was a trained killer and he knew how to fight. He ripped the shoes off and tore the clothes from my back, leaving me bloody and naked on the lawn except for my underpants. Diane's parents were powerless to stop this big raging brute of a man and called the police. Most of the Willowdale cops had worked with my dad in his police days and were drinking buddies of his. Basically, they told Diane's father that I was a bad kid and probably deserved everything I was getting. At this point in my life I really believed I was "a bad kid." I must be. My father told me constantly how "useless" I was and I had come to accept this as a fact.

I crept away in shame, unable to face Diane and her family. Barefoot and half-naked, I walked several miles to the Puglieses' house, where they took me in, cleaned me up and fed me. By this time they were used to seeing me appear at their home battered and bloody. No one wanted to face my father's rage and calling the police did no good—they would just take me back to my father for another beating. I was so ashamed that I couldn't even face the Puglieses so the next morning I borrowed some clothes from Bill and left. I would never go back home again.

I Can't Complain

I'm standin' on the corner, cryin' in the pourin' rain
I'm standin' on the corner, cryin' in the pourin' rain
I'm out here waitin' for my baby, but you know me, I can't complain

My daughter stays out all night, and my son has joined a gang
My daughter stays out all night, and my son has joined a gang
And all the things I told them, just don't seem to mean a thing

I'm standin' on the corner in the pourin' rain
Bought myself a ticket, but I missed the train
I'm downtown, knocked down, broke again
But you know me, pal, I can't complain

I paid my parkin' tickets, now I can't afford a car
I paid my parkin' tickets, now I can't afford a car
Ah, but that don't bother me, pal, you know I wasn't goin' too far

2

GUELPH REFORMATORY

I was now a street kid in Toronto, and street kids need to develop some basic survival techniques. I found that the bakery trucks came around with their deliveries at 5:00 a.m. and I could grab a box of doughnuts before the restaurants opened. That was breakfast. Honest Ed's retail store downtown had racks of clothing hanging outside on the sidewalk and the security guards were usually retirees who couldn't possibly outrun a fast fifteen-year-old. Office buildings usually locked up around 9:00 p.m. after the maintenance crews were finished, and if I crept into the basement by 8:00, I could sleep in the furnace room till dawn. At night I would prowl the empty offices, where there was usually spare change in the desk drawers, and that would get me through the next day. I seldom slept in the same place twice.

I discovered that the used car lots didn't always lock the cars at night and I could sleep in the back seats. That began my life of crime. It wasn't long before I figured that since I was sleeping in the car anyway, maybe I could figure out how to hot-wire it and have my own ride, maybe even pick up a girl at the local drive-in. Of course I got caught. At first I got probation, but after a couple of arrests for vagrancy, joyriding and probation violations, the magistrate, at the recommendation of my father, sent me up to the reformatory at Guelph, Ontario, to "make a man of me." And thus a criminal is born. I was sixteen. In retrospect I believe I wanted to be caught. Being homeless during the winter in Canada is not a pleasant prospect. At least in the reformatory I didn't have to worry about where my next meal was coming from and I would have a roof over my head.

Introduction to the reformatory was a deliberately demoralizing experience. It was all very military. Most of the guards were ex-servicemen and "the joint" was governed by military rules. Incoming inmates were stripped, showered and had their heads shaved. They were issued prison denims, boots, a towel and blanket, toothbrush and comb. Then they were paraded double-time through the cellblock in their underwear, carrying their prison issue while the entire inmate population hooted and hollered at the new "fish." It was a process designed to cut down to size any young smartass who thought he was a tough guy.

At Guelph Reformatory I learned a whole new set of rules. The first thing you learn is that the guards lock and unlock the gates, tell you when to sleep and eat and where you will work. Other than that, the inmates run the joint. If you break the guards' rules you may get a few days in "the hole." Break the inmate code and you can get killed. An elaborate code governs the joint. Inmates have their own pecking order. At the top of the food chain are the "Wheels." These are the coolest and the most deadly of the prisoners. Their denims are always neatly pressed and they are rich in prison currency, called "bales," packs of tobacco that can buy almost anything in jail—extra food, dope, booze, sex, whatever can be smuggled in. Many of the guards were on the take and almost anything was available. In the insulated society of the joint, the Wheels ruled. Even the guards treated them with respect. The institution used these guys to keep a lid on the place. The Wheels ran crap games, took bets on sports and were not to be crossed. Retribution was swift and brutal and the "screws" were usually looking the other way.

The majority of the inmates were solid guys who didn't want to play joint politics. They just wanted to stay out of trouble, build up some "good time" and get the hell out of there. At the bottom of the food chain were the "goofs" and "rats." Goofs were just harmless misfits who could be victimized at will. They got bullied and punched around occasionally but it was never that serious. They would give up their bales and their desserts to pay off anyone who threatened them, and they endured the slaps and the insults without protest. These guys didn't really belong there. They did hard time but they survived. Anyone labelled a "rat" was in deadly peril. He didn't have to actually inform on anyone. A rumour could get you killed. If the screws found out that a guy was being called a rat, he would be taken out of the general population and locked in isolation for his own protection for the rest of his "bit." Suicide attempts were not uncommon in isolation. It's a hard, lonely way to do time.

I was only at Guelph a few months when a guy who was labelled a rat was given what was considered to be a safe job. He ran the elevator in the tower, the central control area in the joint, accessible only to guards and trustees. One morning the rat was found beaten to death, his skull crushed. The weapon used was the detachable steel handle from the elevator mechanism. To the best of my knowledge no one was ever prosecuted for the murder. The wall of silence closed around the perpetrator and the prison officials were none too eager to start pulling guys out of the yard to start a major investigation. That would fire up another round of rat rumours and there would be more violence. No one rats, so the investigation fizzles. They make their own rules in the joint.

The main work detail at Guelph was the Bull Gang at the rock quarry. The "buggy line" on the Bull Gang was a line of perhaps fifty wheelbarrows that went up the hill empty and brought the crushed rock down the hill to trucks that took it out to the highway, where it was used in provincial road projects. The buggy line was ruled by an absolute order. The first buggy was always the top Wheel in the joint. He was followed by his henchmen, who were usually the biggest guys on the gang—iron pumpers with huge biceps, small brains and vicious tempers. The top Wheel seldom fought. He was too cool and never got his neatly pressed denims dirty. He had enforcers to take care of his problems.

The Bull Gang was ruled by a sergeant called "the Dick," a nickname he got because his chiselled profile resembled that of the comic-book character Dick Tracy. He was an ex–Royal Marine commando and the toughest man I ever knew. No one crossed the Dick. He seldom brought troublemakers up on charges—he dealt with them personally. He was a trained killing machine and would take on the toughest inmates who dared challenge him. A fight with the Dick was over in seconds and usually ended with the inmate in the hospital. The Dick ran the Bull Gang with an iron fist and a system of buggy-line protocol. The Wheels were allowed to associate with the Dick and they kept everyone else in their place in the line.

All disputes were settled twice a day at "smoke-up," two fifteen-minute smoke breaks, morning and afternoon, under the supervision of the Dick. The men would form a circle in the pit of the quarry, bales would be wagered and the two guys would have it out bare-knuckled. The smoke-up fights had basic rules: fists only, no boots, no gouging. The fight lasted until one guy quit or was so badly beaten that the Dick had to step in and end it. The winner then took his place in the buggy line. It worked and in a strange way kept the violence to a minimum because if you were called out at smoke-up, no retaliation was allowed. You had it out then and there and it was over. If a loser tried to ambush the other guy later in the yard or in the cellblock, this was a serious violation of the code and he would be attacked by the other inmates. Fighting every day to determine in what order I pushed a wheelbarrow up the hill seemed like an idiotic exercise to me. I didn't really give a damn about the pecking order on the buggy line, so I volunteered for the hammer-and-shovel crew, breaking big rocks into little ones to be loaded into the buggies. It was tough, heavy work but usually the buggy-line guys left you alone. The hammer crew was made up of heavily muscled guys who didn't care about the politics of the buggy line. They just didn't want to be fucked with.

I signed up for the prison boxing squad. We had the dubious honour of having the Canadian middleweight champion, Brian Kelly, at Guelph Reformatory. He was in on an assault beef and the superintendent allowed him to put together and train a boxing team to stage fights every Saturday. The idea was that this would provide a relief for the simmering tension always present in the joint and would in its own way control violence. If you got called out you could always say, "Okay, motherfucker, in the ring on Saturday." Then the inmate code required that the guy fight you, Marquess of Queensberry rules, in the gym on Saturday afternoon. It beat the hell out of going at it with shanks in the yard. The code ruled that if a guy lost a fight in the ring and later attacked you in the yard, he had broken the rules, and retaliation by the other inmates was brutal. Not only did they want to see the boxing matches on the weekend, but there was heavy wagering by inmates and guards alike on the fights, so the combatants were protected by the code.

Brian Kelly took a liking to me and I got a lot of personal attention in my training. The boxing team trained three nights a week and fought on Saturday afternoons. Any time spent out of lockdown was good time in the joint. I was a big, strong middleweight, heavily muscled from swinging a ten-pound hammer all day and no stranger to slipping punches, thanks to a childhood spent as a punching bag for my father. I had a huge reserve of pent-up rage and soon got a reputation as a pretty capable fighter. Reputation is everything in the joint and after a few knockouts no one bothered me anymore. That's the best situation you can hope for in the joint, to be left alone. The guys band together in small groups for protection and friendship, but people come and go in the joint, so most friendships are brief. The place is full of predators, hustlers and con men, always on the prowl, looking for any edge. It's not a place to inspire trust in your fellow man. And at the end of the day you are in your cell … alone.

I was well on my way to spending my life caught in that vicious cycle of recidivism. Here's how the system works. You accept a parole in order to obtain an early release, so you are released three months early with the stipulation that you are on parole for two years. Coming out of Guelph you got twenty bucks and a bus ticket back to where you were arrested. The police are notified that you are back and then you are picked up for some chump charge like vagrancy. Ah, but here's the catch … that misdemeanour constitutes a parole violation, and you are returned to the joint to serve out the rest of your parole—two years. Two years for having no visible means of support. Jobs aren't easy to come by for a reformatory graduate.

The system works for the cops, another conviction for their records. It looks good on paper: another bad kid off the street, problem solved. And if your father is in league with his buddies on the police force, he doesn't have to deal with his embarrassing, no-good son for another two years and *his* problem is solved. Hell, he doesn't even have to visit him. Out of sight, out of mind. I did two stretches in Guelph and never had a single visit from my family. A few friends from Willowdale visited me occasionally and I received letters from my mother, but Fred had written me off and wouldn't allow her to visit me, and in Fred Thomsett's house, Fred's word was law.

My first "bit" was nine months for car theft. I was released after six months with a two-year parole and returned to Willowdale. A few weeks later I was caught sleeping in a closed office building at night and charged with breaking and entering, trespassing, vagrancy and, oh yeah … parole violation. No one bothered to call my father. I don't think he even knew that I was out. A quick court appearance and I was sent back to Guelph to serve out my parole. This time I did the whole bit.

When a guy returns to the joint he is welcomed back like a hero. My stature in the joint was enhanced by my reputation in the ring, and I did pretty easy time that second stretch. I went right back to my job on the Bull Gang and again joined the boxing squad. Brian Kelly had been released by this time and I took over his role as a trainer on the team. I didn't fight much anymore. I didn't need to: my rep was made, no one messed with me and I was developing other interests. I took high school courses and devoured the prison library. I'd always loved books, and in prison not only is there plenty of time to read, but escaping into the fantasy world of literature allowed me to be anywhere but where I was. For a few hours each night I could be in Spain fighting bulls with Hemingway. I could trudge the dust-bowl highways with John Steinbeck and ride the Mississippi riverboats with Mark Twain.

Contrary to the popular image of inmates scratching off their days on a calendar, that's just not how it is. Counting down the days makes your time seem interminable, so you put the "street" out of your mind and concentrate on life in the joint one day at a time. The hardest time is the last few months of your bit, when the prospect of freedom is actually becoming a reality and every day seems like an eternity. Some guys actually go "over the wall" with only a few weeks left in their sentence. They just can't take the waiting, and the idea of life outside the structured environment of the joint is terrifying for them. I was in real danger of becoming "institutionalized" at this point. Life on the street was hard, and I had it pretty good in jail. On the street I was a broke, homeless street kid, but in the joint I had a certain status. Believe it or not, there are guys who are so successful in jail and such a failure on the street that they deliberately keep coming back. *They* are institutionalized.

The only thing I couldn't get in jail was sex, and at eighteen years old my hormones were running wild. Some of the Wheels kept "kids," young inmates who could be used for sex. Kids were pampered and protected by a Wheel or "old man." I never understood the twisted code governing sex in the joint. Among the toughest and most macho guys, a homosexual relationship with a kid was winked at. In fact there was a certain status to owning the prettiest kid in the joint. It didn't mean the old man was gay, and he'd kill you if you suggested he was. He was just doin' what he had to do to survive. He'd get out and go back to his wife like it never happened. What happens in the joint stays in the joint.

The kids played a dangerous game. They had their own social substructure in the joint and they flirted and played the Wheels off against one another. Guys got stabbed over the ownership of a kid. Masturbation was safer. The screws used to tiptoe down the cellblock at night with a flashlight. It was a game with them, trying to catch a guy jerking off. One night a guard we called "Flashlight Freddie" surprised a young inmate masturbating. The guard jumped out in front of the cell and clicked his flashlight on. "What are you doing?" he demanded. Without missing a beat the young man fired back, "Two years, sir." Yeah, the inmate was me.

In 1958 I finished up my two-year stretch in Guelph and again got twenty bucks and a ticket back to Willowdale. I worked odd jobs, from busing tables to delivering telegrams. I lived in cheap rooming houses, bought an old Harley and hung out with Bill and our biker buddies at the drive-in. We joined the Army Reserve for a while, mostly because the legal drinking age in Ontario was twenty-one but if you were in uniform you could get into the Canadian Legion and get a beer at eighteen. So Bill Pugliese and I joined the Reserves, the Irish Regiment of Canada. We took basic training and we went away to boot camp, so I gained some respect for the military. We learned how to march and who to salute and how to clean and fire a rifle, but mostly we hung out at the legion hall and drank beer. That's where all the older neighbourhood guys hung out. It had pool tables and a bar and we got to wear cool uniforms. (Funny how when you're young you want to be older and when you're old you want to be young.) This provided a cover story for me later in life. When I didn't want to explain where I had been during my teenage years, I could always say, "I was in the army." Since I'm telling all in this story, it's time to come clean. It was partly true, but unfortunately, like most lies or half-truths, the story hung with me and even today there are those who believe I had more military experience than I really did.

Willowdale was the worst place for me to be but I had nowhere else to go. Bill and the only other friends I knew were there. My father wanted nothing to do with me, and his buddies on the police force were tipped off that Fred's no-good son was back in town so they were watching me, just waiting for me to slip up. And sure enough I did.

I had gone to school with a guy who I'll call Pete. I honestly can't remember his name. I didn't even know him all that well. Pete got into a fight. Teenage fights were not uncommon in the rough blue-collar suburbs of Toronto. Nothing serious—no guns, knives or anything like that—just an occasional punch-out behind the drive-in. Well, Pete's father had just paid for some expensive dental work for his son, which ended up all over the parking lot. He made Pete press assault charges against the other kid, who I'll call Joe. I ran into Pete at the drive-in a few days later, and in the course of our conversation I said to him something like, "You pussy, shit, we been in fights before, no one ever called the cops. If Joe goes to jail you're gonna deal with me." Stupid macho teenage bluster, but I honestly didn't know I had committed a crime. To me it was just bullshit. Two hours later a warrant was issued and I was arrested. The charges were obstruction of justice and intimidating a Crown witness. I spent the night in jail and went to court the next day. I completely believed the charge would be thrown out of court because, after all, in my mind I hadn't really done anything—it was all just talk. We had all said worse things than that to each other growing up. But I was already an ex-con and the law took it seriously.

Years later I learned that the public defender had called my father and told him about my arrest. He told Fred, "It's not a serious offence. If you'll come to court, I'm sure he'll be home for dinner." My father said, "Fuck him," hung up the phone and called his buddies on the police force. I was taken to court the next morning fully expecting a stern lecture and a warning. The magistrate had also been talking to my father. He read the charges, slammed his gavel down and said, "Two years on each count to run consecutively." The whole process took less than ten minutes. The public defender never showed up for court. After his brief conversation with Fred he just gave up. I didn't even know what "consecutively" meant, so I asked the bailiff. He said, "Four years, son—you're going to Burwash." An hour later I was shackled and on a bus heading for the dreaded Burwash Industrial Farm in northern Ontario, a hellhole I had heard about in Guelph. This was no summer camp. This was serious time in one of the toughest joints in Canada.

A Visit from the Blues

Somebody passed outside my window
Somebody knocked at my front door
Come on in, make yourself at home, old friend
I been waitin' up for you
It's just a visit from the blues

Well just like you said, my baby left me
And just like you told me, I'm so blue
Well old friend, I guess it's me and you again
And there ain't nothin' I can do
It's just a visit from the blues

Hey Mister Blues, you said the sun's gonna shine someday
And everything would be all right
Accordin' to you, we're just waitin' on the judgment day
So how come you come callin' late at night

Come right on in, the door's wide open
Somehow I knew that you would call
It's four a.m.and look who's back in town again
Just an old friend passin' through
It's just a visit from the blues

3
BURWASH

Burwash Industrial Farm was situated in the rugged bush country of northern Ontario about thirty miles from Sudbury and a thousand miles from nowhere. There were few bars and fences at Burwash. The first thing you were told in your induction speech was, "If you want to run, go ahead. There's thirty miles of bush between you and the first sign of civilization. In the summer the blackflies will blind you before you get five miles. In the winter it's twenty below zero with ten feet of snow. Go ahead … run." Burwash was no reform school. It was populated by some of the most violent and dangerous prisoners in Canada. There would be little recreation at Burwash. You worked twelve hours a day, six days a week. The prison was self-supporting and the inmates did all of the work. You cleared brush, built fences through mosquito-ridden swamps, worked on the prison farm—heavy, back-breaking work under shotgun-toting guards.

The introduction to Burwash was brutally simple. Everything was a privilege and all privileges must be earned. You start by having your head shaved and deloused, whether you need it or not, and are thrown into a six-by-eight-foot windowless cell. This is "the Hole," and everything begins and ends here. You must earn your way out of the hole and any infraction of prison rules, no matter how slight, means you start all over again. For starters you are in that concrete box for thirty days. You wear a one-piece smock made of straitjacket material. At night you are given a tick mattress about two inches thick, with no blanket, and the mattress is removed every morning. You are fed a sickening pasty block of nutritionally correct food called "meat loaf" once a day and given a paper cup of water three times a day. The light is harsh and is never turned off. There is a steel mesh–covered air vent about eight feet up on the wall. The solid steel door is seldom opened. Food and water are pushed through a slot. The toilet is a hole in the floor that flushes itself several times a day. A few sheets of coarse brown toilet paper are supplied each day and you are taken to a shower room twice a week. There is no contact and no communication with guards or any other inmates. All conversation is forbidden and any attempt to communicate is punished by a high-pressure water hose poked through the door slot and unleashed on the prisoner.

After ten days you earn your first privileges. You are given prison denims, socks and a blanket at night. The mattress stays in the cell and you are given a Gideon Bible to read. In the last ten days you graduate from meat loaf to regular prison food three times a day, and the lights are dimmed at night. The slightest infraction at any time during this initiation period and you begin your time in the hole all over again. I know of some guys who spent close to a year in the hole.

After thirty days you are moved to "isolation." These are open cells with bars and a window, and you can talk to other inmates. You're allowed thirty minutes a day in the yard for exercise, ten men at a time. You are given reading and writing materials, and for the first time you receive mail. You still have no visits and are not permitted to work—these privileges must be earned. Thirty days in isolation and you go into the general population and are given a work assignment, hard field labour at first, and if you are well-behaved or can afford to bribe the screws, you might advance to a cushy job like the kitchen or the laundry. People don't want to know what goes on in these joints as long as the bad guys are off the street. You are told right off, "You are no longer a person, you are a number. You have no rights in here unless we give them to you. If you have problems or complaints, write them down in a letter, roll it cylindrically and stick it up your ass. Have a nice day."

After a month in isolation I was given my first work assignment, building a cattle fence across a swamp. It was hot, gruelling work. We smeared our faces and arms with kerosene to protect against the swarms of mosquitoes and blackflies that tortured us constantly. The kerosene mixed with sweat and ran into our eyes. My hands blistered and then calloused over. The work was back-breaking but we were just glad to be outdoors and able to talk to someone.

The men lived in bunkhouse-style dormitories. This was a more social environment than a cellblock but also less supervised and far more dangerous. I found that my status at Guelph meant nothing at Burwash. Here I was just a green kid in a world of seriously tough men. One evening after dinner in the mess hall I was walking back to my bunk when I passed a small group of men, the Wheels of Burwash, led by a huge black guy named Joe Paterson. He was only maybe six feet tall but he weighed around 250 pounds. His biceps were bigger than my thighs. He was a vicious fighter and was feared by everyone. Everybody in the joint paid tribute to him in one form or another. Even the guards walked softly around Joe Paterson. As I passed the group one of them made kissing noises and someone said, "Hey, sweet thing, you need an old man?" My time at Guelph had taught me that I couldn't let this pass or word would be all over the joint that I was a pussy and life wouldn't be worth living. I knew the code of the joint and I knew what I had to do. Even though he outweighed me by maybe 70 pounds, I walked straight up to Joe Paterson and threw my best sucker punch, a big looping overhand right that had racked up a half-dozen knockouts in the ring at Guelph. It nailed him right on the button. Joe Paterson didn't even blink. He just smiled at me. I remember thinking, "Oh shit," and the lights went out. I never even saw the left hook that hit me. As I lay on the floor with the room spinning around me someone buried a boot in my side and I heard Joe Paterson say, "Hey, leave him alone. The kid's all right, he's a fighter." The guards swarmed into the dorm and dragged me out. I was charged with fighting. Not much of a fight—all I did was get knocked out cold—but I was hustled back to the hole. Since no one appeared to know who hit me, nothing happened to Joe Paterson. I suspect that the screws were not too eager to bust him anyway.

Back to the hole and the thirty-day initiation process began all over again. I strutted out of the dorm with my best cocky jailbird walk, like I didn't give a shit. You don't dare show a sign of weakness in the joint. "Fuck 'em," I bragged. "I can do this standin' on my head." It was all false bravado. Inside I was shaking. It's a good thing I couldn't get any sharp objects because this story might have ended right then and there. I didn't know if I could do another thirty days in that six-by-eight-foot hell.

A man survives the sensory deprivation and loneliness of the hole by finding all sorts of ways to occupy his time. Push-ups, sit-ups, rolling your socks into a ball and playing catch off the wall … You withdraw into a fantasy world where you're not really in solitary confinement anymore. You're outside the walls of the joint and you're a big shot on the street. You have a Corvette and hot chicks and lots of money. I fantasized about being a rock star like Elvis. But sooner or later reality comes crashing in and there you are back in the hole at Burwash and it seems like you'll never get out of there.

I occupied my time by singing. I discovered that the little concrete room was a natural echo chamber and I began to sing to myself. It was a habit I had picked up from my mother, who always sang. Doing the dishes, vacuuming or driving her car, Mum always sang. She had a pretty, clear voice and her music-school training gave her perfect pitch and a great melodic sense.

One day, through the vent high on the wall, I could hear the men in the exercise yard. One's memory is a strange thing, but of all the thousands of songs I've sung in my life I will always remember the song I was singing that day. It was an old New Orleans tune called "St. James Infirmary Blues." I was singing at the top of my lungs, bouncing my voice off the concrete walls, when I suddenly noticed that the yard was silent. The men were all gathered around the vent and I heard someone say, "Who the hell is that?" Someone else replied, "I don't know, but damn he sure can sing." Looking back I realize that it was a turning point. Someone actually said I did something well. My father's favourite name for me was "Useless," and I had come to accept that as a fact. Now someone had actually said I was good at something.

The screws didn't mind you singing or talking to yourself as long as you didn't try to communicate with anyone else. They knew that if a man didn't have some way to vent he'd go mad and they didn't want to deal with that. Singing became part of my daily ritual. The guys would gather around the air vent and I would belt out the blues. By the time I got out of the hole word had spread all over the joint and my reputation as a singer was made. Now I wanted to sing every chance I got. But singing a cappella just wouldn't cut it. I needed an instrument. In my dorm were four Ojibway kids named Fisher. They were in for signing up for firefighting crews and then setting forest fires. "Damn," I thought, "you must be really desperate for work to do that. That's one of the most dangerous and dirty jobs in the world." One of the Fisher boys, Brent, had a guitar with him when he was arrested. It was kept in a locker in the gym and one afternoon he showed it to me. It was an almost unplayable mail-order Kay acoustic guitar, a real piece of junk. It only had five strings and they were about an inch off the fretboard. Brent knew a few chords and could play a couple of Johnny Cash tunes so I asked him to teach me how to play.

Prison rules prohibited musical instruments in the dorms—guitar strings could be a lethal weapon—so I improvised … Aha! A cribbage board. A guy in the carpentry shop planed it down to roughly the shape and dimensions of a guitar neck, and I drew strings and frets on the mock fretboard. I found a guitar instruction book in the library, *Mel Bay's Guitar Chords*, and began to practice, sitting on my bunk playing chords that only I could hear. In the gym once a week I got to borrow Fisher's guitar for a couple of hours so I could actually hear what I had been practicing. He let me work on the guitar too. I ordered some mail-order strings, took the nut off, ground it down on the concrete floor and reset the neck angle so that it was actually playable.

My first love was the blues. I felt a particular kinship with this music written by men like myself who toiled on prison work gangs. Country musicians like Hank Williams, Johnny Cash and Woody Guthrie also struck a responsive note in my soul. These were dirt-poor working-class hobos with nothing to their name but their music. I knew exactly how that felt. Colour had no meaning to me—white music, black music, it didn't matter. It was all the blues to me. Within a few months my reputation with the guitar had spread through the joint and some of the guys petitioned the superintendent to let me sing at the annual prison Christmas concert. Ironically, big Joe Paterson became my biggest fan and supporter. A few years later, when I was working the bars on Yonge Street, Joe would come in often and catch my set. Years later I heard that big Joe Paterson had muscled the wrong guy and a skinny little drug dealer had shot him dead.

That Christmas I played on a makeshift stage in the gym with a squeaky microphone and the cheap guitar. I played a couple of Jimmy Reed tunes, "Peepin' and Hidin'" and "Big Boss Man." I knew some Robert Johnson, some Leadbelly and of course the prison favourite, a Johnny Cash tune, "I Walk the Line." I played for nearly an hour and the place went nuts. The guys cheered and clapped and hollered for more, and I was in my glory. I loved every minute of it and left the gym that day with a dream. Maybe I could actually do this for a living. Maybe people on the street would react the same way as the guys in the joint. Maybe I could really be a musician. Maybe I wasn't totally useless.

A few months later the Fisher boys were paroled and Brent left me his Kay guitar. "Hell," he said, "you play it better than I ever will, it's yours." Now I was a regular fixture at every prison event. Christmas, Easter, any holiday was an excuse to ask the superintendent for permission to give a concert. I think the screws enjoyed my music too and the institution welcomed any event that could keep a lid on the place. It was understood that any violence would mean the end of the concerts, so everybody was on their best behaviour. Before long I had recruited a little band and there were concerts every month. I lived for those weekend concerts and practiced every chance I got, learning new tunes and even making a few crude attempts to write my own original songs. For the first time I began to believe that my life could be more than an endless cycle of prison sentences. Believe it or not, if that's all you've known you can come to believe that's all you'll ever know. A pat on the back, a little approval, even from a bunch of chronic losers, can work wonders.

I counted down the days and dreamed of someday actually playing in a band. This made my time even harder. Now I had a reason to be out of there and the days crawled by. I tried to keep my nose clean but the violence and the rage always simmering just under the surface in the joint could explode at any time for the slightest reason. One day a fight broke out in the mess hall. I didn't start it but I was right in the middle of it, swinging. This was a serious infraction—a fight involving a large group of prisoners could be considered "inciting to riot." There were about a dozen guys involved. We were all brought up on charges and transferred to Millbrook, a maximum-security joint near Peterborough, Ontario, not far from Toronto.

I did my last six months at Millbrook. It was a sterile, spotlessly clean, super-max facility. Inmates left their cells for only a few hours each day, to work on scrub gangs, on their hands and knees with a scrub brush and a bucket. The rest of the time, eighteen hours a day, was lockdown, but that didn't bother me at all. Inmates at Millbrook were very isolated from each other, so the rules regarding things like musical instruments were more relaxed and I was allowed to keep my guitar. I even had a radio. There was lots of time to practice and learn new tunes. In the spring of 1962 I walked out of Millbrook with twenty bucks in my pocket, a mail-order guitar and a dream. I was going to be a blues singer. I took my one-way bus ticket to Toronto and I never looked back.

Me and Amaretto

Got no home since the roof caved in
Had no lovin' since I don't know when
Just enough money left to last the night
But things look different in the mornin'
How many times have I told myself
It don't help matters when you run your mouth
Rompin' Ronnie Hawkins once told me, son
Things look different in the mornin'

Me and Amaretto and a night of sin
Left me on the floor with my head kicked in
Coulda been the liquor or the barroom light
It all looks different in the mornin'

In walked trouble in a skin-tight dress
We musta got married, but I must confess
Over in Nevada where there is no wait
Things look different in the mornin'
Woke up sleepin' in a heart-shaped bed
Lookin' in the mirror right above my head
Tryin' to remember all the things I said
Cause she sure looks different in the mornin'

4
ROMPIN' RONNIE

It's a sick, empty feeling to be released from the joint, especially if there's no one waiting for you. For nearly four years all decisions had been made for me—when to eat, when to sleep, where I worked. Now, when the gates of Millbrook clanged shut behind me and I was a free man, it was terrifying. I was twenty-one years old and completely on my own. I had this crazy delusion about being a blues musician. But I had no idea where to begin. The only thing I knew for sure was that I would die before going back to prison.

The John Howard Society got me a job as a helper on a plastics extruder at Canada Wire & Cable—dirty, smelly work but it put a roof over my head and allowed me a few bucks in my pocket to pursue what I really wanted to do, play music. A few weeks on the job and I noticed that many of the men were missing digits from their hands. The fine copper wire zinged through the extruder head at hundreds of feet per minute, and one careless move could result in a finger being severed. The men joked and laughed about this in the lunchroom. A missing finger was regarded as a badge of seniority—"Yep, lost this one on ol' number nine back in '54." It was no badge of honour to me. I wanted to be a guitar player and needed all ten of my fingers. I knew I wouldn't last long on that job.

I met a pretty eighteen-year-old redhead from Willowdale named Nancy Hewitt. We double dated with Bill Pugliese and his girl. The four of us were always together. Nancy was completely in love with this guitar-playing rebel with a prison record. I loved her too, but I had another agenda and I really didn't want to get tied down before I had a chance to see what I could do in music. I was determined to get into the music business or die trying. Nancy loved to hear me sing and play and would sit for hours listening to me practice, but I think she always thought that it was just a phase I was going through and that sooner or later I would come to my senses and settle down. She nodded and smiled patiently when I told her of my dream of someday being a musician, but I don't think she ever really believed it. Who ever heard of a rock star from Willowdale? It was a tumultuous relationship. We broke up constantly but we always got back together. It was hard not to in a small town where we saw each other every day and knew all the same people.

I had a steady job, made good money and rented a basement apartment in Toronto. Nancy lived at home with her parents in Willowdale, an elderly couple who'd had Nancy late in life. They were not happy about her hanging out with this tough kid fresh out of prison, but Nancy saw something in me and they always treated me kindly. We were young and in love and, as we had nothing to do but make out in the back seat at the drive-in like all the other kids, Nancy got pregnant. So we did what kids did in 1963—we got married. We were both way too young but it was what you did in a small town where everybody knew everybody else.

We rented the top floor of Bill Pugliese's house in Willowdale and Nancy gave birth to my first daughter, Christine. Nancy was in heaven but I was miserable. I felt trapped. My dreams of being a rock musician were over. I was facing a lifetime of shift work and severed fingers at Canada Wire & Cable. The money was decent but I hated the job. I lived for the day shift when I would have evenings off to catch any of the hot R&B shows that regularly came through Toronto. I bought a used Fender Telecaster and an amp on instalments from the Long & McQuade music store, and in my spare time I began to hang around the clubs on Toronto's Yonge Street, known as "the Strip."

The Strip was a six-block-long row of bars and strip joints populated by a rough crowd of rounders, hookers and hustlers. The clientele consisted of steelworkers from Hamilton, truckers, loggers and miners from Sudbury, in town for the weekend, looking to blow off steam along with their paycheques, and there were plenty of bar girls available to help them do both. Music was being played in the bars on the Strip, mostly blues and country. Johnny Cash or Carl Perkins would be playing at the Edison Hotel one week and the Muddy Waters Band or B.B. King the next. The blues had migrated up from Chicago and Detroit, brought to Toronto by Motown and Chicago blues artists who loved the fact that there was no colour bar in Canada. In the States in the early sixties, black artists played on the black side of town in funky joints and white bands played on the other side of town in the best clubs. But in Canada the R&B acts played anywhere they wanted. They were booked into the top clubs in Toronto and played to mixed audiences. Not only were they accepted in Toronto, but they were idolized by the young Canadian musicians. James Brown, Ike and Tina Turner, Muddy Waters, Bo Diddley, B.B. King, the Temptations, the Four Tops, they all played on the Strip. My personal favourite was the Muddy Waters Band, from Chicago. Willie Dixon, Otis Spann and Muddy Waters, with his bottleneck Telecaster. This was the real thing, raw, unpolished and visceral. This was "The Blues."

I would sit at the bar at the Edison, nurse a beer and soak in the music of the greatest blues band in the world.

The closest thing I had to a religious experience in those days was the first time I saw the Ike & Tina Turner Revue on Yonge Street. When Tina and the Ikettes hit the stage, it was like a body punch. The energy, the fire—it changed my life forever. James Brown and the Famous Flames used to play a roller rink in Toronto's west end. The tightest R&B band in the world, right there onstage in front of me. Every young band in town had a singer trying to do James Brown's dance steps. Wilson Pickett, Jackie Wilson, Sam Cooke, Otis Redding—they all played on the Strip in those days and their music found a home in Toronto.

The king of the Strip was Rompin' Ronnie Hawkins, an Arkansas-born rockabilly singer who had come out of the Memphis scene along with Jerry Lee Lewis, Carl Perkins, Johnny Cash and Elvis Presley. Ronnie brought his Deep South music to Toronto. He had a band built around a couple of guys who came up from Arkansas with him, drummer Levon Helm and Will "Pop" Jones, a honky-tonk piano player. Jones soon left and went back to the States, but Ronnie and Levon loved the Toronto scene and saw opportunity in Canada. They recruited some young local players: Robbie Robertson, Garth Hudson, Richard Manuel and Rick Danko. Along with Levon Helm they became the legendary "Hawks." The Hawks would go into the Rock and Roll Hall of Fame as The Band. This was the Ronnie Hawkins Band, and the young musicians of Toronto absolutely idolized them. To this day I believe they were the greatest rock & roll band ever. Their blend of Canadian country music, Arkansas rockabilly, Chicago blues and Memphis R&B was some of the purest rock & roll I've ever heard.

Ronnie Hawkins and the Hawks played bars all over Ontario but reigned supreme at Le Coq d'Or, a rowdy joint that was at the centre of the Yonge Street Strip. The room was loud and raucous, with a noisy bar on one side and a stage complete with go-go cages on the other. This was Ronnie's base of operations. Upstairs he had his office, a gym and an after-hours club called the Hawk's Nest, where all of his friends would congregate. Kris Kristofferson, Bob Dylan, John Lennon, Frank Zappa—he seemed to know everybody, and you never knew who might show up there.

The Hawks were the role models for every young musician in town. We absolutely worshipped them. They wore mohair suits, so that became the dress code for every young band in Toronto. They got their razor-cut haircuts at a barbershop on Yonge Street, so all the young musicians in town got their hair cut there. Robbie played a white Telecaster, so every guitar player had to have a white Telecaster. They'd add a song to their repertoire and within a week every band in town would be playing that song. Levon would add a cymbal to his drum kit and the next day every music store on Yonge Street would be sold out of that particular cymbal. Once, while loading in behind the club, a truck backed over his crash cymbal and he had to play with a broken cymbal for a few weeks and—you guessed it—young drummers all over town drove their cars over their crash cymbals just to get that Levon sound. To be invited up on that stage to sit in with the Hawks at Le Coq d'Or was the dream of every young musician in Toronto.

On Saturday afternoons many of the bars had matinees. No liquor was served at the matinees, so the underage musicians could hang out and get to know each other and if they were really good they might get to jam with their heroes. I was already in my early twenties so I could get into any of the bars on the Strip, but at the Saturday matinees you might be invited to sit in with the Hawks, and that's where I wanted to be. Ronnie Hawkins was the genial master of ceremonies at the Le Coq d'Or matinees, and one afternoon I persuaded him to let me sing with his band. I think I sang a Ray Charles song, "Night Time Is the Right Time," and a couple of Jimmy Reed tunes. Ronnie was impressed. He took me under his wing and gave me my first paying job in music, singing with his band. Years later Ronnie told me that he had called his friends in Nashville that day and told them, "You won't believe this, but there's a white boy up here in Canada, fresh out of prison and tough as nails, who sings the blues like he was born black."

I quit the job at Canada Wire & Cable and began playing music full-time. Nancy was sure I had lost my mind. I had a steady job with benefits and I was throwing it all away for an uncertain future in a bar band. I only worked with Ronnie when he was in Toronto. When the Hawks went on the road I was unemployed. I didn't care. This was my chance. The first time I stepped onstage with the Hawks I knew I was born for this. I was a lousy plastics extruder operator, but I was really good at music and everyone knew it. Everyone, it seemed, but Nancy. She wanted no part of these rough bars downtown, and who could blame her? I think she still believed this madness would pass and I would go back to my day job and be a decent husband and father, but I was too far gone already. I had tasted what it felt like to be onstage—to be really good at something, to be loved by an audience, to feel a great band kick into an R&B tune and make the whole place come alive. I was hooked and there was no turning back.

In the joint I had learned how to handle myself, which allowed me to hold my own in the brawling bars on the Strip. If some drunken steelworker took exception to the way his girl smiled at me, I was more than willing to discuss it in the alley behind Le Coq d'Or. I've been known to walk off the stage in the middle of a song, knock a drunken heckler on his ass and return before the guitar solo ended. This was par for the course in the bars on the Strip. Even the genial Ronnie Hawkins was no one to mess with in a bar fight, and bar fights were an almost nightly occurrence. Most didn't involve the band. We learned how to smile and keep on playing no matter what was happening. Ducking flying beer bottles was just part of the job. Ronnie kept in shape for his gig at Le Coq d'Or by sparring upstairs in his own fully equipped gym with Canadian heavyweight champion George Chuvalo. These were rough joints.

Having another singer in the band gave Ronnie the opportunity to leave the stage and circulate around the club, playing the backslapping, joke-telling host to the crowds that always packed the place when he was there. He told the same jokes and used the same lines every night: "Son, that girl is so tough, she's got a vibrator with a kick-starter." Everyone had heard them before but it didn't matter—people just loved hearing him talk with that Arkansas drawl. Everybody loved Ronnie. He made everyone feel like they were his personal guests in the club. I learned a lot from Ronnie Hawkins. I learned that this wasn't Burwash and that decking a guy was not always the first option. I learned how to handle an audience offstage and on. Ronnie also had an uncanny ability to spot musical talent. Even after the Hawks left to back Bob Dylan, Ronnie Hawkins always had the hottest rock & roll band on Yonge Street.

If you worked in Ronnie's band, he worked you hard. We would play five shows a night, forty minutes on and twenty off. The band would break at one in the morning when the bar closed, grab a bite to eat and be back at the club by three for rehearsals which lasted till dawn. Then we'd round up the always present bar girls and cocktail waitresses, head upstairs to the Hawk's Nest and party till noon. The band would sleep until around five in the afternoon, eat breakfast and start all over again. Some nights I crashed upstairs at the club. Sometimes the band would pool their money and rent a party room at some cheap hotel and I'd sack out there. On Saturday afternoons we'd play a two-show matinee beginning at one. On Sundays either we'd play a one-nighter somewhere or we'd all collapse and sleep around the clock. My formal education in show business had begun.

We were surrounded by drugs, booze and loose women, and we indulged in them all. If someone wanted to buy you a drink, the club owner expected you to accept it. It was an insult to refuse to drink with the customers and an insult wasn't taken lightly on the Strip. The local hookers and bar groupies were always ready and willing to party with the band and we took full advantage of their generosity. We popped uppers to balance the booze and get through the night and downers to come down after the shows. Liquor and drugs had entered my life, and it would be years before I could finally rid myself of these nasty habits.

By 1964 my marriage to Nancy was hanging by a thread. She was living with Christine at Bill's place up in Willowdale. I paid the bills but I seldom slept there. This was not what she had bargained for. She married a blue-collar stiff who worked nine to five and came home every night. She didn't know this wannabe rock star who hung out in the bars downtown and was doing God knows what all night. She tried to make our marriage work but it was a losing battle. I was living in a different world. I'd been locked up for most of my teenage years and the lifestyle of a rock musician was incredibly seductive. Nancy couldn't possibly compete with all that sex, drugs and rock & roll.

I was singing with Ronnie Hawkins and the Hawks, the hottest band in town, and loving every minute of it. I made many lifelong friends among the young musicians who gathered at the Saturday matinees. One afternoon I met a young left-handed guitar player by the name of Fred Keeler. He came in with a bass player named Scott Richards, who played with Fred in a little R&B garage band called the Shays. They had a keyboard player with his own B-3 and a drummer with a wicked foot pedal. They lived out in the suburbs. They all had day gigs or were still in school and they played high school dances and such on weekends. They needed a singer and invited me to a rehearsal.

Like every other band in town they worshipped the Hawks. They knew all the tunes I sang with Ronnie's band and we clicked right away. Before long we were playing dance gigs at local high schools and shopping plazas. We called ourselves "David Clayton Thomas and the Fabulous Shays." We played R&B by Wilson Pickett and Otis Redding and blues by Willie Dixon and Bo Diddley. I had dropped the "Thomsett" name to put some distance between the prison years and my new life in music. Many of my blues idols had three names—John Lee Hooker, Sonny Boy Williamson, Lightnin' Sam Hopkins. My name just sounded like a blues singer's name. Then a club owner on Yonge Street inadvertently hyphenated my last name on the marquee. I liked it and it stuck. I became David Clayton-Thomas.

Donnybrook

What's all the fuss, what's all the racket
I just came here to have me some fun
Take my beer and hold my jacket
A donnybrook has just begun

Man, this life is crazy, and it makes no sense
We all go round for a while, then we all fall down

You think you're tough, you think you're funny
And you think you've got the world by the tail
You're outta luck, you're outta money
And tonight you're gonna land in jail

Man, this life is crazy, and it makes no sense
We all go round for a while, then we all fall down

5

YORKVILLE AND THE BLUENOTE

Nineteen sixty-four and I was finally a working musician. I sang with Ronnie's band when they were in Toronto, did pickup gigs around town when they weren't and played high school dances and shopping malls with the Shays on weekends. On weeknights I became a regular fixture at every bar and strip joint in town, eager for any chance to sit in with the band and sing a tune or two. I didn't care if I made any money. I just wanted to get up onstage for a few minutes. After years of being told that I was just a number, a nobody, the spotlight and the applause gave me an identity. Onstage I was somebody.

There was a little after-hours club on Yonge Street called the Bluenote. The club didn't open till after midnight, served no liquor and ran till dawn. Once the bars on the Strip closed, the musicians would head for the Bluenote to hang out and jam. It was the only place in town still open. Anyone who was in town, from Motown acts to Chicago blues bands, would end up at this little upstairs club. The Bluenote had a house band called the Silhouettes. At around two in the morning the dance floor would be cleared and the "floor show" would begin. Whoever wanted to get up and sing was welcome, but beware: like at the Apollo in New York, the audience could be merciless if you weren't really good. In that crowd on any given night would be not only the top local entertainers from the bars on the Strip, but you might also find the Righteous Brothers, the Temptations, Albert King, James Brown or Tina Turner.

The Bluenote offered nothing but a great band and hot women but that was enough to draw the biggest names in the business to the floor show. If you were a musician or an entertainer, the cover charge was waived, but you were expected to "sit in." If you didn't, you wouldn't be welcome there again. Leave your ego at the door, get out on the floor and let it all hang out. The crowd was ruthless when faced with mediocrity and the house band was wicked hot, a pure R&B soul machine. Many wannabe singers left that club with their illusions shattered forever. If you had the audacity to step out on that floor, you'd better bring it or they would eat you alive.

I met a remarkable young man at the Bluenote, one who would play a major role in my life and be my friend forever. He played Hammond B-3 organ. His name was Doug Riley but everyone called him "Doc." He was no more than eighteen when I first met him but he was already the undisputed leader of the Silhouettes. A young white kid from suburban Toronto working his way through a music scholarship at the Royal Conservatory, he was the baddest B-3 player I have ever heard. World-renowned organ players like Jimmy Smith and Groove Holmes would drop in at the Bluenote and they would break into a broad smile when they heard young Doc Riley play. Fire and funk, beautifully melodic with a fierce groove—there was only one Doc Riley and there will never be another one like him.

I had seen him play several times but he was always behind the B-3 and he worked the foot pedals like a great bass player. I was surprised the first time he stepped down from the Hammond and joined me at a table. He walked with painful difficulty. He'd had polio as a kid and couldn't walk at all until he was about twelve, and even then wore braces on his legs for years afterwards. When the other kids were out playing hockey and baseball, young Doug Riley was sitting on a piano bench. It wasn't just his astounding chops and considerable musical education that set him apart. It was that intangible thing called soul. If you played with Doc, fasten your seat belt, baby—you were in for the musical ride of your life. There was a fierce intensity and an aching tenderness to his playing. When I sang with him for the first time at the Bluenote, he made me sing better than I ever had in my life and from that moment on we were brothers. Doc Riley would be my best friend and closest musical collaborator for the next forty years.

CHUM Radio was the big pop station in Toronto. One of their disc jockeys, a guy named Duff Roman, heard the Shays and invited us to play at a little after-hours club he was starting downtown. I liked Duff immediately and he was blown away by this white blues band who played John Lee Hooker, Howlin' Wolf and Lightnin' Sam Hopkins tunes. Duff Roman became my first manager and took us into the studio to record a single, a John Lee Hooker tune called "Boom Boom." The song exploded onto the local charts and in a matter of weeks David Clayton-Thomas and the Fabulous Shays was the hottest act in town. The bars on the Strip were now demanding the Shays, and we started headlining on the same circuit that Ronnie Hawkins and the Hawks played.

I was barely two years out of Millbrook and I was becoming somewhat of a local celebrity. I still wasn't making much money but I was becoming well known in Toronto. My songs were all over the radio, we had our first local TV appearances and my name was up in lights on Yonge Street. For the first time I began to believe I could be more than just a working musician. I would have been satisfied with that. It was everything I'd ever dreamed of but now I began to believe I could actually be a star.

Home base for the Shays was the Friar's Tavern, another rowdy joint with go-go dancers and Saturday matinees, right down the street from Le Coq D'Or. We adopted the dress code of the Hawks, mohair suits and razor-cut hairstyles. Freddy Keeler played a white left-handed Telecaster and we worked the same five-shows-a-night routine as Ronnie's band. Both bands were so popular on the Strip that rather than compete with each other, the club owners would stagger our sets so the crowd could catch a set with the Hawks at Le Coq d'Or and then move down the block to catch the Shays at the Friar's. Ronnie and I became lifelong friends. Our bands worked the same schedule and hung out together. Both bars closed at one in the morning so we'd all gather at Fran's Restaurant at Yonge and Dundas for dinner, exchange war stories about the hookers, pimps and rounders who were our clientele, then head back to our respective clubs for rehearsals or to the Bluenote to jam until dawn. We lived the same lifestyle and partied together, no-holds-barred, all-night donnybrooks with the hookers, hustlers and cocktail waitresses who worked both clubs. We bought our mohair suits from the same tailor, played the same kind of music to the same crowds, knew all the same local characters and hung out with the same women.

I was living in a different world by now. I had nothing but bitter memories of Willowdale and I had left it far behind me. I had almost no contact with my family. My life was my band and my gigs. Occasionally I'd see my mother, when I knew Fred wouldn't be there. She was truly happy that I had found some direction in life. My father still didn't get it. To him there was no difference between spending the rest of my life in jail and hanging out in bars with a bunch of no-good rock musicians. I was still just a useless bum. I began to realize that nothing would ever be good enough for him. Unlike most parents, who want their children to succeed, Fred Thomsett resented any success I might have. "So you think you're a star, eh … What makes you think you're any better than me?" How do you argue with twisted logic like that? I didn't even try. I didn't give a damn what he thought. I didn't speak to him for nearly seven years.

The Shays were developing a huge following in Toronto. Young people were packing our dance gigs on the weekends. We had our own fan club and that spring we opened for the Rolling Stones at Maple Leaf Gardens. The little garage band that had only played bars and high school dances was performing for 17,000 screaming fans. We recorded a second single, also produced by Duff, and it was an immediate hit. The song was called "Walk That Walk" and it was my first original composition. This time we got national airplay in Canada and the record came to the attention of Paul Anka and his manager-father Andy Anka. Paul was set to host the NBC rock show *Hullabaloo* in New York City and he was looking for a Canadian band to feature on the show. We got the call.

So off we went to New York in April of 1965, a little five-piece blues band from Toronto with our disc-jockey manager all crammed into a 1960 Cadillac Sedan de Ville, pulling our gear in a homemade trailer. The overloaded Caddy blew a tire on the trip and Duff and I had to change it by the side of the New York State

Thruway. We couldn't have the musicians risk their delicate hands, so the singer and the manager did the heavy work. We made it to New York City, checked into a cheap hotel and prepared for our television debut. A Canadian rock band was unheard of in those days and the *Hullabaloo* producers, knowing absolutely nothing about Canada except that we played hockey "up there," surrounded us with dancers dressed up as hockey players. God, it was awful, but what the hell, we were in New York City and doing something no Canadian band had ever done: appearing on American network television. Welcome to the big time, David!

We were in New York for three days with lots of free time. So I searched out a place I'd only heard about on Bob Dylan records, a mythical place called Greenwich Village. For three days I haunted the clubs in the Village. I saw Frank Zappa and the Mothers of Invention, Carole King, James Taylor, Richie Havens and a band called Jimmy James and the Blue Flames, whose lead singer would later become Jimi Hendrix. It was a creative scene like I'd never known. It was so vital, bursting with energy and possibilities. In Toronto, even with two hit records, we were still playing the bars on the Strip, but this was the gateway to international recognition. I was hooked. I wanted to be a part of this. I wanted to make it in New York.

We returned to Toronto but I was burning with a new fire. What I'd heard in New York was new and exciting, and everyone was writing their own songs. The closest thing we had to Greenwich Village was Yorkville, a two-block-long street of coffee houses that featured blues, jazz, folk and progressive rock. It was a bohemian, artsy Toronto version of the Village in New York. Yorkville Avenue was only a few blocks long, but it was the two blocks between Bay Street and Avenue Road that would become indelibly etched in the history of Toronto. This stretch of Yorkville was lined with rundown three-storey houses that had seen better days. It was these old houses that originally drew the artists to the neighbourhood. The top two floors were rooms for rent cheap, usually by the week. The main floors and the basements were gutted out into larger spaces and in the late fifties were used as art galleries or espresso houses for the beat generation.

By the mid-sixties, the poetry readings and art galleries had given way to music. The coffee houses had become little clubs that hosted every kind of music from folksingers to rock bands. Sidewalk cafés lined the street with their outdoor tables and colourful Cinzano umbrellas bringing people in from the suburbs. The area became so popular that the street had to be cordoned off in the summer and no vehicles were allowed. Tourists jammed the street from sidewalk to sidewalk. The street was lined with tie-dye-draped head shops and T-shirt joints that sold everything from incense and Peter Max posters to hash pipes. That short two-block stretch of Yorkville would be packed with thousands of young people.

At night the club scene took over. There were little basement clubs like the Riverboat, with its pine-panelled riverboat motif complete with faux portholes, a nice, small place that brought in folk and blues talent from Canada and the US. It was here that I first saw Sonny Terry and Brownie McGhee, Joni Mitchell, Gordon Lightfoot, Son House and John Lee Hooker. There were other places that weren't so "nice," like the Purple Onion, the Penny Farthing and the Devil's Den. While the Riverboat audience was seated and polite, many of the other joints had dance floors and were loud and raucous. These places featured local rock

& roll bands with that "Toronto sound," a funky blend of British rock and American R&B.

In Yorkville, artists were actually writing their own music, and this was where I wanted to be. There was one catch, however: there was no money in the coffee houses. They sold no liquor, seated only about fifty people and paid peanuts. I certainly couldn't afford a five-piece band or support a wife and a baby with coffee-house gigs. So in early 1966 the Shays disbanded and went back to their day gigs. Nancy took our young daughter, Christine, to live with her parents, and I moved into a one-room flat on Yorkville across the hall from Joni Mitchell.

There was a real sense of community in Yorkville. The rents were cheap and most of the musicians lived in the neighbourhood. Young artists like myself, Joni, Neil Young, Rick James and John Kay lived in the second- and third-floor flats, working the clubs at night and hanging out in the little cafés along the street by day. I played everything—from folk clubs with an acoustic guitar to rock joints with my Telecaster. I loved Yorkville. This was as close as I could get to that magical scene that was Greenwich Village. I was burning to get back to New York but it wasn't that easy. You had to have a visa to cross the border, a sponsor, a gig to go to. I had none of these so I stayed on in Yorkville, living from gig to gig, rooming with other starving artists. Many times I wondered if I'd made a big mistake. There was still a lucrative scene available to me in the bars downtown but the bars on Yonge Street had a dress code and demanded a certain kind of music. It was a world of mohair suits, top-forty music and drunks. Yorkville was long hair, blue jeans and pot smokers, and Yorkville audiences weren't there for the booze—they were there for the music. Yorkville changed me as a person. The hair-trigger temper that was my survival mechanism in prison and in the brawling bars on Yonge Street was completely unacceptable here. This was an intellectual community. They weren't impressed by my tough-guy bullshit.

I had always been a voracious reader. In the joint I had devoured the prison library: Hemingway, Steinbeck, Shakespeare, Dostoevsky. I had read most of the classics and was delighted to find myself among people who shared my love of literature. I was exposed to innovative thinkers like Marshall McLuhan, Buckminster Fuller and George Orwell. I loved hanging out all night in the coffee houses discussing philosophy, politics, music and art. But the simmering rage that had allowed me to survive the brutal prisons and the tough bars still ran just beneath the surface and I was not one to be provoked. Old habits die hard. I was still capable of lashing out with incredible fury if I felt threatened. It would be years before I learned to control the wicked temper I had inherited from my father, but Yorkville was a good start.

Brainwashed

I woke up one mornin' and I took a look around
Found myself sleepin' in the city dog pound
I told myself this just can't be
In the home of the brave and the land of the free
I finally found my voice and I began to shout
I gotta, gotta tell ya what it's all about
I been brainwashed, brainwashed, brainwashed

Now it pours from my paper and from my radio
Tellin' me what to do and which way to go
White knight chargin' down on me with a lance
Giants in the valley, I don't stand me a chance
Stamp out overpopulation, take a walk in outer space
I gotta, gotta, tell ya what we got to face
We been brainwashed, brainwashed, brainwashed

Down with the hangman, I'd rather fight than switch
Public insulation, don't know which is which
We won ourselves a victory, the casualties were light
Judgin' by the news machine it ain't much of a fight
Sixty million people readin' all about Vietnam
And eighty-five percent of them don't give a [bleep]
They been brainwashed, brainwashed, brainwashed

6

THE BOSSMEN

It was Doc Riley who originally turned me on to the world of jazz. I was drawn to the incredible musical prowess of local players like Oscar Peterson, Lenny Breau and Moe Koffman. International jazz and blues artists like Joe Williams, Jimmy Witherspoon and Lonnie Johnson played regularly in Yorkville. I became friends with a jazz pianist named Tony Collacott. Tony was a young genius who had played with Sarah Vaughan at Carnegie Hall when he was fourteen, and now, in his early twenties, he was a hopelessly burned-out heroin junkie playing the jazz clubs in Yorkville. He was a total wreck, a chain-smoking, pill-popping outpatient at the psychiatric hospital on Queen Street. He was under constant doctors' supervision, self-destructive, suicidal and brilliant. A talent like his wasn't meant to last. It burned so fiercely that it was bound to destroy anyone who was cursed with it. Tony and I would sit up all night long talking about revolutionary new concepts in music. He was obsessed with the fire and energy of rock & roll. Why couldn't conservatory graduates play this music? Look what George Martin was doing with the Beatles—jazz and symphonic concepts applied to rock & roll. Miles Davis was experimenting with using funk and rock grooves in jazz. The barriers between different styles of music were breaking down and it was a whole new world to explore.

Tony Collacott and I gradually evolved an idea. I would write some new songs and he would arrange them using his considerable jazz chops. We put together a band based on this concept. We were called "the Bossmen"—three electric guitars arranged like a jazz horn section and a rock rhythm section built around Tony's madly inventive piano playing, described as something between Bach, Thelonious Monk and Jelly Roll Morton. I contacted Duff Roman and tried to explain what we were up to. I don't think he really understood where we were going with this idea. Then again, neither did we. This was uncharted territory. Duff's record company was just about broke by this time but he believed in me and borrowed two thousand bucks to pay for some studio time.

The result was "Brainwashed," an absolutely insane mix of heavy rock guitars orchestrated by Tony and featuring his outrageous jazz piano. The lyrics were an anti-war primal scream of refusal and outrage. I was influenced by the politically charged lyrics of the anti-war writers—Dylan, Jim Morrison, John Lennon—but underneath my songs was a strong undercurrent of raw blues. Collacott, a conservatory-trained jazz musician, gave the song an edgy avant-garde flavour that was totally unique. No one had ever heard anything like it. It was absolute musical madness, and it became the number-one record across Canada, knocking the Beatles and the Stones off the charts and dominating national radio for an unheard-of sixteen weeks. Even that couldn't save Duff's label, Roman Records. He folded the company. "Brainwashed" was our last release. It was 1966 and anti-war songs were still not fashionable in the States, and without a US release Duff's company couldn't survive. Duff went on to be president of CHUM Radio and founder of FACTOR, a government-backed organization to support Canadian talent. He is a dear friend to this day.

We couldn't possibly make a living in Yorkville with a six-piece band. The clubs were just too small. One-nighters were few and far between around Toronto, and the bars downtown wanted no part of this edgy, outrageous band with their hippie clothes, long hair and junkie piano player. Even with the number-one record in the country, this band was just too "far out" for the Strip. So we embarked on an absolutely crazy venture—we booked a driving tour across Canada. It had never been done before. The distance between gigs alone was daunting, and even in summer the North Country could be hostile and unforgiving. Breaking down north of Thunder Bay could be disastrous. We planned to start out in Toronto and make our way up through northern Ontario, across the Canadian prairies and out to Edmonton. I sold the old Cadillac from the New York trip and we bought a used cab-over bakery van. We built makeshift bunks in the back, loaded up our amps and drums, and headed out.

Our agency in those days was the Bigland Agency, run by a guy named Ron Scribner. I guess they figured if we were crazy enough to attempt a 3,500-mile drive in a bakery van, they would book the dates. No one had ever tried it before, they got their 10 per cent anyway and who knows … we just might make it. We played shows every night, heading north up through Ontario. Barrie, North Bay, Sudbury, Thunder Bay. With the shitty money we were making, most of the profits were going into the gas tank or on food, but we kept going. There was a carrot at the end of this stick: a big gig waiting for us in Edmonton, a full week at the Klondike Days fair for $2,500. That was *big* money in those days—in Toronto we worked five shows a night for $1,000 a week, split six ways after expenses and commissions.

The agency had booked the tour with no consideration for sleep or routing. We played every night in a different town and drove hundreds of miles through the night in shifts to make the next gig on time. By the second week we made it to Sault Ste Marie, Ontario, a minor miracle considering we had driven a thousand miles across some of the most hostile country in the world. In the "Soo" the shit hit the fan.

We were booked in to a quonset-style arena, a big, boomy tin-roofed joint meant for hockey, not concerts. Of course calling what we were doing "concerts" was a euphemism. The promoters booked everything from junior hockey to professional wrestling and bingo. The place was filled with beer-drunk hosers who came mostly to get laid or get in a fight. Since they had zero chance of getting laid, the show usually ended in a brawl. If any of the local lovelies so much as batted their eyes at the band they'd incite a riot, so we avoided the local talent. The show was about half over when the arena was invaded by a gang of toughs, motorcycle guys from across the line in Sault Ste. Marie, Michigan. One of them must have put the moves on a local girl (that's usually how these things got started) and a pier-six brawl broke out. Security consisted of one aging Canadian Legion veteran and he was hiding somewhere. The promoter grabbed the money from the till and ran. The fight was out of control and boiling up over the stage. It had nothing to do with us. We just wanted to get the hell out of there.

We were trying get our gear off the stage and make our escape when I saw little Tony Collacott, trying to protect his electric piano, go down under a whole gang of fist-swinging goons. I waded into them, cold-cocked one of them with the butt end of a microphone stand and dragged Tony, dazed and bleeding, out of harm's way. Now we were in for it! The buddies of the guy I had whacked with the mic stand wanted me. We backed up to the loading ramp, trying to escape. I was guarding the band's retreat with the mic stand as they loaded our equipment out the back door and into the truck, but I was fighting a losing battle. There were just too many of them. Somebody winged a beer bottle at me. It clipped me over the eye and opened up an inch-long gash. I looked desperately into the arena manager's office, hoping to find a way out of there, and standing against the wall behind his desk was a twelve-gauge shotgun. I didn't know if it was loaded or not, but then neither did they, so I grabbed it and, with blood streaming down my face, I yelled at the top of my lungs, "All right, you motherfuckers, who wants some of this!" The fight stopped immediately and the goons began backing away down the ramp, then turned and ran back into the arena to find easier prey. Under the unblinking eyes of the double-barrelled shotgun, we loaded up the truck. In the parking lot I popped the twelve-gauge open. It wasn't loaded. I tossed it into the woods and we headed into the night.

We were battered and exhausted and sometime that night our guitar player drove the van into the ditch on a desolate stretch of highway in northern Ontario somewhere between Sault Ste Marie and Winnipeg. The radiator was cracked, the front axle was broken and the van was finished. There we were, huddled in the wrecked van, shivering in the cold night air by the side of the deserted highway, a million miles from nowhere. At dawn a trucker came by and we flagged him down. He took a couple of us to some little town where we signed the title to the van over to a local who picked up the remaining guys, loaded our gear into a U-Haul trailer and drove us the four hundred miles to Winnipeg.

We tried to check in to a hotel but we looked like hell. We hadn't slept, bathed or changed our clothes for three days. We were bruised and battered by the brawl in Sault Ste Marie, banged up from the truck wreck and were with Tony Collacott, a junkie who looked like one. The desk clerk called the cops. The Mounties arrived and we told them our tale of woe. They were sympathetic until Collacott was frisked and they found the contents of a small pharmacy on him. We were detained for hours while Tony had to prove that he actually had prescriptions for the cocktail of drugs they found on him. Percodan, Demerol, methadone—just a part of Tony's daily diet. Then they checked my driver's licence. I still hadn't legally changed my name yet so my licence still read "Thomsett." A quick check and it was discovered that "Thomsett" was an ex-con. That didn't help matters either. They weren't impressed that we had the number-one rock record in the country.

They finally let us go and drove us back to the hotel, where I tried to contact our agency in Toronto. They were not taking our calls. "I'm sorry, Mr. Scribner is in a meeting. May I take your number?" Apparently the story had gotten back to Toronto and was totally blown out of proportion. The agency had been told by the promoter in Sault Ste Marie—who hadn't paid us yet and didn't intend to now—that I had fired a shotgun into the audience ("It's a miracle someone wasn't killed!") and that the band had been busted for drugs in Winnipeg. Neither story was true, but the agency had disowned us and cancelled the rest of the tour. We had money enough for maybe two nights at the hotel, no transportation and no gig in Winnipeg. That too had been cancelled by the agency. Then an angel came to our rescue. I called the Edmonton radio station that was promoting the Klondike

Days show. I told them about our predicament and they sent us airfare to Edmonton. We played a solid week at Klondike Days, got paid and they flew us back to Toronto. God bless that little AM radio station in Edmonton, Alberta. They saved our lives.

When I arrived home, in my front hall was a box of promotional photos from the Bigland Agency, which were supposed to have been delivered before the tour began, along with an invoice for two hundred bucks. I took the subway up to the agency's office. When I walked in the receptionist tipped off the agents that I was there and they all fled out the back door or locked themselves in the washrooms. I dumped the photos all over Ron Scribner's desk and walked back to Yorkville.

That was the end of the Bossmen. By this time Tony Collacott was deteriorating rapidly. We had to sign him out of the psychiatric hospital for gigs and bring him back afterwards. His brilliant mind was burning out fast and the years of drug abuse were taking their toll on his body. Every time I saw him I was surprised that he was still alive. The Bossmen were doomed to fail. The band was very much a product of Tony Collacott's mad genius and without him it could not exist. The group disbanded, still with the number-one record in the country, and I went back to playing the coffee houses in Yorkville.

Oh Angelina

I've seen some towns I hope I'll never see again
I've known some people who I used to call my friend
I've done some things I know I'd like to do again
And I ain't seen Angelina since I can't remember when

Sun in the mornin', moon at night
Long as I get my lovin' everything's goin' be all right

Oh … Angelina, say when you comin' down from Montreal
I just can't wait …
Oh Angelina I'm only passin' time until you call
Oh yes I am …
Just when I'm gettin' used to bein' on my own
I hear your voice and baby I just can't … be alone

Sometimes I don't know why I do the things I do
Sometimes I just don't care but somethin' gets me through
Sometimes a piece of me's the best that I can do
And it's the things I never say that mean the most to you

Sun in the mornin', moon at night
Long as I get my lovin' everything's goin' be all right

Oh … Angelina, say when you comin' down from Montreal
I just can't wait …
Oh Angelina I'm only passin' time until you call
Oh yes I am …
Just when I get to thinkin' baby it's been too long
I hear your voice and it's like you've never … been gone

7

JONI AND JOHN LEE

After the abortive Bossmen tour I found I had gained a reputation in the Canadian music industry. Now I was rock's bad boy. The story about the shotgun and the mic stand was told and retold and grew with every telling. There were stories swirling around Toronto about how I had single-handedly cleared out a bar on the Strip. Not true, but that didn't matter—people just loved to recount these juicy tales. My prison record, which I had kept pretty much hidden, now became public knowledge. The angry lyrics of "Brainwashed" fuelled my bad-boy image even more. My abilities as a songwriter were completely overshadowed by my tough-guy reputation. Now I was more than famous. I was infamous. My reputation as a badass followed me everywhere and I couldn't fight it. Eventually I gave up trying. Fuck it ... You want a badass, you got one.

I put together a four-piece band called the David Clayton-Thomas Combine. We played the heavy rock clubs around Yorkville, joints like Café El Patio and the Devil's Den. The bass player was a guy named Bruce Palmer who later teamed up with Stephen Stills in LA and formed Buffalo Springfield. The band was loud and aggressive. We played everything from "Brainwashed" to Howlin' Wolf and Willie Dixon. I lived in rented rooms with nothing to my name except my Telecaster and my amp. I had a few offers to play the lucrative bars downtown but I had gone too far to turn back now. There was no way I could go back to mohair suits and top-forty music. My band wore ripped T-shirts and leather pants. Our hair was long, our attitude was tough and cocky, and our music was fierce and rebellious. We smoked dope and chugged whisky onstage. We made the Rolling Stones look like choirboys.

There was one night, and I remember it well. It was the last time we would play El Patio. The club owner came back to the dressing room between sets and told us to "turn it down." The waitresses couldn't hear the drink orders and the customers were complaining. We told him to go fuck himself and pushed him out the door. He came back a few minutes later with the bouncer. "Throw them out," he ordered. The bouncer knew me and he knew my band. "Fuck you," he told the club owner. "You throw them out, I quit." Like I said, it was the last time we played El Patio.

In those days I had a huge crush on Joni Mitchell. I used to jump the fence behind the Devil's Den on Avenue Road, slip in the back door of the Riverboat and stand in the kitchen to worship her from afar, but she paid me no mind. After her show she would sweep past me in her flowing, diaphanous gowns, surrounded by her adoring fans, and I was tongue-tied. I never even spoke to her. I was not worthy. I was a leather-jacketed, Telecaster-playing thug who played in a thunderously loud rock & roll band, and she was this flaxen-haired goddess from the west coast who played an acoustic guitar and sang her delicate melodies in a clear, silvery voice. Her lyrics were pure genius, her songs were beautifully crafted and she was drop-dead gorgeous. I'm sure some nights she could hear my band all the way into the

Riverboat, rattling the glasses on the tables and disturbing her raptly attentive audience. We weren't subtle, baby. We were loud and we were rude.

In later years, our common love for jazz brought us closer together. Joni and I had a couple of musician friends in common, Don Alias and Jaco Pastorius. They both played in her band and with me in BS&T. I was so completely smitten by her that I borrowed a phrase from her song "The Circle Game," the line about "painted ponies," and used it in my song "Spinning Wheel." In 2007 both songs were inducted into the Canadian Songwriters Hall of Fame and I confessed my plagiarism to her. She said she had never even noticed. Maybe she was just being polite but I was crushed. She didn't notice me then and she doesn't notice me now. Ah well, Joni … Life goes on.

Two of my biggest songs were written in Yorkville: "Spinning Wheel" and "Lucretia MacEvil." "Spinning Wheel" was my response to the flower-power songs of the anti-war movement. My time in prison had left me with a tougher point of view than that of my love-generation colleagues. I was more pragmatic about love changing the world forever. I knew there were some really bad people out there, and all the flowers and free love in the world wouldn't change that. It was all well and good to be against violence and to protest the war, but my experience had taught me that sometimes you just have to stand your ground and fight. The message of the song was "Don't get too carried away with the politics of the moment—everything comes full circle in time."

Lucretia MacEvil was a composite of every bad girl I had met in the rough-and-tumble bars on Yonge Street. She'd rather be notorious than ignored. Every funky little bar in every little Ontario town had a Lucretia, a hot little badass who desperately wanted out of her small-town existence, where girls like her were pregnant by the time they were eighteen, their dreams ending there.

I recorded "Spinning Wheel" for a record company in Toronto called Arc Records. Duff Roman's company had gone belly-up. Even with our hit records there was just no money in Canada. There simply weren't enough people in this vast country to support a real record industry, and Duff finally had to give up his dream of owning a record company. I'll always be grateful to Duff Roman. Guys like him, who were willing to mortgage their houses and borrow money from friends to support artists they believed in, are hard to find in this business. At any rate, Arc Records signed me to a contract and gave me a budget of five hundred bucks. I booked a studio and recorded "Spinning Wheel." When I brought them the finished master, they were not pleased. "What's this?" they said. "It sounds like jazz, we can't sell jazz. We wanted another 'Brainwashed.'" They rejected the song, made a show of tearing up my contract and showed me the door.

Three years later, when BS&T's version of "Spinning Wheel" had sold over ten million copies, I was summoned to Clive Davis's office in New York. There were the guys from Arc Records. They were squirming uncomfortably in their chairs. They couldn't look me in the eye and never even offered a handshake. They were claiming prior ownership of the song. The contract I had signed gave them publishing rights and they wanted a piece of the action. They had made a show of ripping up my contract, but of course they had another copy. A lawsuit would have been expensive and time consuming, so Clive paid them off. A deal was arranged to split the Arc payments with Columbia's publishing company. I didn't care—it wasn't coming out of my pocket. But for years this crummy little company that had rejected the song received a slice of the publishing royalties from "Spinning Wheel." Eventually, when Arc went broke, I was able to buy back the publishing rights to the song, but I had learned a couple of valuable lessons. First, have a lawyer read everything before you sign it, and second, there is no shame in the record business.

Yorkville's days were numbered. The city fathers of "Toronto the Good" had determined that Yorkville was a den of iniquity, full of drug addicts, hippies, sex fiends and, worst of all, musicians. They decided to clean it up. The Toronto police swept through Yorkville, arresting anyone who didn't move along fast enough. There were literally dozens of arrests every night and within a few weeks an era had ended. Yorkville today is a fashionable neighbourhood, the once-funky bohemian street now lined with expensive shops and trendy boutiques. It's lovely and prosperous and attracts thousands of tourists, but in my mind we lost something. Maybe the Yorkville I knew could only have existed in those tumultuous, crazy sixties and would be as out of place today as bell-bottoms and tie-dye.

I had become friends with bluesman John Lee Hooker. I had scored a hit in Canada with his song "Boom Boom" years before any other white artists in North America had even thought of recording such songs. The only other people who were playing this music were in England, where the British blues of John Mayall and Long John Baldry was taking hold with British youth. Every time John Lee came to town to play the Riverboat, I would run over between sets at my gig and sit in with him. He liked the way I played his Delta-blues style. I knew all his songs and all those years of practicing with Lightnin' Sam Hopkins and Jimmy Reed records made it easy to play with Hooker.

One night in early '67 he told me he was going to New York to play the Cafe Au Go Go in Greenwich Village. I begged him to take me with him. I was desperate to get back to New York. He agreed, with one condition. He didn't drive. His driver had had trouble at the border and was refused entry into Canada, and his car was still in storage in Niagara Falls. If I would go down there, pick it up and drive it to New York, he would give me a gig when I got there. There were no visas or work permits involved. It wasn't exactly legal but I didn't care. I wanted to get to New York so bad I decided to take a chance. I took a bus to Niagara Falls, Ontario, walked across the border as a tourist, picked up John's Cadillac in Niagara Falls and was on my way to New York City.

I dropped off John's car with some lawyer in midtown Manhattan. I didn't even have a guitar, as carrying a musical instrument across the border would have raised a red flag. I was, after all, only supposed to be a tourist. So I rented a Telecaster and an amp from Manny's Music on 48th Street and took the subway downtown to Greenwich Village. I arrived at the Cafe Au Go Go to find the owner, Howie Solomon, frantic. John Lee Hooker wouldn't be opening at the Au Go Go that night. His agent had booked him on the American Blues Festival tour in Europe and had cancelled the club date in New York. I was sitting on my amp, dejected, nearly broke, with no gig in New York, and Solomon took pity on me. He asked me to play him a couple of tunes. So I played him the John Lee Hooker tune, "Boom Boom." He liked what he heard and asked me if I had a blues band that could fill in for Hooker for a couple of weeks. Even though I had just arrived in town that day and knew nobody I said, "No problem, I'll be back at five," and went looking for a band.

That afternoon I made the rounds of the pizza joints, coffee houses and restaurants around the Village looking for anyone carrying a guitar case or even looking like a musician. I rounded up a ragtag bunch of unemployed musicians and invited about twenty of them to an "audition" at 5:00 p.m. at the Cafe Au Go Go. Then I went back to the club with my rented Telecaster to await the band. Only about half of the guys I had invited showed up but I lucked out. A couple of them had been in a band from Chicago called the Butterfield Blues Band. Their club gig uptown had run out and they were looking to stay on in New York and, even better, they could really play. One of them was a guitar player named Mike Bloomfield who later would record the *Super Sessions* album with Al Kooper and go on to San Francisco to form the Electric Flag. We rehearsed for a couple of hours and opened that night at the Cafe Au Go Go. I was in the music capital of the world, and I was working. I thought I was on my way.

I rented a furnished flat on MacDougal Street and Nancy brought our young daughter, Christine, barely eighteen months old, down from Toronto. I've often wondered why we did that. It was crazy. Maybe Nancy thought she could still save our marriage. Maybe I was trying to show her that I really could make it in the big time. Maybe we were both desperately trying to hang on to something that was gone forever. In any event, it was a really bad idea. The marriage was over and my dreams of glory wouldn't last long either. The gig at the Cafe Au Go Go lasted three weeks, the rent money ran out and I was out of work in a city that is not kind to unemployed musicians.

I was determined not to go back to Toronto with my tail between my legs. And while it was hard enough for me, for Nancy being broke and homeless in New York was impossible. She was a small-town girl from Canada with a new baby to care for and a husband who again seemed to have lost his mind. I had to make it in New York or die trying—most likely the latter. Nancy finally gave up on me, returned to Toronto and filed for divorce. I stayed on in New York. Nancy soon remarried and Christine was adopted. Her name was changed and she was raised by her new family. She wasn't told that I was her father until much later in her life, and that was probably for the best. I was in no shape to be a father. I was absolutely obsessed with making it in New York. I can remember standing at the foot of Fifth Avenue at four o'clock in the morning, like a madman, shaking my fist at the city like it was a living being, screaming "You son of a bitch," at the top of my lungs. "You son of a bitch … You won't beat me!"

Secretive Child

I'm down to nothin' but my music
Workin' on Bleecker Street just to survive
I play my songs and pass the basket
Playin' these blues is bound to keep me alive
Fall down, turn around, do it again

Life ain't easy on the mean streets
Love ain't easy for a secretive child
Let the blues become my refuge
Let the music take me away for a while

Maybe someday I'll be famous
Or maybe I will fly too close to the flame
But I'll be someone you remember
For fifteen minutes you will all know my name
Fall down, turn around, do it again

Life ain't easy on the mean streets
Love ain't easy for a secretive child
Let the blues become my refuge
Let the music take me away for a while

Lyrics by David Clayton-Thomas. Copyright © Clayton-Thomas Music Publishing Inc., 1999.

8

GREENWICH VILLAGE

For the next two years I lived from day to day. Scuffling to survive was nothing new to me—I had been broke and hungry before—but this wasn't Toronto. Being homeless on the streets of New York was something else entirely. I hung out in the Village. It was the centre of the music world in the sixties, with lots of loose girls and cheap gigs and other struggling musicians. I crashed with Village girls when I could and with other musicians when I couldn't, often staying up all night in twenty-four-hour coffee shops. Sometimes a few musicians would pool their meagre resources and rent a single room, then we would use it in shifts, sleeping for a few hours before turning it over to the next guy. I worked any gig I could get. I sang and played my guitar on street corners for spare change, busking on weekends with an open guitar case, around the fountain in Washington Square with all the other out-of-work musicians. Mostly I played "basket houses" in the Village. It was a rite of passage … Everyone did the basket-house circuit.

In the eight square blocks that was Greenwich Village were several little coffee houses. Seating no more than thirty people, these grubby hole-in-the-wall joints served no liquor but you could get a drink called a piña colada, which was basically canned pineapple juice on ice with no rum, for about five bucks—a total rip-off, but that's not why people were there. At one end of the room was a "stage," a six-by-ten-foot plywood riser about a foot high, with a squeaky microphone and a couple of cheap speakers on the wall. Some of the more "lavish" joints actually had a battered old upright piano on the stage. Usually it was missing keys and was so out of tune that a guitar was preferable. We would stand in line along the wall, guitars in hand, waiting for a few minutes of stage time—Richie Havens, John Hammond, Tim Hardin, Dave Van Ronk—anyone trying to make a little rent money. The audiences and the club owners were merciless. If you didn't grab their attention within the first few bars, the microphone went dead and you were hustled unceremoniously off the stage. If you were going over well, you might last as long as one or two songs but you couldn't hog the mic. There was a lineup of other singers waiting to get on. If you stayed on too long, they would begin hooting and hollering for you to "get off the stage." After a couple of songs you took a basket and passed it among the patrons, collecting spare change and an occasional dollar bill. It was a trial by fire and most of the young artists trying to break into the paying clubs in the Village went through it. The paying clubs were the Bottom Line, the Cafe Au Go Go, the Bitter End and the Gaslight. In those places you might actually be seen by a record company. The record execs seldom ventured into the sleazy basket houses. I guess they figured if you survived that scene, you just might be worth listening to.

The wonderful thing about that era was that the entire music industry was centred on that eight square blocks of downtown Manhattan and everybody knew everybody. You could be playing for chump change one night, get spotted by a record company and be a star within weeks. The dream was always dangling right in front of us. We all knew people who were discovered in the Village, signed to a major record deal and a year later were collecting Grammy awards and gold records. That all disappeared in the seventies, when the music industry moved to Hollywood and dissipated all over that spaced-out, soulless town. There was no sense of neighbourhood in Los Angeles. It was every man for himself out there and no one knew anyone anymore.

I got to know some really fine people in the Village. John Hammond Jr. and Richie Havens became good friends and saved my ass more than once when I had no place to live and it was getting cold out on the street. Eventually I moved into a one-room sixth-floor walk-up flat on Thompson Street, right in the middle of Greenwich Village. I was in heaven. After nearly a year in New York City I actually had an address.

Not part of the Village scene but definitely a place to be was a club uptown, on 46th Street, called Steve Paul's Scene. All the heavy bands hung out there. Jimi Hendrix, just back from London with his new band, the Jimi Hendrix Experience, Eric Clapton and his band Cream, the Rascals, the Lovin' Spoonful, the Allman Brothers—everybody hung out at the Scene. I would sit in with anyone who would let me, and eventually Steve Paul noticed me and asked me to put together a house band to back any of the rock stars who happened to drop in looking to jam and hook up with the exotic ladies who were always at the club.

This was a great gig. I got to meet and hang out with the biggest stars in the business. I led the house band in a club that had the hottest babes in town—sleek models from the fashion district, actresses and dancers from Broadway, Andy Warhol girls and movie starlets in from Hollywood. I hooked up with a Warhol girl, a European actress named Ultra Violet. She was ten years older than me, a beautiful and bizarre creature of the night and sexy as hell. I ran around with her for a while, and the Warhol crowd began to hang out at the club. They were a shallow bunch—art-world poseurs who really believed they were trend-setters. The truth is they were just followers, drugged-out syco-phants waiting for Andy to tell them what was art and what wasn't. Warhol himself showed up at the Scene one night. I was ushered over to his table and introduced to him like he was roy-alty. He murmured something like "very powerful" and waved me to a seat. I mumbled something about having to get ready for the next set and fled back to the safety of the dressing room. I thought he was a vampire, sucking the life out of the lost, lonely, drugged-out souls who hovered around him, convinced that he was going to make them all superstars. Creepy—definitely not my scene.

I met a guy at Steve Paul's who would become a lifelong friend. Deering Howe was friends with Jimi Hendrix, knew the Beatles, Clapton, the Stones and nearly everyone else on the six-ties music scene. Deering was good-looking and charismatic, educated at the finest schools, a product of old money, heir to the McCormick-Deering farm machinery fortune. A trust-fund kid with absolutely no interest in entering the family business, he had a lifelong love affair with rock & roll. Deering Howe was the quintessential fan, flying to London for a Stones concert, hanging out with Hendrix in New York, living with the Allmans on their commune in Georgia. He was passionate and knowledgeable about music but he never could play the blues he loved so deeply. That's a gift given to a few and he knew it. Maybe he couldn't play the blues but he was a good friend to those who could.

When Deering Howe went out on the town in New York, it was an event, complete with champagne, beautiful women and an entourage. Everywhere Deering went was a party. I began to cross paths with him around town. We seemed to like the same bands and frequent the same clubs, and I liked him. He was smart and fun to be with, and he loved music with a real passion. I remember jamming on acoustic guitars at his Fifth Avenue apartment with Jimi Hendrix, Mick Jagger playing drums on a cardboard box and Deering recording it all on a cassette recorder. He still has that tape.

Deering Howe was born to big money. He'd known ass-kissers all his life and he could spot a phony from a mile away. I liked this guy and I wanted to be friends, but I also wanted it understood that I was not one of his entourage. One time Deering threw a party on a sixty-foot cabin cruiser he kept moored at the 79th Street boat basin. All night long we cruised around the Statue of Liberty and under the George Washington Bridge, *Sgt. Pepper's* blared from the stereo speakers—Jimi Hendrix, Eric Burdon, myself and Deering with a full crew and a boatload of babes and rock musicians, stoned out of our minds and having the time of our lives. In the morning the boat docked at 79th Street. I had to make my way back to the Village and I was broke. It was drizzling rain and I trudged the eighty-plus blocks back downtown carrying my guitar case, hungover and feeling like shit. Deering found out about this several weeks later and demanded to know why I had walked home. "All you had to do is ask," he said. "I would have put you in a cab." I told him gently, "Deering, I'm your friend, I don't need your fuckin' money."

From that moment on we became friends. I got to know his family and I got to know this exceptional guy. His stepmother, Jacqueline, once told me, "Deering works harder at playing than most men do at working." As the years passed I learned what she meant. Whatever Deering Howe did, he did well, and I respected that. When his passion was deep-sea fishing, he became one of the best, following the black marlin around the world and filling his home with trophies. He was a natural athlete, and when he took up golfing, he excelled at that too, becoming a scratch golfer, playing head to head with pros like Fred Couples.

I still visit Deering and his wife, Barbara, a couple of times a year at their summer home in Maine or their winter place in Florida. He's been at nearly every milestone concert I've ever played and he's a trusted friend and confidant. Deering is usually the first one to hear my new songs even before they're finished. I can always count on him to be brutally honest with me. He's not a musician, but he's an astute listener, and I take his advice seriously. He always tells me straight up when he thinks I'm drifting off course musically ... and he's usually right. The relationship we established way back when I refused to be one of his entourage holds true to this day. He's been there for me through all my ups and downs. We've been deep-sea fishing off Jamaica, toured the funky clubs of New York and crawled the rock & roll bars of Los Angeles, and this story wouldn't be complete without him.

Deering Howe was not the only person I met at Steve Paul's who would have a major effect on my life. It was at the Scene one night that folksinger Judy Collins heard me and told a friend, drummer Bobby Colomby, about me. Bobby and bass player Jim Fielder came in later in the week. When I started singing, Bobby turned to Fielder and said, "Who the hell is that? He sings like Ray Charles." Jim replied, "I think that's the guy Judy's talkin' about." After my set they introduced themselves and told me about their band, Blood Sweat & Tears. They had recorded a debut album for Columbia Records entitled *Child Is Father to the*

Man, but the band had fallen apart due to infighting between founder Al Kooper and guitarist Steve Katz. There were only five guys left from the original nine-piece band, but they still had a record contract and were looking to recruit some new players. First they needed a singer and they asked me if I was interested. I knew a few of the guys from the now-defunct Blues Project and I had heard the early edition of BS&T at the Cafe Au Go Go, but word around town was that they had broken up and a lot of people had written them off. I was extremely interested in this band. I shared their vision of a rock band made up of conservatory-trained jazz musicians. It seemed like an idea whose time had come. Young musicians were coming out of Berklee and Juilliard with master's degrees, well versed in everything from Beethoven to Charlie Parker, but like me had grown up with the music of Chuck Berry and Ray Charles. In many ways it was the fulfillment of the concept that Tony Collacott and I had envisioned with the Bossmen in Toronto. I would have joined them right then and there but fate and treachery intervened.

I was still technically in the US illegally and the immigration department finally caught up with me, tipped off by someone who really didn't want me to get the gig with BS&T. I don't know who turned me in but they knew exactly where to find me. At four in the morning, INS agents crashed into a crib I shared with bass player Harvey Brooks and took me away in handcuffs. Ordinarily they would have politely asked a Canadian without a visa to get his documentation straight, but one check of my prison record and once again I was automatically a dangerous criminal. I spent the night in lock-up and was deported back to Canada. My two years of struggle in New York seemed to have been in vain.

Friday the Thirteenth Child

Friday the thirteenth child, Mother nearly died in pain
And you never look over your shoulder
Friends and family you'll never see again
Friends and family you'll never see again

Friday the thirteenth child must be somewhere roads don't run
Put another day over your shoulder
Make it shine like silver, warm like the mornin' sun
Shine like silver, warm like the mornin' sun

I'm havin' the time of my life and yours, my life and yours
Livin' the life life intended me for
And God knows you can't do no more

Friday the thirteenth child, there's a rabbit dyin' by the road
And another day over your shoulder
Shines like silver, Lord, but it weighs like gold
Shines like silver, Lord, but it weighs like gold

9

COLOMBY
AND KATZ

After being deported from the US I returned to Yorkville, back to little coffee-house gigs, stoned on pot and hash and psychedelics. This was the age of acid and all musicians in rock & roll were experimenting with hallucinogens, trying to expand their consciousness. I was just trying to numb the crushing disappointment of being kicked out of the States. I had gambled everything on making it in New York and I had been so close.

The two guys from BS&T didn't give up on me, however. Jim Fielder and Bobby Colomby got an immigration attorney on the case and began the legal process of petitioning me back into the US. They felt that I was the right singer for their band and they had the weight of CBS on their side. The first BS&T album had been on Columbia Records and was a critical, if not a huge financial, success. Columbia's president, Clive Davis, felt that with the band's superb musicianship, Bobby's business smarts and the right singer, Blood Sweat & Tears was poised to blow the lid off the music business.

I had never committed a crime in the US and my deportation was on a minor technicality. The BS&T people were successful in obtaining a temporary visa for me, and soon I was on a plane back to New York. They got me a room at the Chelsea Hotel, on 23rd Street, and I prepared to audition for Blood Sweat & Tears. The band rehearsed in a fifth-floor loft above the Cafe Au Go Go. This band was a killer. The musicians were great jazz players who were well versed in the blues and R&B. Most of them had never heard me sing. They just knew that Colomby and Fielder were hot on me. The first song I chose for the audition was Al Kooper's "I Love You More Than You'll Ever Know," from the band's first album. By the end of that first song there was no doubt that something was happening here. One look around the room and I knew from the band's faces that I had the gig. My vocal style and my jazz and blues background were perfect for this band. Colomby would later say, "We never heard anyone sing like that, he was incredible." That first rehearsal was magic—there was absolutely no doubt that I was the right singer for this band.

We all went across the street to the Tin Angel café for dinner after the rehearsal and everyone knew we had something very special. That rehearsal had revealed a very different kind of band. It had traditional elements reminiscent of Basie and Ellington, an edgy modern jazz sound echoing Miles and Coltrane, a pop edge with shades of the Beatles, and running through everything was a funky undercurrent of the blues. I had never heard anything quite like it. But right from that first meeting I was aware that there were political stresses within the band. There was still a fair amount of bitterness toward the recently departed Al Kooper. The guys didn't feel that he had the vocal chops to sing with this band, and apparently there had been an absolute war for control between Kooper, Katz and Colomby.

The guys told me a funny story at dinner that evening, about the conflict between the founding fathers of the band. It seems they were booked to play Bill Graham's Fillmore East right after the release of their first album. Graham put the band's name up on the marquee: it read "Tonight, Blood Sweat & Tears." Kooper saw the sign and had it changed to "Al Kooper's Blood Sweat & Tears." Later that day Katz passed by the theatre and saw the sign. He had it changed to "Al Kooper, Steve Katz and Blood Sweat & Tears." The next day Colomby called and Bill Graham put his foot down. He was running out of letters. Kooper's and Katz's names were removed and the sign once again read "Blood Sweat & Tears." It sounds funny today, but this is the egocentric mess I was stepping into. I heard many more stories about the epic battles between Kooper, Katz and Colomby. There were even hints that Kooper may have been involved in turning me in to the INS when it was suggested that I might replace him. I have no proof of this but it made sense at the time. After a knock-down, drag-out war between the founding members, Kooper had quit or, as rumour had it, was forced out by Katz and Colomby. They now owned all rights to the name "Blood Sweat & Tears," a fact that was to overshadow my life for years to come.

Steve Katz was somewhat standoffish at that first meeting. I had the distinct feeling that he wanted me to know that he was a power player in the group and that he was still not completely sold on me as the band's singer. I didn't pay much attention to him at the time—the positive energy around the table more than made up for his skepticism. I felt an immediate connection with these guys. They were pure musicians. They based their opinion of me not on my past but on what had just happened in that rehearsal loft across the street. They were all about the music and didn't give a damn where I came from.

Trumpet player Lew Soloff was also new to the band. He had been recruited to replace Randy Brecker, who left in the midst of the power struggle between Kooper, Katz and Colomby. Lew was the quintessential New Yorker, talkative and likeable, a baseball fan ready in a big-city minute to give you the stats and history of his beloved Yankees. Lew and I bonded right away. We were the new guys, so we really had no interest in the old politics of the band. We just wanted to get on with the new music. Bass player Jim Fielder was a laid-back, easygoing Texan and I was immediately comfortable with him. I knew we would be friends. We spoke the same language musically. We talked about the Chicago blues of B.B. King and Muddy Waters, Motown and Memphis, Otis Redding, Aretha Franklin and Ray Charles. Arranger and sax player Freddie Lipsius was a creative dynamo already bubbling with ideas for new charts. His enthusiasm was contagious. Freddie wanted to find a piano right then and there and start working on new tunes. Bobby Colomby was over the moon. He was the guy responsible for bringing me into the band, and that first rehearsal had proven him right. "I knew it," he told the band. "That was amazing—wait till Clive hears this."

We opened at the Cafe Au Go Go a couple of weeks later and Clive Davis came in to see us with a group of people from Columbia. The look on his face said everything. He was completely blown away. He came backstage after the set and said, "How soon can we get this into the studio?" In his 1974 autobiography, *Clive: Inside the Record Business*, he described his initial impression of hearing me that night at the Cafe Au Go Go: "He was staggering ... a powerfully built singer who exuded an enormous earthy confidence. He jumped right out at you. I went with a small group of people, and we were electrified. He seemed so genuine, so in command of the lyric ... a perfect combination of fire and emotion to go with the band's somewhat cerebral appeal. I knew he would be a strong, strong figure."

Word spread around New York like wildfire and within a few weeks there were hundreds of people lined up around the block waiting to get into the Cafe Au Go Go, which seated only about two hundred people. We played there at night and recorded by day at Columbia's studio on 52nd Street. We basically recorded the set we were playing in the Village, a combination of unrecorded songs left over from the early band, like "More and More" and "You Made Me So Very Happy," and new tunes, like "Sometimes in Winter," a beautiful ballad by Steve Katz; "And When I Die," written by Jim Fielder's girlfriend, Laura Nyro; one of my original songs, "Spinning Wheel," which I had brought with me from Canada; and a jam-session tune called "Blues Part Two," which consisted of my lyrics and an arrangement written by the band collectively. They brought in a producer named James William Guercio, who later went on to produce a string of hits for another horn band, Chicago. He was a fine producer and very helpful in the studio, but the arrangements and the repertoire were determined at the little club in Greenwich Village every night. If a tune connected with the audience we recorded it … simple as that.

The self-titled album *Blood Sweat & Tears* was released in September 1968 and literally exploded onto the national charts. By Christmas we had the number-one record in the country. It was propelled to the top of the charts by a massive promotional campaign by Columbia and an intensive tour schedule from the band. We worked our asses off to promote that record. The band played nearly every night. We were everywhere—colleges, clubs, arenas. We had one of the best concert bands in the world and we knew it. We knew it every night when the show left people stunned by the power and precision of the band. It wasn't arrogance—we were damn good, and we knew it. When people like Janis Joplin, Jimi Hendrix, Eric Clapton and Jack Bruce came backstage after the show visibly shaken by the music this band was putting out, we knew it. In a business dominated by power trios like The Who, Cream and Hendrix, this band stood out. The arrangements were beautifully written, the arrangers obviously Juilliard- and Berklee-trained. The charts evoked Ellington and Basie with just a hint of Broadway. It was a New York City band. The bravura Broadway brass and the Village Vanguard rhythm section were the sound of the city. These guys could play salsa in Spanish Harlem one night and soul music at the Apollo the next. I brought my rhythm & blues roots to the band. The blues kept the music grounded. People could relate to the blues. The blues allowed this somewhat esoteric band to hit the audience right in the heart. It was powerful. It was different. It was magic.

The undisputed leader of the band was drummer Bobby Colomby. Athletic, good-looking and clever, Bobby was not only a great drummer, but also an excellent basketball player. He had been an all-state guard at City College of New York, where he had majored in psychology and business. Raised by his mother, who he adored, Bobby came from a family steeped in jazz. His brother Harry was a manager who listed people like Miles Davis and Thelonious Monk among his clients. Bobby's first drum kit had been given to him at six years old by none other than Philly Joe Jones.

I had seen Bobby play a few times before I met him that night at Steve Paul's. I became aware of him when he was with African folksinger Odetta. He played with fire and personality, and he stood out immediately. I met him briefly on a little pickup gig in the West Village and I liked him. He was bright, articulate and one hell of a drummer. I'll always be grateful to Bobby. He saw my raw talent and went to bat for me against impossible odds, even against the wishes of his partner Steve Katz. I looked up to Bobby. He was the smart, fast-talking New Yorker, and I was the hick kid fresh in from the backwoods of Canada. He grew up in the music business and knew the ropes, while I was still ignorant of concepts like management publishing and record-company politics.

As much as I liked and respected Bobby, I really didn't care for Steve Katz, and the feeling was mutual. First of all, I came from a tradition of the great blues guitarists—B.B. King, Albert King, Otis Rush. My guitar heroes were Clapton, Hendrix, Duane Allman. I was not impressed by Steve Katz as a musician. He was a pretty good folk guitarist and a decent harmonica player, but musically he was way over his head in that band of killer musicians. I didn't really understand why he was in this band, but the reasons soon became apparent. He had been the rhythm guitar player for the Blues Project and had come into BS&T with Al Kooper. Katz owned a piece of the name and hence a piece of the Columbia recording contract. In addition, his brother Dennis was the group's attorney and co-manager. To me it was obvious that Steve Katz's presence in this band of superb musicians was more political than musical.

Katz didn't like me either. He didn't want me in the band from the get-go. He thought that I was a crude ex-con and that my immigration problems were more trouble than they were worth. He wasn't wrong, on both counts. At that time in my life, fresh out of the tough bars of Toronto and not too far removed from the reformatory, I was not the most sophisticated man about town, and the INS certainly was a pain in the ass. Columbia and our management people disagreed with Katz, though. With our records taking off and big-money offers starting to roll in, they didn't want to rock the boat. They had a winner and they were willing to do whatever it took to keep me in the band.

Steve Katz fancied himself a radical, always spouting off about racial discrimination, the tyranny of the US government and the plight of the underclass. He'd never gone hungry, been homeless, worked a brutally hard job or been beaten down by the system a day in his life. I agreed with him on many of his issues, and I actually admired his commitment to his ideals, but his open animosity toward the establishment was over-the-top. I had to deal constantly with the establishment. I was still in the US on a visa that had to be renewed for every gig. Management was dealing with the INS on a weekly basis, and I was paying some very expensive immigration attorneys who were fighting to keep me in the US. Thumbing your nose at the government was easy for Steve Katz, but it could be fatal for me. I had little patience for this limousine liberal who formed his radical opinions by reading the *Village Voice*. Steve Katz and I were oil and water, and we were never destined to get along.

Then something happened that confirmed everything Katz believed about me. Shortly after I joined the band, someone tried to steal my Telecaster. One night after our show at the Cafe Au Go Go I stopped in at a little bar on Bleecker Street to have a beer with a couple of musician friends in town from Toronto. We had only been there for a few minutes when I saw this junkie-looking guy headed out the door with my guitar. I went after him with my two buddies right behind me, grabbed my guitar case and we had a little tugging match. I got the guitar away from him and he took a swing at me. I swung the case up and caught him in the face with the butt end of it. He staggered back. I dropped the guitar and waded into him, catching him with three or four good shots, and he went down. My Canadian buddies and a well-meaning bartender rushed over to help and we all went down in a pile, me on top of the would-be thief, with my friends and the bartender on top of me. The guy twisted his head around, got his teeth into my ear and bit a piece of it clean off. I wrestled one arm free and landed a few more punches before I was pulled off him. In the confusion the junkie ran out the door and was gone. The locals took me to the hospital, where the doctors bandaged up my ear, shot me full of antibiotics and gave me a prescription for the pain. Then my friends took me back to the Chelsea Hotel. This incident completely horrified Steve Katz, and my image as a brawling ex-convict was forever cemented in his mind.

The very next day the band left on a tour around New England. I removed the bandages every night and performed with my hair combed down over my mutilated ear, stoned out of my mind on painkillers and booze, but every show was a knockout. Then on the last night of the tour I walked into the dressing room to find Katz complaining that he couldn't go on. He wasn't feeling well and thought he was "coming down with something." I was disgusted. I had gone out there and performed night after night with a chunk bitten out of my ear, in horrendous pain, and had never let the band down once, and now he "wasn't feeling well." He wasn't going to get any sympathy from me. I snapped at him, "Suck it up, asshole, it's showtime," and slammed out of the room. Not the smartest thing to say to the guy who was essentially my boss, but I'd had enough of Katz and his condescending attitude. Steve went on and did the show but obviously we would never be friends.

A few weeks later the band booked its first tour of the west coast. We were still relatively unknown outside the New York area and the promoters needed to drum up some press. It was no secret by now that I had spent time in prison and, rather than cover it up, some genius at the record company decided to cash in on my bad-boy reputation and arranged for the band to do a free concert for the inmates at the California state penitentiary at Chino. Steve Katz loved this idea. I think it really appealed to his image of himself as a radical activist bringing his political views to the downtrodden victims of an unjust system. Columbia's publicists latched on to the fact that I had done time and used it to generate publicity, later booking us into joints like New York's infamous Rikers Island. I was never completely comfortable with this and eventually I put a stop to it. But here we were booked into Chino, and at the time I had no problem with it. In fact, I was kind of excited to see the inside of a joint again—especially since now I could walk out whenever I wanted to. So one afternoon they bused us up from Los Angeles to play the show at Chino.

We stepped off the bus right into the yard at the joint. There were maybe a hundred inmates in the yard when we arrived. The event was heavily guarded, with rifle towers and razor wire everywhere. These were seriously dangerous guys with venomous eyes, pumped-up biceps and gang tattoos. They were all trying to look as bad as possible. That's just how it is in the joint—you'd better look bad or someone will make you his bitch. I wasn't intimidated at all. Hell, I'd seen all this before. I jumped off the bus and walked right out into the middle of the yard, slapping high-fives and chatting easily with the toughest of the inmates. They recognized immediately that I wasn't some condescending social-worker type sent there to help the poor downtrodden victims of the system. They hate that. The men in the joint have a sixth sense for weakness, and they knew by my jailhouse tattoos and by the way I carried myself that at one time I had been one of them and we were brothers. They gathered around me, high-fiving and embracing, everybody talking at once. Contact with the street was a luxury, and the guys couldn't wait to tell their stories, to spend a few minutes with someone from the outside world.

At one point I looked back across the yard. The other guys were off the bus and were uneasily shaking hands and talking to the inmates, but they weren't straying too far from the security of the bus. And who could blame them? For someone who's never been in one of these joints, it's a scary experience. Through the tinted windows of the bus I saw the white, drawn face of Steve Katz. He wasn't getting off the bus without an escort. I was out there all by myself, in the middle of the yard, surrounded by black militants, swastika-tattooed white Aryan Brotherhood types and Latino gangbangers. I burst out laughing. "Well, mister radical activist," I thought, "mister champion of the down-trodden. Here they are, come and say hello." Steve stayed on the bus until showtime and then had an escort to and from the stage. Even during the show he looked scared to death. On the ride back to LA, most of the guys were subdued. It had been a heavy experience. Katz couldn't stop talking. "God, did you see that? David just walked right out there. Christ, I wasn't going out there. Did you guys see that?" For the first time there was a grudging admiration in his voice. For the first time he had an inkling of what my life had been and he was genuinely shaken by it. Welcome to my world, Steve. This isn't some abstract editorial in the *Village Voice*. This is the real thing.

Nobody Calls Me Prophet

Nobody calls me prophet, nobody hears me call
Nobody calls me mister, I'm nobody's child at all
Nobody calls me brother, nobody calls me son
And nobody calls me prophet till my prophesies are done

Never been known to swear upon the gospel
But I've sure been known to swear by what I've seen
Never been known to know where I am goin'
But I sure been known to know where I have been
Sure been known to know where I have been

Somebody's life is wasted, somebody's war is won
Somebody's back is breakin', somebody's favor's done
Somebody calls me brother, somebody calls me son
But there ain't nobody calls me prophet till my prophesies are done

Lyrics by David Clayton-Thomas. Copyright © Lady Casey Music, 1972.

10

THE ORIGINAL BS&T

The power structure in Blood Sweat & Tears very much dictated how decisions were made. Bobby Colomby and Steve Katz were the sole owners of the BS&T name, and Katz's brother was our manager. In theory everyone in the band had an equal voice in the decision-making process, but in reality the business of the band was controlled by Colomby and Katz and everyone else was basically an employee. Relationships can be contentious enough in a four-piece rock band where every member is essential to the sound of the group. The Beatles without John or Paul or the Stones without Mick or Keith is unthinkable, but BS&T was a nine-piece band, and the individual members were less important to the overall sound. Still, in the original lineup there were certain members who were so talented that they were absolutely essential to the success of the early band.

In a horn band the arrangers are extremely important. It was their genius that was largely responsible for the unique sound of Blood Sweat & Tears. We had two very different and very gifted arrangers, Dick Halligan and Fred Lipsius. I liked and respected them both but for quite different reasons. Dick was a tall, scholarly, pipe-smoking academic. A multi-instrumentalist, he played most of the brass instruments, particularly trombone, and was a fine keyboard player. The Hammond B-3 work on the early records was Halligan's. Dick wrote the classic arrangement for "God Bless the Child." I loved his completely original approach to songs that had been previously recorded, like James Taylor's "Fire and Rain," Steve Winwood's "Smiling Phases" and Laura Nyro's "And When I Die." Jagger and Richards's rock anthem "Sympathy for the Devil" became a classical tour de force in Halligan's hands. Hindemith, Prokofiev, tritones, unorthodox voicings never before heard in rock were all part of the powerful musical arsenal of Dick Halligan. When a tune was presented to Dick, he pretty much worked alone. Once the key and the groove were established, he would disappear for a few days and the arrangement would come back completed—always perfect, always totally appropriate, but with very little input from the writer. I would hand Dick a cassette tape of a new song with a vocal accompanied by my guitar, and that was the end of our collaboration; the rest was all Dick Halligan. I didn't mind this arrangement. He was brilliant, and he made my songs better— that's all that counted. I had so much respect for Dick that I would give him this latitude. My personal relationship with Halligan was very much like our musical relationship. He was a shy, somewhat aloof man, hard to really get close to, but I liked and respected him.

The arranger I worked best with on my original compositions was Fred Lipsius. Most of my original material went to Freddie, who played alto sax and piano in the original band. He was a gentle, sensitive soul with an air of childlike wonder about him. Enormously gifted with an extensive musical education from Berklee in Boston, Freddie was nonetheless wide open to new ideas and musical experiences. He seemed to appreciate instinctively that what rock & roll musicians like me had to say musically wasn't being taught at Berklee but that even if we weren't conservatory-trained, there was worth and value to our ideas. This is a rare thing. Some conservatory guys can be a little snobbish about their musical education, and many dismiss self-taught musicians as crude, untrained and beneath their lofty musical standards. Coming into this band of highly educated musicians was a daunting and sometimes humbling experience. I was a saloon-trained rock singer, and musically I was in way over my head.

Collaborating with Fred Lipsius was like taking a course at Berklee. He was a natural teacher. No question was too dumb to be patiently explained. He was fascinated by the freshness of the ideas we relatively unschooled musicians came up with. When I worked with Freddie it was a back-and-forth collaborative process, with him sometimes calling me in the middle of the night bubbling with enthusiasm about an idea he had for one of my tunes. Where Halligan would pretty much ignore the guitar tracks on my demos and write his own interpretation of the song, Freddie would find a guitar line and expand upon it, often building an entire score from a single lick. A perfect example is "Spinning Wheel." I had cut a demo of that song in Canada long before I went to New York, and listening to the tape today I can really appreciate the genius of Fred Lipsius. Those signature horn lines were all contained in the guitar parts on the original demo. Not that Freddie copied them, he just realized that they were an integral part of the composition. He extracted them and expanded upon them and made the song infinitely better. He would often corner me in the dressing room before a show, his eyes burning with a fierce creative intensity, and shove a guitar into my hands. "Play me that lick again," he would say. "I want to see what notes you're using." Then he would watch my hands as I played the guitar part while he scribbled furiously on his score pad. "Damn!" he'd yell to the entire room. "You see that? A Berklee cat would never use those notes. He was taught how to play properly."

That was Freddie, filled with wonder at the way we self-taught musicians found ways to express ourselves. He was totally devoid of musical prejudice. He loved the creative anarchy of rock & roll. He went right to the heart and soul of the song. While Halligan was consistent and reliable, Lipsius was erratic and unpredictable and sometimes took weeks agonizing over a single idea. I appreciated the talents of both Dick and Freddie, and having two very different arrangers working on tunes gave a certain freshness and diversity to the band's music. When it came to working on my own original tunes, however, I must confess I much preferred working with Freddie. It was in some ways a painful process, kind of like collaborating with Vincent Van Gogh, but when the process was over the results were well worth the agony of the creation.

Then there was Lew Soloff, the quirky, eccentric little trumpet player who I used to room with on the road. I once called him, in my best Monty Python voice, "A horrible little man," a remark that Lew delights in reminding me of to this day. That was my relationship with Lew. I liked him and he knew it. We traded insults and practical jokes, hung out together and were friends. Onstage that "horrible little man" became a monster. He was and still is one hell of a trumpet player, with a fierce attack, a big bold tone and a huge musical vocabulary. Lew possessed that rarest of gifts in a trumpet player: he was a wicked high-note specialist who could also solo eloquently. There was a note written in the Fred Lipsius arrangement of "Spinning Wheel," a nearly impossible high double G at the end of the trumpet solo. That one note personifies Lew Soloff. Only a handful of trumpet players in the world could hit that note following that long, demanding solo. Lew took it personally. Glaring fiercely into my eyes over the bell of his horn each night, he would suck in a deep breath and nail it. It didn't matter if he was sick or tired or his lip was sore, Lew Soloff came to play every night. God, I respected that, and I loved him for it.

Jim Fielder was one of my favourite guys in the early band. A tall, lean, laconic Texan with a slow Southern drawl, his country-boy personality concealed a keen intellect and an enormous musical talent. He came to New York as a graduate of North Texas State University in the late sixties to play with Frank Zappa's radical experimental band the Mothers of Invention. I saw Jim in those days on Bleecker Street at the Garrick Theater with Zappa's band. That rhythm section, with Aynsley Dunbar on drums, Frank Zappa on guitar and Jim Fielder on bass, absolutely blew my mind. They affected a lot of people that way. This was some of the most radical music I'd ever heard. The tunes were bizarre and yet always musical. The band was unpredictable but amazingly tight and precise, and I thought Jim Fielder was the most original bass player I'd ever heard.

Working with him onstage was a joy. He was solid as a rock, had great time, was always consistent and at the same time was furiously creative. In the studio you could always count on Jim to insert just the right bass lick at the right time to make the song work. Offstage I bonded with him immediately and probably spent more time with him than with anyone else in the band. We were both basically country boys in the big city, Jim from Texas, and me from Canada. The rest of the band were native New Yorkers and had their own very New York point of view. Their humour was quick and cynical, their backgrounds full of stories about Yankee games, stickball and neighbourhood rivalries that Jim and I didn't really relate to. When I finally left New York and moved to Marin County, Jim wasn't far behind me. After five years in the big city, Texas Jimmy Fielder was still a country boy at heart.

Trumpeter Chuck Winfield was a fine player, but we were never that close personally. He played second trumpet in the original band, but any competent horn player could have played in his place. Soloff was the star of the trumpet section. Winfield hung with Steve Katz and they had little in common with me.

I had hoped, coming into the band, that I would be playing with Randy Brecker, a giant of a trumpet player who had been in the original lineup, but that was not to be. Upset by all the infighting between Kooper and Katz, easygoing Randy bailed out just before I got there and started his own band, Dreams. We became good friends in later years and I confessed to Randy that I had hoped he would be in the band. He told me that if he'd known I was coming, he probably would've been.

The original trombone player was Jerry Hyman, a sweet guy but not a great player. He worked in a bookstore in the Village and used to play with BS&T a couple of nights a week just for fun. When the band exploded onto the international scene, Jerry tendered his resignation. This wasn't what he'd had in mind. Jerry is now a successful chiropractor with a practice in Los Angeles. Musicians can be ruthless, and just like in any team sport, if a guy ain't cutting it, the other guys might not say anything but the whole team moves to the opposite end of the locker room. Jerry made the right call, and I respect him for being a man and not just hanging on for the money once the band hit it big. He walked away with his dignity intact. Jerry was replaced by trombone virtuoso Dave Bargeron, a great musician with tons of experience. Bargeron came in and gave the band an enormous lift. A powerful section player and a show-stopping soloist, he was just what the band needed.

My favourite Dave Bargeron story took place at Lincoln Center. The band was scheduled to play the hallowed Metropolitan Opera House, something no rock band had ever done. It was a controversial booking. There were many who felt that rock at the Met was a sacrilege. I had heard a rumour that Leonard Bernstein might attend the concert. I mentioned in an interview with the *New York Times* what an honour it would be to have Bernstein in the audience. The day of the show, there it was in the *Times*: "Singer David Clayton-Thomas says Leonard Bernstein will be at BS&T concert." Steve Katz went ballistic. "How could you embarrass us like that?" he cried. "No way Bernstein will be there." The night of the concert, many in the audience were still skeptical about BS&T playing the Met, and you could feel the tension in the air. Dave Bargeron had a trombone solo early in the show, stage front and centre, and sitting in the front row was none other than Leonard Bernstein himself. The young trombone player stepped up to the microphone, gave his slide a dramatic flourish, then did something I'm sure he had never done before in his life. He lost his grip on the slide and it clanged to the floor, right in front of Leonard Bernstein. There was a moment of stunned silence in the audience while Dave died a thousand deaths. As Dave bent over to retrieve his slide, Bernstein stood and gave him a solitary standing ovation. Then the entire theatre, as one, came to its feet and cheered and applauded.

Bargeron proceeded to play a barnburner of a trombone solo. There had been a somewhat stuffy atmosphere in the hall until that moment, but Dave Bargeron broke the ice and we went on to play one of our most memorable concerts ever.

That was the original band—an unorthodox mixture of rock, jazz and classically trained musicians that could only have existed in this radical time in history. It was an offbeat mix of musical personalities ranging from hardcore blues artists like myself to conservatory master's graduates like Dick Halligan and Berklee-educated jazz musicians like Fred Lipsius. We probably never should have been in the same band, but we were and somehow it worked. Much of the credit for putting this unique cast of characters together must go to Bobby Colomby. We envisioned a band that defied musical categories, and he had the musical chops to hold it together and the business smarts to make it all work.

It was a Greenwich Village band. Its roots were the Village Vanguard and the Bitter End. Its music came right off the streets of New York, an edgy blend of rock and salsa, the blues and jazz. The sound of the band was the sound of the city—the roar of the subways, the discordant blast of the taxi horns, the frenetic energy of the city sidewalks. This wasn't an LA band with surfer roots and a laid-back attitude. This was big-city music, hard-charging and fierce. When BS&T hit the stage, it was about as subtle as a punch in the solar plexus. All music was political in the sixties, and the politics of Blood Sweat & Tears was the politics of the Village, radical, outspoken and angry. It was the *Village Voice* and *Screw* magazine. It was demonstrations in Washington Square Park, kids getting their heads busted at Columbia University. It was Bleecker Street with its coffee houses and pizza joints. It was the East Village with its jazz clubs and junkies. It was New York City in the sixties, and you had to be there to understand what that meant. We were there, right in the thick of it.

We Were the Children

Went to the river and I came back dry
Went to the mountain and I climbed so high
Came to the city and I don't know why
Talked to the children, I just had to cry
The children dyin' and it makes no sense
A wicked bitches' brew of violence

Brother to brother, son to son
Sister to sister, I'm callin' out to everyone

We were the children who would save the world
Now we're livin' in a world gone crazy
We were the children who could stop the war
Now that war is ragin' round us every day

I lost my brother to a drive-by gun
He saw it comin' and he tried to run
Another mother lost another son
Just another number when the day is done
Another brother and it makes no sense
A wicked bitches' brew of violence

Lyrics by David Clayton-Thomas. Copyright © Clayton-Thomas Music Publishing Inc., 1972.

11

WOODSTOCK
AND MILES

Nineteen sixty-nine was pretty much a blur, a sensory over-
load with the media all over us. Overnight we were stars.
We came right out of Greenwich Village onto the international
stage, and we were the darlings of the New York press. I was on
the cover of the *Village Voice* and every concert was reviewed by
the New York newspapers and trade magazines. It seemed like
one night we were playing a little club in the Village and the next
night we were headlining shows at the Fillmore East, with Jethro
Tull, the Allman Brothers and Creedence Clearwater Revival
opening for us. We had the number-one album in the world and
the big-money offers were rolling in.

Three hit singles came from that first album, generating
enormous airplay worldwide. In 1969 you couldn't turn on a
radio without hearing a BS&T song. The first was "You Made
Me So Very Happy," a remake of a Brenda Holloway Motown
tune with a beautiful Dick Halligan arrangement. That was followed by my original tune "Spinning Wheel," BS&T's biggest-
selling single ever, then "And When I Die," a Laura Nyro song.
All three songs were in the top ten at the same time. In addition,
"God Bless the Child" had become an anthem for the activist
movement protesting the Vietnam War.

Young people in the sixties were becoming increasingly aware of the waste and futility of the war, and the band was deeply involved in the peace movement. Greenwich Village was the epicentre of the anti-war movement and we came right off the streets of the Village, so our music was adopted as a symbol of their frustration. Word was on the street in New York that something big was going to happen. We didn't know when or where, but somewhere in the New York area was a good bet. New York City was the headquarters for the music industry and music was the voice of the peace movement.

I'm often asked about my memories of Woodstock. History has painted the festival in bright colours, like a Peter Max poster—three days of love, flowers and peace. History has also conveniently marginalized the anger that drove 600,000 young people to march on a little town in upstate New York. It was primarily young people who were being brought home in body bags from "'Nam," and the flower-power generation had had enough.

The biggest acts in the music business were booked to play Woodstock, but we had no idea just how big the event would be until we flew into LaGuardia Airport that Sunday morning and found ourselves stranded, unable to get upstate to the concert and unable to get home to Manhattan. The New York State Thruway was jammed to a standstill from Albany to Kennedy Airport. Many of the guys had wives, girlfriends and families stuck somewhere out on the Thruway on their way to meet us at the concert. This raised the anxiety level even higher. It was doubtful that we would make it to Woodstock at all that night. On Saturday afternoon the governor of New York declared the festival a disaster area and mobilized the National Guard. The promoters immediately commandeered a couple of National Guard helicopters.

They feared, and rightly so, that if the artists didn't show up, the anger that ran just under the surface of this movement would explode and New York State would have to deal with a half-million pissed-off young people.

We had been on tour all summer so big concerts were nothing unusual for BS&T, but now the full impact of this momentous event began to register. Finally, after we'd been at LaGuardia for nearly eight hours, a bus with a police escort, complete with sirens and flashing lights, took us to a motel forty miles from the site. From there, a National Guard helicopter flew us to the concert.

It was a frantic scene of mud, drugs and chaos. We played to the largest crowd of the festival sometime after midnight on Sunday night. It was estimated at close to 600,000 people. We were dropped backstage an hour before our set. LSD, pot and hash were everywhere. I remember seeing Steve Stills and Levon Helm briefly backstage, but we were being hustled around by stage crews who were desperately trying to keep the show on time. An exercise in futility—they were already running hours behind schedule. The fences had been trampled by the thousands of fans who thought it should be a free concert, and backstage security had broken down completely. I drank some orange juice backstage, and I'm certain it was laced with something. By the time we stepped onstage that Sunday night and I looked out over that sea of people, I was on another planet. But who cared? Everyone else was too.

The managers were in screaming matches with the film directors about cameras onstage. No one was paying for their tickets. That meant there was no money to pay the bands and no guarantee that they would be paid if a movie came out of this. The promoter, Michael Lang, was holed up in a trailer trying to mollify a dozen angry managers. There had been out-of-pocket expenses to get their acts to the festival and the managers wanted their money. Under normal circumstances they would not put a band onstage until they were paid, but this was not an option at Woodstock. How do you tell a half-million people that their favourite act won't be appearing? There was always the fear that this thing could turn ugly. A few local cops and a handful of state troopers couldn't possibly control a gathering of this size, and no one wanted to see armed National Guardsmen turned loose on the crowd. The music was the only thing keeping a lid on the place, so the show had to go on.

The only leverage the managers had was to forbid filming until they were paid. Albert Grossman, who managed Bob Dylan, The Band and Janis Joplin, was throwing cameramen off the stage. The Band was on right before us. We hadn't seen each other since our Yonge Street days and now here we were, with two of the hottest bands in the world, at the largest concert in history. They were amazing, but Grossman pulled the plug on the camera crew. They were never recorded … Smart move, Albert. Bennett Glotzer and Dennis Katz, who managed BS&T, came storming out of the trailer and ordered the cameras turned off after our second tune. Another brilliant managerial decision. They cut us out of our moment in history because they wanted to be paid. Hey, they're businessmen—you can't take history to the bank. No money, no filming. The artists were very aware of the historic nature of this moment, but the business negotiations were out of our hands. We had 600,000 people to entertain.

We played an hour-long set at around 1:30 in the morning. It was a great show and the people showed their love for this New York City band. Blood Sweat & Tears was the sound of the city with its Broadway horns and jazz roots, and this was largely a New York audience. We were playing to our hometown fans. The band was on fire that night. After a thunderous reception and one encore, it was over. Following BS&T at around four in the morning was Crosby, Stills, Nash and Young. I caught their first two songs and then we were hustled back onto the helicopter. They were still onstage as the chopper circled out over the site and then we were gone. After CSNY the festival began to empty out. I'd wanted to stay and see Jimi Hendrix but he didn't get on until ten the next morning. Jimi's manager had insisted on him closing the show, another brilliant managerial move. By that time there were only a few thousand people left to witness his iconic national anthem, but at least it was filmed.

The remarkable thing about Woodstock was that in the three days of the festival, with nearly 600,000 people packed into that farmer's field, there was not one reported instance of violence. In spite of the rain and the mud and the shortage of water, food and toilets, in spite of the impossible conditions and with virtually no police presence, no one was murdered, no one was assaulted. That would have betrayed everything the love generation stood for. Besides, everyone was too stoned to fight. It may have been anger and frustration that brought people to Woodstock, but it was the music that kept them peaceful and the love that will be remembered.

Nineteen sixty-nine, the summer of love. It was the year of the mega-festivals. In Atlanta we played to over 100,000 people packed into a plowed field in the scorching Georgia sun. Some idiot spiked the water coolers with LSD, and long lines of ambulances were taking away kids who were freaking out and hallucinating. That summer marked the end of the giant festivals. They began with the best of intentions and gave voice to the frustrations of the anti-war movement, but the greed of the promoters was their undoing. The gigantic shows were unmanageable and years of litigation followed every event, so the promoters eventually gave up on them.

In 1970 we became the first rock band to headline the Newport Jazz Festival, another controversial booking. Jazz purists were opposed to this band with its hit records and rock reputation playing the premier jazz festival in America. We were well received but the concert ended in chaos, with tens of thousands of fans breaking down the fences and mobbing the previously well-behaved jazz festival. For years afterward the city refused to have rock acts at the festival.

Our appearance in Newport was followed by a cross-country tour with the other stars of the festival—Miles Davis, Cannonball Adderley, B.B. King, Thelonious Monk and Nina Simone. We travelled by bus—not the luxury coaches of today, but seated buses travelling from town to town … four big buses full of jazz musicians criss-crossing America. It was the Newport Jazz Festival on tour. In Ohio we were the Buckeye Jazz Festival. In Texas we became the Longhorn Jazz Festival, in Pennsylvania, the Keystone Festival and so on. We spent nearly six weeks on the road, packed into hard-seated buses without the luxury of bunks or private compartments, so it was inevitable that someone would get on someone else's nerves.

By the third week on tour, Nina Simone had a bug up her ass about me, a white boy, having the audacity to sing "God Bless the Child," a Billie Holiday song and a black anthem. At first I was confused and hurt by her attitude. I adored Nina Simone. I had listened to everything she had ever recorded and would stand by the side of the stage every night to hear this lady sing. She was one of the all-time greats and I desperately wanted her approval. Every night when she came offstage, I was there to tell her what a great performance it was and how much I admired her, but she completely ignored me, and after a few nights of being snubbed I decided that, legendary artist or not, I wasn't going to take any more shit from her. I stopped trying to approach her and a distinct chill developed between us.

One night after a great BS&T set I came back to the dressing room. The crowd was still screaming for more and everyone was complimenting us on a great show, but Nina was furious. She snapped at me, "What do you know about black pain?" I snapped right back, "What do you know about where I came from?" Nat Adderley stepped between us and told her gently that the song said "God bless the child"—not the black child or the white child, but just "God bless *the* child." Other members of the tour pointed out that the song had probably been heard by more people because we recorded it than had ever heard Billie's recording. That pissed Nina off even more. "This white boy's making all this money off a black woman's song," she said. She never acknowledged the fact that the Billie Holiday estate was making millions from BS&T's recording of her song. None of these racial overtones had even occurred to me. I idolized Billie Holiday and was just flattered that so many people thought I did her song justice.

The next day Nina sent a petition around the bus. It asked George Wein, the promoter, to remove the song from the show. I watched as the letter was passed around the bus. Big Cannonball Adderley read it, looked back at me, smiled and passed it on without signing it. It was then passed to Miles Davis. The respect for Miles even among this legendary group was unquestioned, and I knew him to be notoriously militant about black causes. "Oh shit," I thought, "here it comes." Miles read the petition slowly, got up and walked down the bus toward me. All eyes were on him but he walked right past me without even looking and stood in front of Nina Simone. He bent down until his nose was an inch from hers and said in his soft, raspy voice, "Nina, leave the boy alone." Nina just sat there in shocked silence. No one talked back to Miles Davis. Miles turned and walked back up the aisle, and as he passed me, behind his ever-present shades I caught just the faintest twinkle in his eye. The subject of me singing "God Bless the Child" was never mentioned again. For the rest of the tour, every time I sang that song I would notice Miles and Monk and Cannonball, along with several other members of our troupe, seated by the side of the stage. One night I was surprised to see Nina Simone among them. She was a woman of tremendous presence and dignity. She stood and applauded briefly for that one song, smiled at me and returned to her dressing room. Miles had made his point.

As the Newport tour continued across America, some really warm friendships developed. I became close friends with a couple of guys from the Cannonball Adderley Quintet, Roy McCurdy and Larry Willis. When "Cannon" died in Gary, Indiana, a few years later, Larry and I were at his bedside. Both Larry and Roy would go on to become members of BS&T. Willis and I toured the world together for over five years.

Growing up in Canada, I had never paid much attention to race, but the Newport tour was an eye-opener. The Nina Simone incident wasn't the only episode that brought home the reality of race in America. In the late sixties there were still huge parts of the States that were racially divided. Black musicians checking in to a posh hotel in Dallas, Texas, still brought hostile stares. Which brings us to my favourite Miles Davis story.

Behind Miles's serious demeanour there was a wicked sense of humour, and in Dallas I got a glimpse of the wit and intelligence of the man. We were in a tenth-floor hotel room one afternoon— me and Willis, Cannonball and Miles, along with some local musicians—just hangin' out watching some football. The locals had brought some cocaine. Suddenly there was a knock on the door. Someone said, "Who is it?" A voice said, "Police! Open up." Oh shit! The bag of coke went out the window, we hurriedly swept any evidence off the table and Miles opened the door. It was this goofy roadie from B.B. King's band, laughing his ass off … yuk yuk, very funny. We rushed over to the window and looked down. There on the roof of the cab stand in front of the hotel, hidden from view, was the bag of coke, still intact. Unfortunately, the windows over the cabstand were in the main dining room. Remember, many of the players on the Newport tour were black, and how the hell could anyone, let alone a black jazz musician, walk into the main dining room of one of the finest hotels in Dallas and casually climb out the window? For two days we pondered the problem. I would come back to the hotel in the middle of the afternoon and there would be a half-dozen heads hanging out the windows, staring wistfully down at the bag of coke. Then Miles had a stroke of genius. He sent a couple of the local brothers to a hardware store, where they purchased a pair of overalls, a mop and a bucket. They walked into the restaurant with their best Stepin Fetchit walk, climbed out the window, threw the coke into the bucket and shuffled on out of the dining room. I asked Miles later how he ever came up with such an idea. He said, in his soft whispery voice, "Hell, David, no one ever pays any attention to a nigger with a mop and a bucket in Texas." I loved that man, and from that tour on we had a special relationship. In subsequent years, when we had the chance to appear together, we always enjoyed a private chuckle about Dallas. Miles shared the bill with BS&T many times in the late sixties and early seventies—Madison Square Garden twice, Newport twice, several international jazz festivals. He loved our band and we, of course, idolized him. Once a jazz critic who was something of a purist asked Miles why he compromised his standards by appearing so often with a "rock band." Miles replied, "All I know is there were a lot of trumpet players out of work before this band came along." When asked what he thought of this new music, referring to fusion jazz, his reply was typical Miles Davis. He said, "There ain't no new music, there's only eight notes and two of them repeat." Miles had a gift for saying a lot with a few words.

We had many memorable concerts in those early years, but a couple stood out for me because they were in Toronto. The first was a pop festival at Varsity Stadium. It was my first appearance in my hometown since I'd left nearly three years earlier, and it was a triumphant homecoming. The kid who had been struggling in little clubs on Yorkville came home to 15,000 screaming fans in a football stadium. My face was plastered all over the Toronto newspapers, and my parents were in shock. My father, who had maintained for years that I was a useless, no-good bum and would never amount to anything, was suddenly silent. My mother, who always told me that I had a special gift and always believed that someday I would be somebody, was so happy I thought she would burst with pride. They didn't come to that show. It was a two-day festival, a mini-Woodstock. Traffic was jammed to a standstill for miles around the downtown stadium, and bringing family into that melee was impossible.

The following year we returned to Toronto to headline at a sold-out Maple Leaf Gardens. I invited my parents to that show and made sure they had VIP seats. The concert was a great one—we tore the place up. The crowd wouldn't let us off the stage that night. We came back for encore after encore. The show was nearly three hours long and I was on fire. I couldn't get enough. Backstage after the show Fred grudgingly mumbled something like "not bad"—high praise for him. He stood stiffly off in a corner of the dressing room, surrounded by throngs of young people clamouring for a few seconds with the star of the show. He looked uncomfortable and out of place among all these young rock & rollers that he had always referred to as "goddamn long-haired freaks."

My mother was the hit of the evening in the dressing room. Chatting with the guys in the band, press people, fans, she charmed everyone. She had always been a much more social person than Fred and tonight she was in her glory. I'll never forget my mum's face that night. She was literally glowing with pride. Later she pulled me aside and we had a private moment. She was a small, pretty lady barely five feet tall. She stood on her tiptoes and took my face in both her hands and, her eyes welling with tears, said, "You showed them, darling, you showed them. I'm so happy for you." Moments like this are worth all the standing ovations and encores in the world.

Lucretia MacEvil

Lucretia MacEvil, little girl what's your game
Hard luck and trouble, bound to be your claim to fame
Tail shakin' home breakin' truckin' through town
Each and every country mother's son hangin' round
Drive a young man insane, Evil that's your name

Lucretia MacEvil, I bet you think you're doin' fine
Back seat Delilah, with your six-bit jug of wine
I hear your mother was the talk of the sticks
Nothin' that your daddy wouldn't do for kicks
Never done a thing worthwhile, you're just an evil woman child

Devil got you, Lucy, under lock and key, ain't about to set you free
Signed, sealed and witnessed on the day you were born
No use tryin' to fake him out, no use tryin' to make him out
Soon he'll be takin' out his due, what you gonna do

Lucretia MacEvil, honey, where you been all night
Your hair's all messed up, girl, and your clothes don't fit you right
Daddy Joe's payin' your monthly rent
Tells his wife he can't imagine where the money went
Dressin' you up in style, evil woman child

Words and music by David Clayton-Thomas. © 1970 (renewed 1998) EMI Blackwood Music Inc. and Bay Music Ltd.

12

GRAMMYS AND GROUPIES

Blood Sweat & Tears was on a roll. In 1970 we attended the Grammy Awards at Lincoln Center. We were nominated that year for an unprecedented ten Grammys and won five. I was elected by the band to accept all five Grammys on their behalf, and the big one, Album of the Year, was presented by none other than Louis Armstrong, "Satchmo," himself. The entire evening was like a dream. Remember, it was 1970 and there was no shortage of booze and weed and coke backstage at the Grammys. Record-company execs kept a vial of coke on their desks in those days. It was one hell of a party and I indulged in everything. Girls were still crashing at my Chelsea townhouse a week after the event. I was young and horny, and after years of being locked up I really let it all hang out. A few years earlier I had been on my hands and knees with a scrub bucket in Millbrook, and now here I was onstage at Lincoln Center, with Louis Armstrong and an armful of Grammy Awards ... Man, this life is crazy.

Nineteen seventy was a year of incredible concerts. With three hit singles in a row and the number-one album in the world the promoters were all over us. We played gigantic stadium and arena shows and every one of them was sold out. Five Grammys, *DownBeat* and *Playboy* jazz-poll winners, the George M. Cohan Award (Entertainer of the Year), gold records ... The awards and accolades were flowing, and for a brief moment I really believed that my past was behind me. But one TV show showed me how wrong I was.

We were invited to appear on the *Dick Cavett Show*, supposedly to talk about the Grammy Awards. I was all prepared to talk about how honoured and proud we were when Cavett absolutely blindsided me. His first question was, "So David, I understand you have a prison record?" I froze like a deer in the headlights. I hadn't come here to talk about this. I mumbled "Yeah" and Cavett went in for the kill. "So what were you in for?" I was paralyzed. I didn't know what to say. The prospect of dragging out my troubled past on national television was terrifying. He sensed blood and went for the jugular. "C'mon, tell us, David. What did you do?" I just sat there and glared at him. Inside I was seething with anger. Why did the bastard have to bring this up? Now, in this moment of triumph, just when I thought those years were behind me? I was here to talk about our Grammy appearance and the great band I was so proud of, not the hellholes where I had spent my teenage years. I had pushed those places into the furthest recesses of my mind. I never talked about those years, even with my closest friends. If you have lived through this kind of horrific experience, the last thing you want to do is relive it. Now this muckraker was dredging everything up in front of the whole country. Cavett realized I wasn't going to answer. There was an awkward silence and he cut to commercial. I walked off the show. He's lucky I didn't break his jaw. Today, of course, I would handle it differently. I'd make a joke, snap off a cute line and deflect the interrogation. But then the wounds were still too fresh and I was too green to understand how the media operates.

For years afterwards I refused to do talk shows or live interviews. I avoided any situation where I could be ambushed like that again.

The Hollywood Bowl, Royal Albert Hall, Carnegie Hall, the most prestigious venues in the world were clamouring for BS&T. We were the hottest concert ticket in the world and it seemed like it would last forever. But politics raised its ugly head.

When the shocking news of the massacre of the students at Kent State on May 4, 1970, hit the papers, it galvanized the youth of America and the frustration turned to anger. Within days of the shootings, Blood Sweat & Tears was on the campus at Kent State playing a free concert to raise money for the families of the fallen students. Now we were more than just a rock band— we were part of a political movement, and that put us squarely on the government radar. The Nixon administration was extremely unpopular with the youth of Vietnam-era America, and "God Bless the Child" had become somewhat of an anthem for the anti-war movement. Every popular figure who was involved in the movement, from Jane Fonda to John Lennon, was considered a "dissident" by the administration and came under government scrutiny, but Blood Sweat & Tears had a weak spot. I was still in the US on a work visa, and that visa had to be constantly renewed. Furthermore, I was a convicted felon with a prison record in Canada and had previously been deported from the US.

So the State Department offered us a deal. If BS&T, the darlings of the underground and one of the most popular groups in the world, would do a UNESCO tour of Eastern Europe and ostensibly generate some goodwill for the Nixon administration, then I would be given permanent residency in the US. If not, my visa would not be renewed and I would be deported. They play hardball in Washington, and either we played ball or we were finished. It was a stupid idea. No rock band was going to restore the credibility of the Nixon administration with the youth of America. But they were so removed from reality in Washington that they really believed this would work. The problem was that they had us in a box: agree to their bullshit plan or find a new lead singer. We had no choice. Without me there was no Blood Sweat & Tears, and everyone in the business knew it. The State Department rationalized their idea by pointing out that American jazz musicians had done these cultural exchange tours for decades. Louis Armstrong would tour Russia, and the Bolshoi Ballet would come to America. Benny Goodman, Duke Ellington, Count Basie, everyone had done it. We would be considered cultural ambassadors and would be honoured in a high-profile send-off ceremony in Washington, DC. To their credit, the entire band except for Steve Katz stood firm behind me. Steve, the band's resident radical, felt that this open cooperation with the US government would cost us our following with the underground press. He had a point. The activist wing of the anti-war movement regarded any collusion with the government as a sellout, and we knew they wouldn't be pleased, but the way we were selling records, our image as an underground band wasn't going to last long anyway. With our hit singles all over the radio and with the visibility of the group in the mainstream press, it was hard to argue that we were still an "underground" band.

We had been used by the anti-war movement to promote their agenda. Now we were being used by the government to promote theirs. Steve may have envisioned himself as a spokesman for the radical movement, but most of us were baffled that a rock band could be the catalyst for such controversy. We'd been involved in protesting the Vietnam War and we were outraged by the shootings at Kent State, but we didn't consider ourselves to be political figures. We were just musicians. The guys in the band may have been solidly opposed to the war, but they were still loyal Americans and they were honoured to be named as cultural ambassadors. The jazz musicians in the band said, "Hell, all the jazz cats have done these tours. What's the big deal?" They didn't realize that rock bands in the sixties were held to a different standard. They put the issue to a vote. The band could have fired me and the problem would have gone away, but they elected to stand behind me and face the derision of the underground press. I attended the ceremony in Washington wearing a T-shirt with a large peace sign on it. The State Department people were pissed. They told me to get rid of the shirt and I refused, but the damage was already done. The counterculture screamed "sellout." The anti-war movement was furious at us, but we were trapped. Do this controversial tour or the beautiful music-making machine we had created would be finished.

Steve was right: we were a huge target, and the underground press turned on us mercilessly. We were accused by *Rolling Stone* magazine of collusion with the government and selling out to the establishment. The irony was that *Rolling Stone* was paying millions of dollars a year in corporate taxes. They couldn't exist without doing business with the government either. Now that's collusion … *Rolling Stone* was the establishment. What hypocrisy.

Rolling Stone was just the beginning of a barrage of bad press that seemed to come at us in waves over the next two years. Suddenly my political opinions were of interest to the press. I couldn't believe anyone cared about what I thought, and as a Canadian I had to very careful about criticizing America. I was, after all, a guest in their country and my status was tenuous at best. Until now interviews had been mostly about music. Now they were laced with loaded questions about the war and politics. Even my sex life was speculated about. As the most visible member of the band, I had attracted the attention of the media, and with my juicy past there was plenty for them to talk about. The media are ruthless. There's not a corner of one's life they won't dig into. In New York I became accustomed to the sight of tabloid reporters poking through my trash cans every morning. It seemed like everybody had an agenda, and overnight I had to be very careful about what I said and who I associated with. One such association was about to blow up in my face.

Like most rock bands we were surrounded by groupies. Young, good-looking girls were everywhere and we enjoyed them as one of the perks of stardom. In a way it was compensation for the high-pressure life we were living, and we regarded them as a reward for all the pieces of ourselves that we were giving to the world. Patty was one such groupie. I had met her in the Village when we were still playing at the Cafe Au Go Go. A curvy young blonde, she had already been involved with many of the rock musicians in the Village and in fact had dated Steve Katz before I met her. Bobby tried to warn me about her, telling me to beware, she was "bad news," but she was hot and sexy and I foolishly ignored his warnings.

Then the band exploded into the big time. Money was rolling in and I rented a nice three-storey brownstone in Chelsea. In spite of the warnings from Bobby, Patty moved in with me. I was seldom there in those tumultuous early days and Patty was spending money like water. It didn't take me long to realize that she was now the head groupie in New York. She was living with the hottest rock star in town, showering money and gifts on all her friends and still chasing after any celebrity that passed through town. She really was bad news. I broke up with her. She packed up whatever she thought was hers and moved out. I changed the locks on the Chelsea townhouse and thought I had seen the last of Patty, but no such luck. She had lost her meal ticket, and with nobody to pay for her party lifestyle she became incredibly vindictive, the groupie from hell. She would show up at all hours screaming obscenities in the street outside my townhouse and demanding to be let in. I kept the doors locked and refused to see her. Thank God I was out of town most of the time. I just hoped she would move on, find another rock star on his way up and leave me the hell alone.

On the day we were to leave on the highly publicized Eastern European tour, I met the band at Kennedy Airport. Surrounded by the press, State Department officials and fans, I was arrested by detectives from the NYPD as the band was boarding the plane. The timing was no coincidence: someone had orchestrated this. I was taken downtown in handcuffs and soon found out what it was all about. Patty had filed assault charges against me, claiming I had threatened her with a gun. The police had checked me out and again my teenage prison record had come back to haunt me. In their eyes I was no longer a celebrity. I was just an ex-con with a gun. I'll never know for sure how much politics were involved in my arrest. The Village radicals were outraged that we were cooperating in any way with the US government, and Patty certainly ran with this crowd. I'm sure she had plenty of encouragement in filing this totally bogus charge.

The police obtained a warrant to search my house in Chelsea, and of course they didn't find a gun. I had never owned a gun and that became evident also. Neighbours testified to Patty's screaming episodes in the street outside my house and the band rallied to my defence, swearing to the fact that I wasn't even home when this alleged assault happened. The police realized they had been duped and immediately released me with apologies. That, of course, was barely mentioned in the press. The next day I flew to join the band in London to begin the State Department tour, but the public damage had already been done. I hoped I had seen the last of Patty. Unfortunately, that was not to be.

Hell or High Water

Oh it's lonely late at night
When the rain is fallin'
Wonder where my baby is
I wonder if she's missin' me
It's a little too late I know
But you can't blame a guy for callin'
All I need is one more chance
One more chance
Oh baby come home
Oh … I promise, girl

Hell or high water
Push comes to shove
Next time I'll be there
When you're reachin' out for love
I just want to say I'm sorry
Baby come home …
Oh … and here's what she told me now
She said …

Can't put the ring back in the bell
Don't even try
Can't get no water from the well
Once it's run dry
And you can't take back the heartache
No matter how hard you try

13

EASTERN EUROPE

The Eastern European tour was at once sublime and ridiculous, uplifting and terrifying. In Yugoslavia the fans greeted us with peace signs and with tears in their eyes. They were so grateful that we were there. Our music had already penetrated the Iron Curtain through Radio Free Europe and black-market record sales. People would accost us on the street and clasp our hands with tears streaming down their faces, saying, "Thank you, thank you for coming, we never thought we'd live to see this, God bless you." The audiences in Yugoslavia were wonderful, standing and cheering and waving the universal peace sign, chanting, "Peace USA, peace USA."

The first three concerts, in Belgrade, Zagreb and Sarajevo, went without a hitch. The people were starved for Western music and showered us with flowers, encores and standing ovations. We were followed wherever we went by throngs of adoring fans and surrounded constantly by beautiful girls. We had a great time in Yugoslavia and we thought, "So this is communism? This ain't so bad. The people seem happy, the chicks are gorgeous, this is great. I'd like to come back here someday." Yugoslavia was the most progressive and democratic of the Eastern European countries. There were jazz clubs and a bustling nightlife, and the young people wore jeans and colourful shirts just like back home.

Then we entered Romania and we could hear the Iron Curtain slam shut behind us. It was a scary place. Armed soldiers were everywhere and we were tailed constantly by KGB types. We were told by the promoters to be careful: our hotel rooms were bugged and we would be under constant surveillance. In Bucharest I took a picture of a beautiful old bridge over the river. Out of nowhere came a couple of Party officials, who stripped the film from my camera. That was a "military" bridge and pictures were forbidden. The entire country seemed painted in shades of grey, stripped of colour. Even the lighting in the hotel seemed to be on half wattage. The people were grey, the buildings were grey, the food was grey. It was a dark and unhappy country. The fans may have been happy to see us, but the Ceauşescu regime certainly wasn't. The promoters had sold the idea to the government by telling them that we were a "jazz band." They were thinking maybe Dave Brubeck? Now they were pissed that the "jazz" concerts were turning into rock events. There would be no Woodstock in Ceauşescu's Romania.

One moment determined the fate of our appearances in Romania. We were to play two concerts in a gigantic sports arena in Bucharest. There was a dramatic point in our show when the lights were dimmed and Dick Halligan played a dark, almost *Phantom of the Opera* Hindemith-style organ solo all by himself in a single spotlight. At the end of his solo he would play a long crescendo reminiscent of the mangled chord at the end of the Beatles' "A Day in the Life." As the chord rose to its climax, I would stride across the stage with a large gong and throw it into the air. It would sail across the stage, and when it struck the floor the band would explode into the opening of "Smiling Phases." At the first show, when I threw the gong, the audience of 12,000 people went crazy. They rose to their feet screaming, "Peace USA, peace USA." They loved the complete freedom and anarchy of that gesture. It was pretty tame stuff, really, next to bands like The Who, who totally destroyed the stage at the end of their shows. But it was great fun, rock & roll theatre, and the audience loved it. The concert that night was sensational. The Ceauşescu government, however, was not amused.

The next day we were rousted out of bed in the morning and were escorted by uniformed Party officials to the Communist Party headquarters. We were taken to a large, heavily fortified grey stone building, where we sat for several hours on hard wooden benches in a hallway while the Politburo decided what action would be taken. Apparently my flinging the gong across the stage had struck a raw nerve with the Communist Party. In Romania such spontaneity was not allowed or tolerated. Many of the New Yorkers in the band were Jewish, and this was a frightening moment for them. Anti-Semitism was still very present in Eastern Europe, and to be sitting for hours in this cold stone hallway under the expressionless gaze of armed soldiers, completely at the mercy of a mindless bureaucracy, was terrifying. This is how it must have been for their parents and grandparents, many of whom were Holocaust survivors. Finally the government's decision was handed down. I would be allowed to strike the gong as long as it stayed mounted on a stand, but flinging it across the stage was absolutely forbidden. We thought this was hilarious. The Romanian government had deliberated all day over a fuckin' gong. The tension lifted and we laughed all the way back to the hotel. Surely they weren't serious! We were naïve. We had no idea just how serious they were.

We had a day off, then we were to play a second concert at the same venue. The gong had become a national issue. A photo of me with the infamous gong was all over the newspapers. Press people thronged around the hotel clamouring for interviews with the outrageous rocker who had thrown a gong across the stage. Would he throw it again tonight? became the big question. The gong had become a symbol of their yearning for freedom. Young people would come up to me in the street with tears in their eyes, begging me not to cave in to this government tyranny. "Please throw the gong tonight," they would plead. "Please. Please." We had a band meeting and came to a mutual agreement. They were not going to tell us how to run our show. This government inter-ference with our music ran counter to everything we freedom-loving Westerners believed in, and the fans desperately wanted me to defy this bureaucratic stupidity. The Jewish guys in the band were particularly defiant. Evidence of anti-Semitism was everywhere in Romania, from the empty, boarded-up synagogues to the frightened look on the faces of people we would meet on the street. They'd pull a Star of David from their shirt and whisper, "Juden?" their eyes darting around looking for informers. There was no "official" government policy regarding Jews; that wouldn't look good in the international court of public opinion. No, they were too devious for that. Jews were simply not given any meaningful employment by the regime and were consigned to the most poverty-stricken ghettos in Bucharest. At the band meeting, when he was asked to voice his opinion, the usually upbeat, wisecracking Lew Soloff had a look in his eyes I had never seen before. "Fuck 'em," he muttered quietly. "Fuckin' Nazis."

Backstage on the second night we were mobbed by media and fans. They were concerned with just with one question: "Will you comply with the Communist Party's edict or will you throw the gong for freedom?" When Halligan began his organ solo, a deathly silence fell over the arena. Will he do it, or will the Communists prevail? That was the issue on everyone's mind. I had no idea what I was going to do, but when the moment arrived and I was to strike the gong, everyone in that 12,000-seat arena held their breath. I looked out over the crowd of desperately unhappy young people, some with their hands clasped in prayer, their eyes pleading with me not to give in. I looked back at Lew Soloff, mouthed silently, "Fuck 'em," and tossed the gong across the stage. The place exploded with joy. The entire audience came to their feet and began cheering, "Peace USA, peace USA." Then all hell broke loose. The military government was ready for this. Doors slammed shut all around the arena, trapping the people inside. Suddenly, club-swinging police in riot gear were everywhere. Vicious attack dogs were unleashed on the audience. The power to the stage was cut and the concert ended in chaos. Dozens of young people were injured and maybe even killed—I may never know. I sat huddled on a bench backstage, devastated, crying for the havoc I had naïvely unleashed, crying for the young people of Romania. Jim Fielder threw his arms around me and hugged me tight with tears streaming down his face. "It's all right, David," he cried, "it's all right."

We were filming the tour for a feature film. National General Pictures and a crew of British cameramen were travelling with us. They filmed everything—the brutality, the attack dogs, the kids being beaten mercilessly by the police. The Romanian government wanted the film. They tried to intimidate the film crew, saying they had audiotapes of the crew in their hotel rooms with local women and threatened to expose them. The British crew laughed at them. "Go ahead," they said. "Can I get a copy?"

The next day we were escorted to the airport by armed soldiers and were unceremoniously kicked out of Romania. It wasn't funny anymore. The Ceauşescu regime was deadly serious about any demonstration of freedom in that desperately imprisoned country. They X-rayed the film cans at the airport. The National General guys raised a huge commotion. The cameramen were yelling at the impassive border guards, "You're destroying a million-dollar film!" It was a diversion. The guards X-rayed the film cans, but the Brits had already outfoxed them: they had switched the film. The real footage was already on the plane, loaded in earlier that day with their gear and labelled as blank film stock. They got the film out of Romania, but it disappeared after that and hasn't been seen since. I've often wondered where that film is. I guess someone thought it would be an embarrassment to the Nixon administration, who came up with this idea in the first place. A bloody riot was not what they had in mind when they appointed us "cultural ambassadors," so they buried it. Years later, when the people of Romania dragged the body of Ceauşescu through streets of Bucharest, I felt a moment of satisfaction.

On to Warsaw and one last show in a historic old concert hall. Poland was already hungry for freedom and democracy, and you could feel the Iron Curtain beginning to disintegrate years before the Berlin Wall began to crumble. Polish youth wanted blue jeans and rock & roll. Word of my defiant gesture in Bucharest had already reached Warsaw and I was welcomed like a hero. The audience that night was wonderful and we all reached down deep to deliver one last memorable concert. I have been to Poland several times since and that concert is still indelibly etched in the national consciousness. On the flight home I saw a look in the eyes of the band that reminded me of men returning from battle, an empty, dull look. We were done. We had seen too much and we were numb. It was a brutal, exhausting experience and the band arrived home emotionally drained.

Our next album, *Blood Sweat & Tears 3*, had just been released. It was already a certified million-seller and we had two more hit singles on the charts—another of my songs, "Lucretia MacEvil," and Carole King's "Hi De Ho." Columbia wanted visibility for their hit-making machine and our management felt we needed to overcome the bad press generated by the State Department tour, so instead of giving us a few weeks to recover and allowing the political smoke to clear, they took us straight into Madison Square Garden for a sold-out moratorium concert protesting the Vietnam War. For the most part the audience was supportive, but the concert was marred by Abbie Hoffman and a handful of followers carrying signs calling us "CIA pigs." They marched to the front of the arena and began pelting the stage with dog shit. They were immediately hustled out of the Garden, but of course pictures of the Abbie Hoffman incident made the news. Not the standing ovations and the encores from 15,000 fans, but this clown and his little band of radicals with their hands full of dog shit. Maybe it wasn't cool to be patriotic in the sixties, but after what we'd seen in Romania, we were so happy to be back home in the USA that we wanted to get down and kiss the ground. CIA pigs? It sounds almost comical today, but that's how it was in the radicalized America of the time.

The band had by now completely lost its underground status. The press hammered us and it hurt. The band that couldn't do anything wrong in '69 couldn't seem to do anything right in '71.

The band that had won three consecutive DownBeat Jazz Awards was now derided by the critics as a jazz pretender. The band that had won an unprecedented five Grammy Awards was now ridiculed by *Rolling Stone* magazine as "commercial crap." The band that had revolutionized the music industry in 1969 was solidly mainstream. Now, just like *Rolling Stone* magazine, we were a multi-million-dollar tax-paying business corporation. The jazz-rock band from Greenwich Village and the little underground music magazine from San Francisco had both crossed over into mainstream America.

Steve Katz may have been right about alienating the underground press, but he was dead wrong in assessing its effect. The kids out in middle America didn't give a damn about the underground press. In fact, all the publicity we were getting just brought them out to concerts in greater numbers. They were drawn by the controversy, saw a great band and went home to buy even more records. An entire generation may have been united in their opposition to the war, but the vast majority of young people were still proud Americans and regarded characters like Abbie Hoffman as left-wing nuts. In any event, our concerts were still selling out and our records were still topping the charts.

With the Vietnam War drawing to a close, the radical underground in Greenwich Village lost its focus and drifted aimlessly into the drug-riddled club scene uptown. It wasn't about the "cause" anymore. It all morphed into one big drugged-out dance party. Studio 54 and mind-numbing disco music replaced the Cafe Au Go Go and the socially conscious music of the sixties. The music industry itself was undergoing cataclysmic changes. The record companies that had cashed in on the anti-war movement sold out to giant multinational media conglomerates and moved their headquarters to LA. The big business corporations that were so despised by the flower children of the sixties had spread their corporate tentacles across America, and now they owned the music business.

After the Madison Square Garden incident and the Patty debacles, I wanted out of New York as quickly as possible, but Patty had one last card to play. She was pregnant and filed a paternity suit against me. Of course, for the right amount of money it could all go away. I honestly didn't know if I was the father or not, but I refused to be blackmailed. If I acknowledged the paternity I would have "the groupie from hell" in my life forever. I hired a high-priced lawyer and prepared to fight the suit. More bad press. By the time a hearing had been arranged, the lawyers had uncovered some facts. The timeline was shaky at best. When Patty got pregnant she was no longer living with me and there were plenty of other musicians around the Village who admitted to having sex with her during that time, so the case fell apart. It was thrown out of court and Patty was at last out of my life. I wish I had listened to Bobby and never got involved with her in the first place, but what's done is done. Thank God it was finally over.

There were two more paternity suits that year, both from women I'd never met. As word leaked out about my prison record, it attracted opportunists who smelled deep pockets and would trump up charges against me for anything, knowing that on a cross-country tour we couldn't come back to Podunk to fight a court case so we'd probably just pay it off. It's the cost of doing business in the big-money world of rock & roll. Even some of the guys in the band got hit by fallacious lawsuits. Of course, there was always a price to make it all go away. I was especially vulnerable. Anyone who goes into court with a criminal record has two strikes against him already, and the bottom-feeders knew it. It's not just a prison record that makes you vulnerable—any well-known person has to be careful. There are hustlers out there who will take any opportunity to get them into a compromising situation. We had a full-time lawyer to deal only with nuisance suits. Sometimes it's cheaper to just pay a few thousand dollars and avoid the publicity and expense.

Nothing in my life so far could have prepared me for the treachery and deceit that big money brings. In jail I knew who my enemies were. Now it was my friends I had to worry about. They could inflict the most damage and I'd never see it coming. I had all sorts of new friends. They told me that I was a musical genius and that I had to surround myself with people who understood how special I was. I knew it was all bullshit, but sometimes when you are buried in bullshit you can start to believe it, and in show business there are people who have bullshit down to a fine art. I was quickly learning that the trials and tribulations of my youth were nothing next to the complexities I was now facing. It was confusing and frightening, but there was no time to be afraid. I had to suck it up every night, step out on that stage and be a rock star. I bluffed my way through it with alcohol and the cocky bravado that had helped me survive in prison, but deep inside I was scared. Everything was spiralling out of control. I felt like a feather in a hurricane. I really didn't understand what was going on around me, and I had no idea how to handle it.

In a few short months I had gone from penniless musician to millionaire pop star, from a little club in Greenwich Village to Lincoln Center. I had been presented with Grammy Awards and lawsuits. I had been honoured in Washington, DC, and arrested in New York City. I had been tossed out of Romania as a threat to national security and welcomed as a national hero in Poland. I had performed for hundreds of thousands of people at the largest concert in history and I'd had dog shit thrown at me at another. Our music had been called "groundbreaking" by some and "commercial crap" by others. I had experienced triumph and tragedy. I had been praised and reviled, both totally out of proportion to who I was as a person. Trying to stay balanced in this storm of contradictory opinions was next to impossible. I knew instinctively that believing your own press was the road to disaster, but my image had become such a large part of who I was that it was all I had. I was desperate for some peace and solitude. I needed to make some sense of all this, but when you're caught in the follow spot of fame, there's no place to hide.

Last Chance

Come on, mama, let's get out of here, I know a place put a smile on your face
Days are lazy and the nights are clear and you won't find a prettier place
Sweet mama, come and take my hand, I think I'm ready to get out of the race
Let me take you to another land where the people live an easier pace

Headlines, deadlines, hard times
Don't mean nothin' down there
Slow dance, romance, last chance
Let's get out of here

Now it's a real peculiarity the way the sun puts a smile on your face
I just need a little clarity and everybody to get out of my face
Sweet mama, don't you be concerned about the world and the nuclear race
Here I am with all my bridges burned and a goofy lookin' grin on my face

I been thinkin' 'bout the life round here, it's about to come apart at the seams
Every year becomes another year, it's getting harder to remember my dreams
Sweet mama, come away with me, there's another world awaitin' out there
And we'll go sailin' on Brazilian seas with the sun and the wind in our hair

14

SAN FRANCISCO

I fell in love with San Francisco the first time we went there to play Bill Graham's Fillmore West. The city had an almost mystical quality to it, quite the opposite of the gritty reality of New York. I had visited Janis Joplin at her home in Marin County, and San Francisco seemed like a refuge where the New York press couldn't touch me. Janis and I had been pals since the first time we met at a Columbia Records convention in Puerto Rico. We were both on Columbia around the same time, played many of the same gigs and had a mutual respect for each other. I liked Janis. She was a hard-living, hard-drinking blues singer, but she was honest and plain-spoken and had come up from the same rowdy bar scene in Texas that I had graduated from in Toronto. We were kindred spirits and we both loved the blues. We were both a little rough around the edges but we understood each other.

In 1971 I gave up my brownstone in Chelsea and bought a lovely house in Corte Madera, a few miles from Janis's place in Larkspur. Actually, once we were neighbours we saw very little of each other. We were both on tour constantly in those days. We were seldom home at the same time, and I was more likely to run into Janis out on the road somewhere. But there was always a party going on at Janis's house in Larkspur whether she was there or not. Her doors were never locked and no one really knew who was living there and who was just passing through. Janis was a very insecure girl. She needed constant reassurance and had to have people around her all the time. She couldn't say no to anyone, and the local dirtbags took advantage of her generosity. Janis's place became a hangout for Hell's Angels, homeless Haight-Ashbury types, drunks and drug dealers. They stole her memorabilia and smashed her furniture, hocked her gold records, trashed her cars and conned her out of money. In the end she was a prisoner of her own entourage. I visited her in Larkspur one more time but it was an ugly scene. I never went back.

The Bay area was a lovely place to live in those days, still relatively unspoiled, with rolling hills stretching up into the wine country of Napa, Sonoma and Mendocino. Corte Madera sat on the slopes of Mount Tamalpais just a few minutes from the redwood trees of Muir Woods. I loved the redwoods. In the muted light of the forest, the ground soft and spongy underfoot, I found quiet and solitude. The gigantic trees seemed to put everything into perspective, dwarfing the troubles of the high-pressure world that I now lived in. The view from the deck of my house was spectacular, with the Golden Gate Bridge and the city of San Francisco looking like something from a picture postcard. I would drive up to the top of Mount Tamalpais and spend hours gazing out over the incredible vista stretched out before me. I found a measure of peace there, far removed from the madness that had exploded around me in New York.

California is car country. In New York a car was unnecessary, an expensive nuisance. Parking was always a problem. Cabs and the subway were far more practical. In Toronto I had never been able to afford anything more than an old beater. But in California a car is not only a necessity, it's who you are. You're known by what you drive. Here I developed a passion that would be with me for the rest of my life, a love affair with high-performance automobiles. I once joked to a Toronto newspaper, "I fell in love with fast cars from the first time I stole one." Just a joke, but not far from the truth. I can chronicle my life by what I was driving at the time, and my cars became an integral part of my life story. It all began with my first sports car, purchased soon after I arrived in San Francisco. It was a green 1969 Jaguar E-Type, a British racing coupe with a saddle-leather interior—a perfect car for northern California, nimble enough to handle the winding mountain roads and fast enough for the freeways. I was hooked. My favourite pastime was exploring the California countryside in my sleek Jag. Coming home after a whirlwind tour, it was a perfect way to unwind, and I loved driving. I even took a few courses in high-performance driving at the Bondurant School.

Then one day, while shopping in Mill Valley, I saw the most beautiful automobile I had ever seen, and my passion became an absolute addiction. It was a 1957 Mercedes Benz 300SL roadster. Sitting at the back of a dusty used car lot, a little banged up, covered in dust and with spiderwebs lacing the interior, she had obviously been abused and neglected—a queen who had seen better days. The graceful lines of the car, the aggressive stance, the huge white enamel steering wheel ... I knew that under the dirt and neglect she was still royalty. It was love at first sight. I bought the 300SL on the spot for $5,000 and limped her home, misfiring and spluttering. She was hopelessly out of tune and only firing on about four cylinders. I shipped her down to Barris Kustom Industries in Riverside, California, and had her completely restored to her former glory. Three months later I flew into LA and picked her up. The car was like new, the body cherried up and repainted, the engine totally rebuilt, new upholstery, convertible top, carpeting, everything done to factory specs. The queen was ready to rule the road again. She was a royal beauty turning heads wherever we went, but under that regal exterior beat the heart of a full-blown race-bred high-performance car. On the road she turned from an elegant queen into a snarling animal.

In addition to the five grand I originally paid for the car, I had spent over $10,000 on the restoration, a lot of money in 1971. I drove that car all over California. I'd come home from the road, throw an overnight bag in the 300SL and take off, tooling the powerful roadster along the winding highways of wine country or down Route 1 to Los Angeles. The car had no AC or power assist. Windows, top, steering, brakes, everything was hands-on manual. There was an AM radio but I never used it. With the top down and the wind whistling in my ears, the sound of that finely tuned engine was all the music I needed. A few years later, when I left California for Toronto, I knew the car would be impractical in Canada. The road salt and the harsh winters would ruin the beautiful roadster, so I reluctantly sold the Mercedes for $35,000 to actor Steve McQueen, who had a stable of 300SL roadsters and gullwings. When he died she went into the Harrah's auto museum in Reno, and I visited her there a few times. Thirty years later I came across the car again, at a classic auto dealer in Nyack, New York. They were asking $275,000 for her.

Jim Fielder, Fred Lipsius and I moved to San Francisco around the same time. We all bought homes in Marin County. Freddie, Jim and I were close friends, and we all wanted to get away from the pressure cooker that was New York City. The band had grown up fast in those first few years. All our illusions about show business had been shattered. That didn't mean we loved it any less—we were all hooked on performing—but we had become cynical about "stardom." These guys were serious musicians. The glitz and glamour of rock stardom was embarrassing to most of them. We were surrounded by bullshit and politics, and these were smart guys. They hadn't gone to Juilliard to be rock stars, but the money and the acclaim were hard to walk away from. The only thing that remained untainted by the business was the music, and we made some of our best music at that time. We clung to the music like a drowning man clings to a life preserver.

The next album was recorded in San Francisco in 1971. *BS&T 4* was considered by even our harshest critics to be our best ever. With Freddie, our arranging genius, Jim, the rock of our rhythm section, and me, the principal songwriter, already in California, and with the band battered by three years of high-pressure touring and intense media scrutiny, bringing the boys out to San Francisco to record seemed like a great idea ... and it was. We couldn't be touched out there. Even the native New Yorkers were ready for a break from the city. We enjoyed the laid-back feeling of San Francisco and even stopped the relentless touring while we were recording. The album was produced by Bobby Colomby and engineered by Roy Halee, the technical wizard behind Paul Simon's records. It contained another hit single, "Go Down Gamblin'." I played lead guitar on that one. The guys felt the tune needed a raunchy blues guitar, and Steve Katz couldn't play the blues to save his life. It was the last time I would ever play guitar with the band.

Again Katz and I would butt heads. I think one of the underlying reasons for the friction between us was that we both played similar roles in the band. We were both songwriters, but I was writing the hits. We were both singers, but there was no doubt in the public's mind who the voice of Blood Sweat & Tears was. We were both guitar players, and now Katz felt I was stepping on his toes in that role also. I was having enough problems with him as it was, so I gave up playing guitar with the band. I was much more useful as their lead singer. I enjoyed the freedom of being able to roam the stage and work the audience without being tethered to an amp. Besides, I was basically a blues guitarist, and the music of BS&T was now reaching far beyond the blues. I could carry my load as the lead singer, but the truth was I just wasn't versatile enough to be the full-time guitar player with a band who played everything from Monk to Mozart. Even though he'd never admit it, Steve Katz wasn't the right guitar player for the band either. He was way over his head musically. The band needed a Larry Coryell or a Mike Stern, but Katz owned the name and you couldn't argue with that.

We had a great time recording *BS&T 4*. The band was focused on the music and sheltered from the furor that raged around us in New York, but all too soon the album was done and the record company wanted us back on the road to promote it. The band was now under the direction of Larry Goldblatt, a smart and savvy business manager who had replaced the original managers, Bennett Glotzer and Dennis Katz. I was never privy to exactly why Glotzer and Katz were let go. There were stories swirling around the band about mismanagement of money, but that, like much of the band's business, remained between Katz and Colomby. Goldblatt presented us with a deal to play a week in Las Vegas, something that no rock band had ever done. With our counterculture status in tatters anyway, we all said, "What the hell, let's go for the money," and we signed to play Caesars Palace, the pinnacle of big-time show business. *Rolling Stone* again howled in protest, screaming "sellout." Most of us didn't give a damn. Caesars was offering us a huge amount of money, and by this time the so-called underground press was beginning to bore us. We had taken so much abuse from them that it was becoming a joke. We just couldn't take it seriously anymore.

Go Down Gamblin'

Born a natural loser, can't recall just where
Raised on pool and poker, and a dollar here and there
Blackjack hand, dealer man, better pay off that last bet
A two-bit hand of twenty-one is all I ever get

Go down gamblin', say it when you're runnin' low
Go down gamblin', you may never have to go

Down in a crap game, I been losin' at roulette
Cards are bound to break me, but I ain't busted yet
Cause I been called a natural lover by some lady over there
Well, honey, I'm just a natural gambler, but I try to do my share

Go down gamblin', say it when you're runnin' low
Go down gamblin', you may never have to go

Words and music by David Clayton-Thomas and Fred Lipsius. © 1971 (renewed 1999) EMI Blackwood Music Inc. and Minnesingers Publishing Ltd.

15

VEGAS AND SAMMY

Las Vegas in the sixties was a different place. The mob ran the town, and say what you will about "the boys," they ran the town with class. Frank and the Rat Pack ruled the showrooms, and you didn't get in to see Mr. Sinatra without a jacket and tie. The Circus Maximus room at Caesars was the most prestigious showroom in town. There had been a few attempts to introduce rock on the Vegas Strip, but to date they had never been successful. Rock acts may have been big with the young people, but they didn't bring in the high rollers, and that's how success in Vegas was measured in those days. The showrooms seldom broke even and they weren't expected to. The house count was all that mattered. The casinos made their money on the tables and they paid huge dollars to the acts who brought in the big money gamblers.

Show people were treated like royalty in Vegas. The top floor of the hotel was always the entertainer's suite. Artists in those days were booked into the casinos with long-term contracts and lived in those opulent suites for months on end. Anything the entertainers wanted was on the house … women, food, booze, everything was available on room service courtesy of the boys. We were even given money to blow in the casino. The bosses knew the presence of a celebrity at the tables would attract the high rollers.

Tickets for the showrooms were hard to come by. Not everyone could get in to see the big names. You had to know somebody and have the means to tip the maître d' generously. The best tables went to the highest bidders. There was real prestige in having a ringside seat at Caesars. The town catered to the rich and famous, and those lucky enough to get tickets for a show dressed for the occasion. The high rollers wore tuxedos and evening gowns. No T-shirts and flip-flops at Caesars. It was glitzy and glamorous, and the town will never be like that again.

In the late seventies Vegas went corporate. It became a big family-oriented theme park. Large corporations like Disney and MGM now owned the casinos and they ran the town with a different philosophy. The bottom line was all that mattered and even the showrooms had to earn a profit. Dress codes were dropped to sell more tickets, and today the once-glamorous showrooms are full of tourists in baseball caps and cut-offs. The high rollers gave way to old-age pensioners gambling away their Social Security cheques at the slot machines. The floor space taken up by a high-stakes baccarat table could be occupied by a dozen nickel slots. It's all about the numbers. In the old Las Vegas they didn't care if the showroom was full just as long as the high rollers were happy and blew big money in the casino. In this new Las Vegas they catered to the tourist, and show tickets were given away with the price of the junket. A million people dropping a few bucks each was worth more to them than a big spender dropping a few hundred thousand. We played Las Vegas in the last days of the golden era. It may have been sneered at by the underground press, but to headline at Caesars Palace meant you had arrived.

The engagement at Caesars was a complete triumph. On opening night the royalty of show business were present. For six nights we lived in a dream. The band was unbelievably hot and I was in my glory. Every night the audience was dotted with the faces of legendary actors, musicians and entertainers—Frank Sinatra, Bill Cosby, Dean Martin, Elizabeth Taylor, Count Basie, Duke Ellington, Sammy Davis Jr. Hollywood turned out in droves for BS&T at Caesars Palace. Backstage I was hobnobbing with people I had known only from the movies. Every morning my message box was filled with congratulations from the biggest names in show business. We were the hottest ticket in town. Conventional wisdom of the day said that rock & roll would never sell tickets in Vegas. That week changed the town forever. It paved the way for Elton John, the Rolling Stones and countless other rock acts to play Las Vegas showrooms.

I first met Sammy Davis Jr. during that great week at Caesars Palace. He was not exactly considered to be hip by the young people of the seventies, and when he came backstage after the show at Caesars I wasn't all that impressed. I knew he was a big Blood Sweat & Tears fan and performed several of my songs in his show, but everyone was doing BS&T songs in those days. A few weeks later the band got an offer to play the Greek Theater in Los Angeles, co-billing with Sammy. The show was to be billed as "Mr. D and BS&T." Some of the guys, especially our resident radical, Steve Katz, were dead set against it. "Sammy Davis just isn't cool, man. For Christ's sake, he hugged Richard Nixon. We don't need any more publicity like that." Most of the band felt that it was a great honour to co-bill with such a legendary per-former. Sammy really wanted to make this show happen and he seemed like a nice guy, so I thought, "What the hell, let's do it." After Eastern Europe and Caesars Palace our underground image was shot anyway.

The agreement was for two nights at the Greek, equal billing. One night Sammy would open and the next night we would. The first night I didn't really get to see his show. I arrived forty-five minutes before BS&T was to go on and was immediately sur-rounded by press and celebrities. Sammy's show had just finished. We went on last and brought the house down. We had just come off a record-setting gig at Caesars and a sold-out concert tour across the States, and the band was hot. We did two encores that night, and when I came back to the dressing room Sammy was waiting. He had watched the entire show. He gave me a big hug and said to me, "Wow! Thank God you can't dance." We laughed about that but I guess I was a little full of myself that night, with the dressing room crowded with movie stars and media. The next night we went on first and again tore the place up. After another killer show, again with multiple encores and standing ovations, I was thinking, still full of myself, "Let's see you follow that, little man." I decided to stay and watch Sammy's show from the wings, and I watched a miracle happen right in front of my eyes. That "little man" grew into a giant. He had the audience in the palm of his hand. He had complete control of the stage. He was unbe-lievably poised and graceful. He could dance, he could sing, he could act. Each song was a dramatic performance of heart-breaking intensity. He was magnificent. He was Sammy Davis Jr., and now I knew what that meant. He had spent his entire life on the stage, and he handled it like a master. He closed with

David in wartime England, 1943

Biker Bill—Bill Pugliese,
Willowdale, Ontario, 1962

The Thomsett family (left to right): Fred, John, Freda and David,
Willowdale, Ontario, 1948

Exclusive Acta Recording Stars

Ron Scribner Agency Ltd.
P.O. Box 277, Willowdale, Ont.

DAVID CLAYTON THOMAS
& THE FABULOUS SHAYS

The Fabulous Shays (left to right): Scott Richards, Brian White, John Weatherall, Fred Keeler and David, 1964

David and Duff Roman, 1964

With Rompin' Ronnie Hawkins at Le Coq d'Or, 1967

The original BS&T (left to right): Lew Soloff, Jerry Hyman, Fred Lipsius, Dick Halligan, Jim Fielder, Bobby Colomby, David, Chuck Winfield and Steve Katz, 1968

Deering Howe, 1971

California dreamin', Brentwood, 1973
(Courtesy of Gems/Contributor; Collection: Redferns)

*On a CBC-TV special,
Toronto, 1973
(Courtesy of the CBC Still
Photo Collection)*

*BS&T in 1976 (left to right): Forest Butchtel, Danny Trifan,
Tony Klatka, Mike Stern, Dave Bargeron, Don Alias, Bill Tillman,
Larry Willis and David*

The Canadian BS&T in Capetown, South Africa (left to right): David, Peter Harris, Bobby Economou, Earl Seymour, Lou Pomamti, Wayne Pedzwiatr, Bruce Cassidy and Vernon Dorge, 1980

David and Ashleigh, Rockland County, New York, 1983

Jennifer and Ashleigh, Newport, Rhode Island, 1986

Doug Riley (left), David and Tony Klatka, Beartracks Studios, Suffern, New York, 1998

David at the Montreal Jazz Festival, 2006 (Courtesy of Dominique LaFond)

James Taylor, Joni Mitchell and David at the Songwriters Hall of Fame, 2007
(Courtesy of Grant Martin Photography)

Ronnie Hawkins, Ashleigh, David and Ronnie's daughter, Leah, 2009

"Mr. Bojangles." As he tipped his hat and struck a pose, the single spotlight faded to black and there was a split second of silence. The entire audience caught its breath. Then the lights came up and he was gone. It was a moment of exquisite theatrical timing, and it hit me right in the heart. The Greek Theater erupted in a tumultuous standing ovation and I found myself applauding and crying uncontrollably, the tears pouring down my face. Next to him I was a bumbling amateur with too high an opinion of himself. I had just watched a consummate entertainer at work, and it was a humbling experience. I stumbled back to his dressing room, pushed my way through the crowd of well-wishers and grabbed him in a bear hug, still crying. "My God," I said, "that was amazing. You were incredible." I was probably a little over-the-top but I didn't care. I had just witnessed something very special and I had to know how he did it. Sammy freed himself from the embrace of this big awkward Canadian, smiled that lopsided Sammy Davis Jr. grin and said, "Come up to Vegas next week and we'll talk."

I did just that, the next week and many times thereafter. I sat in the audience at the Sands and watched the master at work. I got to know his musical director, George Rhodes, and Murphy Bennett, his stage manager. Most of all I got to know Sammy. He was a wonderful, generous man and he spent hours with me talking about the craft. I learned more in an hour watching that "little man" onstage than I learned in all my years of performing before or since. He invited me to his palatial home in Beverly Hills and we would spend hours watching old films of people I hadn't even been aware of. Sammy as a child with the Will Mastin Trio. The Nicholas Brothers, Fred Astaire, Gene Kelly and Judy Garland. Singers like Mel Tormé, Nat King Cole and Sinatra in his prime. We would study those films, with Sammy interjecting comments like "See, look how he moves, effortless. If you work too hard, you'll make the audience nervous. It's all got to look easy." Or about Sinatra he'd say, "Listen to his phrasing. He learned that from the horn players in the Dorsey band. You've got a great horn band. Listen to them. Learn to breathe with them."

I learned many things in those evenings with Sammy. I learned that there was more than just tricks of the trade to what he did onstage. It came from something deep inside the man. He didn't just sing a song, he lived it. When he sang "Mr. Bojangles," he transformed himself into Bojangles Robinson onstage. He completely inhabited the character. I learned that a song was more than just notes and words that rhyme. It was a story, a play with all the elements of a great script—characters and plot and drama. All the great songwriters, from Cole Porter to Bob Dylan, had this gift. They were more than just musicians, they were storytellers. I learned that being a performer was not just something you did, it was who you are, and if you didn't have that kind of commitment the audience would see through you instantly.

Years later Sammy was dying of cancer and was making a last personal appearance in Toronto at a private charity event. He was still giving of himself right up until the end. I caught up to him at the airport the next morning, before his flight left for Los Angeles. Murphy Bennett and George Rhodes took me to the first-class lounge to see Sammy. The cancer had ravaged him, and his diminutive body looked even smaller than ever. I wanted to thank him for everything he had done for me, but my eyes welled up once again. He put a thin, wasted hand on my arm, smiled that lopsided Sammy Davis Jr. grin and said, "I know, David, I know." A few days later he was gone. I often wondered why he gave so much of his time to a young singer, and something he told me has always stayed with me. Once I showed him a glowing review where the writer talked about me like I was the second coming. Sammy wasn't impressed. He had seen a lifetime of great reviews. He said, "David, there'll always be people to tell you how good you are. It's the ones who tell you how you can be better that you should listen to." Much later in life I would learn how rewarding it was to mentor young talent, to pass on the traditions and the knowledge that had been passed to me. If ever again I hear some young smartass know-it-all tell me Sammy Davis Jr. wasn't cool, he'll have to answer to me.

Fifteen Minutes

Must be wild in LA, well, TO's pretty much the same
I seen your face in the paper, seems like everybody knows your name
And your friends are all famous, just for what I'll never know
Ah but everyone loves them, on the late late late late show

There'll be stars in your eyes and a star on your door
There'll be guards round your mansion, but you won't live there anymore
Now you can sell your life story, reinvent yourself again
Spend the rest of your life just lookin' for fifteen minutes of fame

Now you can smile till it hurts and you can laugh away a tear
Make sure all your friends tell you what you want to hear
And they will all call you Baby and they will play games with your mind
And there'll be no time for thinkin' about the ones you left behind

There'll be stars in your eyes and a star on your door
There'll be guards round your mansion, but you won't live there anymore
Now you can sell your life story, reinvent yourself again
Spend the rest of your life just lookin' for fifteen minutes of fame

Lyrics by David Clayton-Thomas. Copyright © Clayton-Thomas Music Publishing Inc., 2007.

16

ELVIS AND EARTHQUAKES

I met Portland Mason that week in Las Vegas. She was the daughter of actor James Mason, and she was Hollywood royalty. I was introduced to her after a show midway through the week, and that first night we sat up until dawn holding hands and talking in the coffee shop. I had never met anyone like her— beautiful, smart, well-educated, with an easy laugh and eyes you could drown in. From our first meeting this elegant Hollywood princess with her Beverly Hills mansion and her Rodeo Drive clothes and this rock & roll hoodlum with his leather pants and reform-school education were head-over-heels hopelessly in love.

Portland lived with her mother, Pamela, and her younger brother, Morgan, in Los Angeles, while I was living in northern California, so I spent the next several months driving the Mercedes up and down the Pacific Coast Highway, Route 1, easily one of the most beautiful drives in the world. South out of San Francisco, through the redwoods to the rugged Big Sur coastline, with the Pacific Ocean crashing against the rocks, the seals barking hoarsely and the gulls wheeling against the incredibly blue California sky. The two-lane highway twists along the shoreline, sometimes hundreds of feet above the jagged rocks. The gnarled pines of Monterey give way to the fertile flatlands of the San Joaquin Valley and towns with exotic Spanish names like

San Luis Obispo. Down through the rolling hills and the palo-mino ranches of central California, the parched yellow hills gradually softening into the lush tropical growth and the palm trees of Santa Barbara. Then along the beaches of Malibu with their bikinis and sun-bleached surfers and on into LA with its freeways and its madness. This small-town boy from Canada had never seen anything like it.

Portland's parents were divorced and her father, James, was living in Switzerland. Nearly a year would pass before I would meet the legendary actor. My first meeting with him was both embarrassing and unforgettable. He was in LA for a few days and Portland and I arranged to have lunch with him at a seafood place in Malibu. Having grown up in a family of Brits, I was somewhat in awe of meeting the great James Mason and I was understand-ably nervous. All went well until I had to excuse myself to visit the men's room. I was attempting to wash my hands when the faucet came on full force, splashing water all over the front of my chinos. There I was with a large wet stain on the front of my pants and I had to walk back to the table. I looked around the washroom desperately for a solution and then I had it. On the wall was one of those hot-air hand dryers, but it was too high to reach with my soaking wet crotch. I didn't want to take my pants off in case someone came in, so I improvised. I pulled a trash can over to the dryer, turned it upside down and clambered up on it, frantically fluffing my pants in the hot-air blast. It was working. The pants were slowly drying. Then I heard the door open behind me. I didn't even have to look—I just knew. It was James Mason. He walked slowly past me to the urinals and as he unzipped his pants he looked at me teetering on the trash can apparently humping a hand dryer. With typical British reserve and in that trademark

James Mason accent, he said one word: "Riilly." I lost my footing on the trash can and fell on my ass on the bathroom floor. James burst out laughing and helped me to my feet. We returned to the table and, class gentleman that he was, he never mentioned the incident in the bathroom. We visited him later in Switzerland and James and I had a private laugh about my debacle in Malibu, but to the best of my knowledge he never told Portland about my pratfall. Like I said, a class gentleman.

When Blood Sweat & Tears played the Hollywood Bowl, Portland's mother, Pamela, the Grand Dame of Beverly Hills society, threw an after-party that was the talk of the town. I danced with Elizabeth Taylor, shot pool with Milton Berle, traded stories with Sammy Davis Jr. and received words of wisdom from Groucho Marx. I believe he told me, waggling his ever-present cigar, "Remember, son, money can't buy you love, but it can sure buy you a bunch of good-lookin' broads."

I took Portland on tour to Europe and we were mobbed everywhere by paparazzi. They tried to scale the balcony of our hotel in London. The daughter of James Mason and her rock-star boyfriend were big news in England. In the frenetic whirl of concert tours and travelling with Portland to Europe, Hawaii and New York, the house in Marin County was sometimes empty for weeks on end. Mostly I flew in and out of LA and stayed at the Masons' home in Beverly Hills. Finally, in late 1971, I decided to sell the place in San Francisco and move to LA.

I bought a beautiful home in Brentwood, a sprawling ranch-style bungalow in Mandeville Canyon. The house wrapped around a large kidney-shaped pool and sat on a lushly wooded hillside with orange and lemon trees and flowering gardens. The property was at the end of a short cul-de-sac and was very private.

Visitors had to be announced from the front gate, and the grounds were completely fenced. A red brick walkway wound around the pool and up to the lovely stucco-and-glass house. In San Francisco I had filled my house with Mexican-style furniture. I loved the solid rough-hewn look of the Spanish-oak pieces, and they fit perfectly into the house in southern California.

Having grown up with a kennel in the backyard, I always wanted to have my own dogs, but my nomadic lifestyle had made that impossible. Now that I was settled in a nice home I began searching for a couple of dogs to share the property in Brentwood. As a boy I had read a wonderful novel about an Irish setter called Big Red. I had always loved the handsome breed, so I bought two purebred setters, Lady and Casey. They were magnificent animals from championship stock, and I paid a small fortune for them. I brought them home as pups and they would share my life for years to come. Lady was an elegant, fine-boned female with a beautifully feathered copper-coloured coat and a gentle, obedient personality. Casey was a large raw-boned male close to eighty-five pounds with a big, bony head and a rambunctious nature, always getting into trouble. I called him "Knucklehead." I loved them both and took them everywhere with me. I bought a Ford surfer van with a fridge and a bed in the back. I'd stock up the fridge, throw some dog food and water dishes in the van and take off for days at a time, camping out with my two beautiful, high-spirited dogs, exploring the Big Sur coastline, the mountains of Yosemite, Baja and the inland deserts. I loved buzzing around Hollywood in the 300SL roadster, top down, with both dogs in the passenger seat, noses in the air, their ears flapping in the breeze. I purchased the dogs with an agreement that the breeder would be allowed to show them. They were from a long line of championship show dogs, and soon my home in Brentwood was filled with blue rib-bons and "Best of Show" trophies from all over California.

Brentwood was a small slice of paradise and I should have been in heaven out there. I had all the trappings of stardom. Several flashy cars, including an SS Camaro and a Jensen Interceptor, had joined the 300SL and the camper van in my garage. I had a beautiful home furnished in Spanish oak, com-plete with a billiard room, a studio and a home office, the walls covered with gold records and awards. I should've been happy but I wasn't. The entire music industry had relocated from New York to Los Angeles in the early seventies, and the idyllic landscape of lush vegetation and palm trees disguised a seamy underbelly of ruthless show-business politics. Returning home to LA after high-pressure concert tours gave no respite from the business. It was like jumping from the frying pan into the fire. It's one thing to visit LA, but living there for the rest of your life is something else entirely. All the clichés are true. It's a meat market, a town full of users and phonies attracted to the money and glamour of the stars. The super-famous are so isolated by their fame that they surround themselves with an entourage of ass-kissers. There is a virtual industry of ass-kissers in Hollywood. They determine your position on the "A" party list ("Oh, you weren't at Elton's party, but darling, everybody who is anybody was there"). It's an unreal town, and at this point in my life, although I didn't realize it at the time, I had a tenuous hold on reality.

One sad, funny story stands out as a microcosm of how fame can corrupt absolutely and how far from reality you can get when you are surrounded by people who tell you only what you want to hear. It was 1972 and the band was in town to tape the *Andy Williams Show* at the CBS sound stage on Beverly Boulevard.

Word was all over the studio that Elvis Presley was in the building, and everybody was trying to catch a look at the legend. He was surrounded by heavy security and the floor he was working on was off limits to everyone. Even the elevator was fixed to not stop at that floor without a special key. At the coffee machine I ran into a musician I knew from Memphis. His name was Ronnie Tutt, and he was Elvis's drummer. I asked him what it was like to work and travel with "the King." He said it was a totally unreal world—there were no words to describe it. He looked at his watch and said, "You want to know what it's like? C'mon, I want to show you something." Ronnie led me down to the loading docks where the heavy equipment was brought into the studio. It was an enormous room with twenty-foot doors that could roll up to accommodate tour buses and tractor-trailers. We stood in a dimly lit stairwell where we couldn't be seen and Ronnie said, "Shhh, now watch this." There were two black Cadillac stretch limos parked in the garage with uniformed drivers by the doors. A door at the back of the dock opened, and there was Elvis, with the trademark sideburns, the "Elvis" sunglasses, the white jump-suit with the turned-up collar, surrounded by bodyguards, who hustled him into the back of one limo. About four of the body-guards jumped into the car, the huge doors rolled up and the limo screeched out the building and hung a right onto Beverly Boulevard. "Wow," I said to Ronnie. "That's impressive." Ronnie said, "No, you don't get it. That wasn't him. That was the decoy." A moment later Elvis himself appeared, surrounded by the familiar faces of the "Memphis Mafia," with Colonel Tom Parker at his side. He got into the second limo and hunkered down. A blanket was drawn over him to protect him from the prying eyes of the paparazzi and hysterical fans. The bodyguards got in the back with Elvis, the Colonel got in the front seat, and again the doors rolled up and the limo peeled out of the building, this time taking a hard left, and Elvis was gone. I said to Ronnie Tutt, "The poor guy can't go anywhere." Ronnie laughed. "David, you still don't get it. There's nobody out there." We walked out into the parking lot, and sure enough it was deserted except for a couple of little old ladies waiting for Carol Burnett's autograph. They had staged this elaborate security charade for so long that it had become a way of life. I wonder how long the King stayed huddled under that blanket before Colonel Tom told him, "It's all right, son, it's safe now."

That's just how it is in Hollywood, a complete fantasyland. I wonder today why there wasn't one person in Michael Jackson's entourage, one person he could trust, who could tell him, "That's enough, Mike, the nose looks fine." My heart goes out to the young girl singers who go from the Mickey Mouse Club directly into that meat grinder called Hollywood, and then people wonder why, with all their money and success, their lives go spinning out of control. When your whole worth is measured on the Richter scale of fame and publicity, who can you trust to keep your feet on solid ground?

In 1972 I experienced my first earthquake and it scared the hell out of me. I woke up one morning and immediately sensed that something was different. My dogs, who usually slept at the foot of my bed, were nervously pacing the room, the hair on their backs standing on end, their ears laid back. Casey was growling, a low rumble deep in his chest. Something was wrong and the dogs knew it first. The usual early-morning cacophony of birds and insects was absent. The sky outside my bedroom window was a strange mustard colour and the leaves on the trees were etched against the sky, motionless. The air was heavy and everything was deathly still.

Then BOOM! The first shock hit. Dishes crashed off the shelves in the kitchen and pictures flew off the walls. My bed jumped a foot off the floor and heavy oak furniture shuddered across the room. I jumped out of bed and ran into the front yard, the earth shaking under my feet. The water in the pool sloshed over the deck, the water level dropping instantly by a foot. I fell to my knees on the lawn and gathered the dogs in my arms, looking frantically for something to hang on to, but everything was shaking and moving. Nothing was stable. It was like trying to stay balanced on a bowl of Jell-O. There were several after-shocks and then it was over. I walked back into the house. It was a mess. Broken glass and dishes were everywhere, pieces of furniture had been thrown clear across the room, my heavy slate-bedded pool table had moved six feet across the room and was jammed against the wall. There were cracks in the walls and ceilings and several windows were broken. A large armoire containing my TV and stereo equipment had toppled over and smashed a couple of my guitars. The phones were dead and the power was out, so I sat in the yard and hugged my dogs. They were shaking and whining, and soon the sirens and flashing lights of the rescue services appeared on my street. It took months to repair the damage to the house and some precious memorabilia was lost forever. One of the guitars had been with me since my Yorkville days and now was reduced to kindling.

To me the '72 California earthquake was symbolic of how far from home I really was. In Canada the solid granite rocks of Muskoka and the hundred-year-old pines hadn't changed since my grandfather had settled that country. In California nothing was solid—my life, my relationships, my home. Even the ground under my feet couldn't be depended on to remain stable. I think I knew, from that moment on, that I wouldn't be spending the rest of my life in LA. I needed the stability of the east coast. I missed the changing of the seasons, the buds blooming in the spring, the warm summers on the Muskoka lakes, the leaves turning in the fall. I even missed the crisp, cold Canadian winters, the hockey games, the evenings by a crackling fire, the snow heavy on the pines outside my window. I missed New York, with its gruff no-bullshit people, the pizza joints, the Broadway shows and the jazz clubs in the Village. The perfect unchanging California climate was beginning to depress me. Every day was just like the next. My body was tuned to the changing seasons and I missed them. Most of all, I missed the people I had known all my life. They weren't impressed by fame and gold records. I was still just Dave from Willowdale. Their advice was solid and dependable, untainted by show-biz politics and the A-list party scene. The California quake shook me to my core, and I knew beyond a doubt that I wouldn't last out there.

Yesterday's Music

Opened my eyes, early this mornin'
And I found myself all alone
Sweet tastin' midnight, still on my tongue
And a touch of tomorrow in my bones

Opened my eyes early this mornin'
And whole round world was turnin' cold
Sweet tastin' midnight still on my tongue
Was it borrowed, was it bought or was it sold

I can still hear yesterday's music, it's the same old, same old melody
Someone belongs to everyone and no one belongs to me
I can still hear yesterday's music, it's the same old, same old melody
Someone belongs to everyone and no one belongs to me

17

THE SPLIT

Portland Mason was completely at ease in Beverly Hills while I was way out of my element. She played the celebrity game with the best in her own carefully controlled environment. The phonies never got past the gates of her Beverly Hills mansion. People like Portland and Sammy were born to celebrity. It's all they'd ever known and they handled it well. I was still a relative newcomer to the game and I had a lot to learn. Hollywood is all about "the Business." It's the only thing that matters in that town—everybody has an agenda. It becomes impossible to know who's for real and who is just playing you. After a while I just didn't trust anyone anymore, and that's no way to live. Not only was Portland at home in Hollywood, but she was uncomfortable anywhere else. In LA she was protected by her family's money and status. She could never be happy in Toronto or New York and I couldn't imagine spending the rest of my life in Los Angeles. I was really beginning to miss the east coast. In New York I could always drive up to Bill's house for a few days, hang out with Doc or visit my mum, but on the west coast I was lost. I was a long way from home.

At the same time a difficult situation was developing in the band. With Freddie and Jim still in San Francisco and the New York guys all living in the affluent suburbs with their wives and families, the band was coming apart. It wasn't the same as when we all lived in Manhattan and hung out together every day.

Furthermore, I'd been fronting the band for three years and had contributed greatly to their success and yet I was still basically an employee. The ownership of the name was still in the hands of Katz and Colomby. I had approached them many times about being included as a full partner but could never seem to pin them down to a firm answer. Steve Katz, in fact, wanted me gone. He felt that the Eastern European tour had cost us our counter-culture following and that I had brought too much bad press to the band. He wasn't wrong on either count. The State Department tour had cost us our underground status, but then so had selling twenty million records. The band had taken on a world of problems when they elected to go with an ex-con Canadian with a checkered past, but it was my songs and my performance onstage every night that helped vault them into international stardom. There were some who believed that I was the band's downfall and others who thought that without me they'd still be playing on Bleecker Street. I guess there was validity to both points of view.

I wish I had a "Brady Bunch" upbringing and that my immigration status and my criminal record hadn't forced the band into so many difficult situations, but on the other hand you didn't find the passion and soul I brought to the band on *The Brady Bunch*. That was tempered in the fire of a brutal childhood, the despair of prison life and the years of singing in tough bars on Yonge Street.

There was no love lost between me and Steve Katz. He never wanted me in the band in the first place and I thought the band deserved a much better guitar player than he was, but we both brought something special to the band, and who knows—without my voice and Steve's business connections, maybe it all would never have happened. There are so many variables in this business, including just being in the right place at the right time. My animosity toward Steve has softened over the years and I have come to realize that I probably owe as much to him as he does to me, but at the time, in the heightened emotion of our larger-than-life existence, we really got on each other's nerves. Bobby tried to ease the friction between me and Katz but that was impossible. We just didn't like each other.

Things were complicated further by our own out-of-control egos. With the band riding high on the charts, everyone seemed to be knee-deep in ass-kissers who were telling them whatever they wanted to hear. "It's your guitar playing that made the band what it is, Steve," or "Clayton-Thomas was nothing until he met you, Bobby." I was surrounded by people in LA who were telling me, "You're the star, David, you don't need those guys." And we all began to believe the bullshit.

I was the most visible member of the band, and for anyone who wanted to take a shot at the big target that was BS&T, I was the bull's-eye. The other guys could retire to the anonymity of their country estates between gigs and nobody knew who they were, but I was the voice and the face of Blood Sweat & Tears, and I was out there in the public eye all the time. As the royalty cheques began to roll in from the millions of record sales and the airplay we were getting around the world, it became apparent that as the principal songwriter I was making more money than the rest of the guys. That fuelled the resentment in some quarters even more. Technically, Steve Katz was still my boss, but I was making a lot more money than he was and Katz hated that.

Larry Goldblatt openly sided with me when it came to the issue of a partnership, which didn't endear him to Steve Katz. Larry believed that if they didn't cut me in, it was only a matter of time before I walked, and that would be the end of the band. Katz maintained that replacing me would cause no more problems than replacing a horn player. But Larry dealt directly with the promoters every day and he knew who was carrying the show night after night—and it wasn't Steve Katz. Goldblatt was also advising the band to slow down and be more selective in our bookings. He felt that we were in danger of overexposing ourselves and that the band would have more longevity if we just backed off on the touring for a while and focused more on recording. He pointed out that after our first blockbuster album, it took nearly three years to complete the next one due to touring commitments. During that time Chicago had pumped out three albums and had eclipsed us in record sales. Goldblatt advised taking fewer gigs and getting back into the studio.

Steve Katz played this political card for all it was worth. He knew the majority of the band would never agree to less touring. They were making their money on the road and they had bills to pay. He also knew that the relentless touring was wearing me down. My voice was taking a terrible pounding. We didn't have the sophisticated monitor systems that we have today. BS&T was a big belting band and we were playing arenas and stadiums. Some days I couldn't talk until late afternoon and then I would croak my way through the show that night, my voice hoarse and ragged. I lived with the constant fear that I would step out onstage one night in front of thousands of people and my voice would be gone. Finally I gave Colomby and Katz an ultimatum. I was tired of being an employee: I wanted in. I needed to have a voice in the decision making. The band had to slow down or I was leaving. This, of course, was exactly what Steve Katz wanted.

The band split into two distinct factions. One side, led by Katz, wanted to tour even more aggressively. If I couldn't handle it, they'd find someone who could. The other faction was led by Bobby Colomby and Larry Goldblatt. They knew you don't replace a lead singer like you would a horn player. Colomby told Katz, in no uncertain terms, "If David leaves, we're in trouble. In the public mind he is Blood Sweat & Tears." Goldblatt told him flatly, "The act just isn't bookable without David." The majority of the band sided with Colomby and Goldblatt, but Katz was relentless. He was politicking constantly to replace me, and I began drinking heavily. At the time it seemed to be the only way I could numb the tensions swirling around me and pump myself up for the shows. The bad habits I had picked up in the bars on Yonge Street were now threatening to destroy me. Of all the drugs I've used in my life, liquor is the most destructive. I felt like I was losing my grip on everything that mattered to me. Blood Sweat & Tears, the crowning achievement of my life, was tearing itself apart. The love of my life, Portland Mason, was slipping away from me and I felt powerless to stop either. I had money in the bank, a hefty royalty income and a million-dollar home in Brentwood that I never lived in. I was burning out but there was no stopping the money-making machine that was Blood Sweat & Tears.

We were on the road constantly. It was out of control. Nobody cared about the future of the band anymore. It was every man for himself. I had my songwriting royalties and Bobby and Steve owned the name, but everybody else earned 100 per cent of their money on the road. I think the rest of the guys sensed the end coming and wanted to get as much money out of the band as they could before it collapsed, so they opted for even more touring. We went through the concerts on cruise control, but the tensions in the band crept into the music and the gigs weren't fun anymore.

Finally, late in 1972, I gave my notice. I had a talk with Bobby after a gig in New Orleans and met with Clive Davis a few days later in San Francisco. I told them that I couldn't go on. Katz and his cronies were getting to me, and the brutal tour schedule was killing me. I was burned out and I needed a break. If Lew's lip gave out or one of the guys had a family obligation, they just sent in a sub for a few days and the show went on, but I had to be there for every concert and, like I said, the shows weren't fun anymore. As for ownership in the band's name? Well, that just wasn't going to happen. Bobby might have elected to cut me in, but Steve Katz … never. He had considerable influence, given his ownership in the name, and he was happy to see me go. He got rid of Al Kooper and now was getting rid of me.

Even though I had officially quit the band, there were still months of gigs that had to be played out, contracts that had to be honoured. I wish I could have just walked away clean but it wasn't that simple. My split with the band tore it right down the middle. Larry Goldblatt told Katz and his friends that they were committing career suicide. If I left he couldn't book the band anymore. The promoters simply wouldn't buy a BS&T without David Clayton-Thomas. Goldblatt tried to convince them to give me a break from the road for a while and maybe this disaster could be averted. Steve Katz began a campaign to get rid of Larry too, accusing him of embezzling money and manipulating me. I saw no evidence of Goldblatt mishandling money and, if anything, Larry was trying to hold the band together. He knew we would both pay a huge price if I left. DCT without BS&T was just as hard to book as BS&T without DCT. But Goldblatt also knew that there was no way he could change my mind. I was exhausted and things had already gone too far. He made a last-ditch effort to save the band from itself, called a meeting without me and advised Colomby and Katz to cut me in as a full partner. Of course if they did that, then everybody would want a piece, and that just wasn't going to happen. He also advised the band one more time to cut back on their touring. He was fired.

After I left, Colomby and Katz continued their war for control of the BS&T name and eventually Colomby won. I presume he paid Katz off. Now he was the sole owner of a million-dollar trademark that was practically worthless without the voice that sang all those hits. Before he left, Katz complained to *DownBeat* magazine, "No matter how interesting we tried to make the music the audience still wanted to hear David Clayton-Thomas." Larry Goldblatt had tried to tell him this would happen and he was fired for his trouble. My closest friends in the band, Jim Fielder, Lew Soloff and Freddie Lipsius, told Bobby that there was no BS&T without me, and they quit also. That began an exodus that eventually included Dick Halligan and Chuck Winfield. In a few short months all that was left of Blood Sweat & Tears was Bobby Colomby, a trombone player and a name.

Bobby and I had begun production earlier that year on a solo album for Columbia. I think they felt if they gave me a solo project it would stop me from leaving BS&T. But a solo career wasn't the problem. I would have been happy to play with the band forever if I had some share in its future. It was Steve Katz and the brutal tour schedule that drove me to quit. When I gave my notice, Bobby turned the half-finished project over to LA producer Joel Sill and turned his attention to trying to salvage what was left of Blood Sweat & Tears. My solo album was released on Columbia but it received little attention. Clive had decided to back the new BS&T. Bobby recruited a new band and recorded an album entitled *New Blood*. He brought in heavyweight jazz players like Joe Henderson, Don Alias and Larry Willis. The musicianship in Colomby's new band was superb. He could afford to hire the best players in the business, but they never managed to find a singer with a really distinctive sound and the record tanked.

I returned to LA and tried to get my life back together. I had broken up with Portland, split with BS&T and was alone and isolated with my beautiful Irish setters and my million-dollar home in Brentwood. I wanted to leave LA, but I was too exhausted by the drama of the past few months to even think about selling the house and starting all over again. I just wanted to stay in one place for a while.

Larry Goldblatt moved to LA and became my manager. We put together a small band made up of some of the top session players in town, and I brought in a couple of old friends from Toronto, guitarist Kenny Marco and keyboard player William "Smitty" Smith from the Canadian band Motherlode. Smitty and I wrote a bunch of new tunes at the house in Brentwood and recorded a very funky album for Columbia called *Tequila Sunrise*. Goldblatt hooked me up with producer Mike Post, later of *Hill Street Blues* fame. They felt I needed to establish a different sound, since BS&T was still out there touring and recording, so they decided not to use the trademark BS&T horn section on this album—in retrospect, probably not a wise decision. The public was used to the sound of my voice with that big brassy sound, and Columbia wasn't ready for a new direction. They wanted another Blood Sweat & Tears and had already decided to put their money behind Bobby and that million-dollar name. Columbia dropped my contract.

Larry negotiated a new deal with RCA and we recorded an album called *Harmony Junction*. It was a fine album, but it was overshadowed by the knowledge that I was losing my friend and manager. Larry Goldblatt had never been in the best of health. He suffered from diabetes and a multitude of other health problems and he never truly recovered from being fired by BS&T. As the manager of one of the biggest acts in show business he had been a power player. Now people weren't returning his phone calls. Rumours of him being fired for embezzling money were swirling around the business. They were completely untrue but people love to talk. The fight to clear his name and establish a solo career for me was just too much for him. His health was deteriorating rapidly. One of the last deals Larry cut for me was for an unforgettable week in Brazil, where we won first prize at the 1972 Rio Song Festival. We took the festival by storm with a funky salsa tune Smitty and I wrote, called "Nobody Calls Me Prophet." It was the first American song ever to win at the Rio Festival. There was a sizeable cash prize and Larry negotiated international publishing deals that would pay dividends for years to come. We had a great week together in Brazil but it was bittersweet. Over dinner on the last night in Rio, in our moment of triumph, Larry told me that his health problems were more serious than he had let on. He feared he didn't have much time left and he had to take care of his family. He wouldn't be able to continue as my manager. I was devastated. I thought the world of Larry Goldblatt, and I'll never forget the loyalty he showed by standing up for me against Katz and his cronies, even putting his job on the line for what he believed in. In this business of back-biters and opportunists, the integrity of a Larry Goldblatt is a rare thing.

We returned to LA and within a year Larry was hospitalized. He died a few months later. I tried to carry on but I wasn't doing well in Los Angeles. There simply wasn't enough work out there for me. The agents and promoters wanted the marquee value of the BS&T name. Once more I was up against the power of that name. Without Larry to represent me I was really on my own in LA. I was lost out there. I spent a lot of time in the bars on the Sunset Strip, drank too much, dated a few B-list movie starlets and in general was going to hell in a handbasket. I learned another hard lesson in Los Angeles. When you're in town for a big concert, LA loves you, but familiarity breeds contempt, and when you're just another lonely rock star hanging out at the Rainbow Bar and Grill night after night, that town will eat you alive. Luckily my time in Hollywood was just about over.

You're the One

I've been racing with the risin' sun
Always goin' where I'm comin' from
I'm still waitin' for my ship to come
And I've been hopin', Darlin', you're the one
You're the one, found me on this rocky shore
Gave me everything and more
You're the one, all I do I do for you
Cause one and one ain't always two, you're the one

Never knew what I'd been lookin' for
And why they left me always needin' more
Never asked where love was comin' from
But I've been hopin', Darlin', you're the one
You're the one, stopped me on the brink of time
Gave me reason, gave me rhyme
You're the one reason for this song I sing
The reason I do everything, you're the one

Words may fail me, but I swear it's true
No one moved me till I came to you
No one touched me and I touched no one
But I've been hopin', Darlin', you're the one

Lyrics by David Clayton-Thomas. Copyright © Lady Casey Music, 1974.

18

BS&T PART TWO

O n a trip to Mexico City in 1973 I met a group of young
Canadian tourists on vacation. They were from Toronto
and we hit it off right away. They were heading for Acapulco, and
when my gig in Mexico City was over I joined them. Among
them was a twenty-two-year-old York University film student
named Terry Nusyna. Coincidentally, she was from Willowdale.
Beautiful, intelligent, talented, and in a bikini on the beach in
Mexico, she turned heads everywhere she went. She had a body
to die for ... tall and lean, with long legs, full breasts and long,
straight, sun-streaked hair down to the middle of her beautifully
tanned back. Terry Nusyna was a knockout! She was vacationing
with her boyfriend in Mexico, so nothing happened at the time,
but we both knew that something was going on. The air crackled
with electricity every time our eyes met.

After a few days in Acapulco, Terry and her friends returned
to Toronto and I went back to my rock-star pad in Brentwood. A
few more tequila-soaked nights at the Rainbow Bar and Grill and
a few more mornings of waking up with self-absorbed, empty-
headed starlets and I knew I had to get out of Los Angeles. I got
up one morning, made arrangements to board my setters with the
breeder until I could send for them, threw a bag in the Camaro
and started driving east. When I got to Las Vegas I called my
lawyer in LA and told him, "Sell the house, sell my cars, pack up

my belongings and put them in storage. I'm heading for Toronto. I'll call you when I get there."

My life had come full circle in a few short years. Toronto seemed a safe refuge for me. I needed to be with my friends, Bill and Doc and the people I had known all my life. Within a few weeks I had rented a house in Willowdale, just a few miles from McKee Avenue, where Bill and I had grown up. My parents had long since left Willowdale and were living in Schomberg, about thirty miles to the north, so I didn't have to deal with my father on a daily basis and could still see my mum whenever I wanted to. Willowdale felt like a good idea. I was trying to find the person I had lost in Hollywood in the tornado of fame and flattery that had swept me up in the past few years, and back where it all started seemed like a good place to begin. Besides, Terry Nusyna, the beautiful film student I had met in Mexico City, was a Willowdale girl.

Willowdale as a town no longer exists—don't look for it on a map, you won't find it. It exists only in the memories of the people who grew up there in the fifties and as a general reference point. The little outlying towns have been swallowed up by the sprawling metropolis known as the City of Toronto. The rolling farmland has been chopped into half-acre lots. The postwar subdivisions have been plowed under to make way for high-rise office buildings and luxury condos. The houses Bill and I grew up in are gone. The family-owned stores, restaurants and service stations have given way to modern malls and department stores. Busy superhighways slash through the once-tranquil farmland.

I sent for my furniture, my guitars and my dogs and settled into the house in Willowdale with absolutely no idea of what I was going to do next. That winter I lost one of my beloved setters.

Lady, unfamiliar with her new territory after being raised in the completely fenced Brentwood property, ran across the highway and was hit by a car. The elegant show dog from California just couldn't adjust to the congested suburbs and roaring highways of southern Ontario. I drove around for hours that night looking for her. I finally found her around 3:00 a.m., by the side of the highway several miles from the house. I was heartbroken. I buried her in the yard behind the house, and now there was just Casey and me.

I had the phone number of one of the tourists I had met in Mexico, Terry Nusyna's boyfriend. So one day I called him up and said, "Hey, let's get together." I'll be the first to admit that I had an ulterior motive. The vision of Terry in that awesome bikini was never far from my mind. On my drive across country from California to Toronto, I had thought of little else. It wasn't long before I connected with Terry and the sparks flew. Within a few weeks she had moved into the house in Willowdale and we were crazy in love. It was intense, it was sexy and it was great!

I hadn't toured much in the past year and I missed the rush of performing live. The royalties from all those songs I had written for BS&T meant that I really didn't need to tour, but I was still a performer at heart, and staying at home writing was just not enough. Even so, one of my best compositions was written during this period. It was a love song for Terry entitled "You're the One." My old friend Smitty was in town for a couple of days and we wrote the song on a Fender Rhodes in the living room of the house in Willowdale, with Terry curled up on the sofa. With Terry's help the emotional wounds from the past few years began to heal and I realized that leaving Blood Sweat & Tears had been an enormous mistake but perhaps it wasn't too

late to put it right. In 1973, David Clayton-Thomas without the
BS&T name was really hard to sell. The songs and the voice may
have been mine but the name on the records said "Blood Sweat
& Tears." That's what the concert promoters were buying, and
that was owned by Bobby Colomby. Bobby had the opposite
problem. He could sell the name to the promoters, but come
showtime the fans expected to see David Clayton-Thomas. Like
it or not, we still needed each other.

I called New York and got in touch with a guy named Fred
Heller. He had been a tour manager in the Larry Goldblatt years
and was now managing Blood Sweat & Tears. He told me Bobby
had a whole new band but confessed that they were in trouble.
By 1974, three consecutive albums for Columbia had tanked,
and what bookings he could get with the weight of the still-
powerful BS&T name weren't going well. He asked me if I'd be
interested in coming back to the band. I told Fred things weren't
going that well for me either but that there was no way I was
coming back if Steve Katz was still involved. Heller assured me
that Katz was gone. He'd been replaced by a superb guitar player
from Sweden named Georg Wadenius. Larry Willis was now on
keyboards. I knew Larry from the Cannonball Adderley Quintet.
He was an outstanding musician. Bill Tillman was on sax and
flute—another great player. Tony Klatka was writing the charts
and playing second trumpet. Tony had been with Wayne
Cochran's C.C. Riders, one of the best R&B bands in the world.
Forrest Buchtel had joined the band. He'd played first trumpet
with Count Basie. Percussionist Don Alias was now in the band,
a giant of a player. Bobby Colomby and Dave Bargeron were the
only ones left from the original band. It was an impressive lineup
and I knew most of the players, but I still had serious misgivings

about stepping back into the political cauldron that had been BS&T. Fred Heller assured me that this was Bobby's band now and he would love to have me back. Bargeron called me and asked me to at least consider it. Heller offered to fly me to Milwaukee that weekend to make a guest appearance at one of their concerts. They were touring with three lead singers at the time—Jerry Fisher, Jerry LaCroix and Luther Kent, all fine singers—but they were singing their hearts out every night to audiences that kept demanding David Clayton-Thomas. It wasn't their fault. I respected every one of them as vocalists, but the audience expected to hear the voice that was on the records. Making it extra hard for the singers was the fact that they were mostly singing songs that I had written.

I flew into Milwaukee and caught up with the band at the concert hall. They were already onstage when I arrived and Heller met me backstage. Damn, they sounded good, in some ways maybe even better than the old band. Wadenius on guitar was everything I had wished Katz could have been and more. He was a guitar hero in Europe and now I knew why. He had it all. He played the blues like Stevie Ray Vaughan and jazz like Larry Carlton. I was blown away. Big Texas Billy Tillman was awesome! Six foot three, 250 pounds of screaming alto sax player. The horn looked like a toy in his huge hands, and goddamn he could play. Larry Willis, Don Alias, Tony Klatka, Colomby, Bargeron ... It was an incredible band.

The show was about two-thirds over and no one in the audience expected me to be there, so when they announced "Ladies and Gentlemen, Mr. David Clayton-Thomas," there were a few seconds of stunned silence and then, as I walked onstage, the place erupted. The entire audience was on its feet before I had sung a note. We launched into "Spinning Wheel" and the place went wild. Their three lead singers knew this was the real thing and graciously left the stage. I think they were relieved to see me. They were tired of battling public opinion and answering the question "Where's David?" every night. They watched from the wings as we tore the place up. We played all the hits. "And When I Die"—Dave Bargeron brought the house down with a tuba solo. "Lucretia MacEvil"—Bill Tillman and I ripped into a scat trade that had the whole place on its feet. We did one encore, "You Made Me So Very Happy." The audience stood and cheered and applauded until we came back onstage. We did a second encore but it wasn't enough for the crowd that night. They wanted more. We had run out of tunes to play so we jammed a twenty-minute blues, improvised on the spot. The band was grinning from ear to ear. It just felt so good. As we finally left the stage, I caught Colomby's eye and he grinned. No doubt about it: we were back.

I was on top of the world again. I had one of the best bands in the world and I liked these guys. This was Bobby Colomby's band. Everyone was on salary and I didn't want to know what they were being paid. Heller and Colomby offered me a deal that worked for me. I got a straight percentage of the gross off the top every night. The expenses and politics of running the band were their business. My money was sent directly to Canada, where I had a lawyer and an accountant to keep track of everything. I still had no ownership in the name, but this was a sweet deal. It provided me with a handsome income without having to deal with all the petty politics that had plagued the original band, and I could live in Canada with Terry, away from the pressures of New York.

Fred Heller was a Larry Goldblatt protégé and had learned from past experience. The band couldn't be allowed to dictate the tour schedule. He knew the name was of no use to anyone if they burned my voice out. He was much more selective about our bookings and allowed time for writing and recording new music. Colomby had built a recording art studio at his home in New City, New York, and in the next three years we recorded two fine albums there, produced by Bobby, *New City* and *More Than Ever*. They sold well but the emphasis was no longer strictly on recording. Columbia Records was putting out so many BS&T reissues and greatest-hits compilations that the new records were in competition with our own multi-million-selling catalogue. Besides, the trail that we had blazed in 1969 was now full of great horn bands like Tower of Power, Chicago, and Earth, Wind & Fire. As a recording band we were submerged in a wave of our own creation, but it didn't matter. We had a sensational concert band and were touring the world playing the most prestigious venues and leaving audiences wildly happy. I was writing new music for the band and making a ton of money.

Georg Wadenius eventually married and returned to Sweden. He was replaced by Mike Stern. Jaco Pastorius had just completed his first solo album, produced by Bobby at the studio in New City, and he joined the band. The rhythm section now consisted of Larry Willis on piano, Mike Stern on guitar, Jaco on bass, Colomby on drums and Don Alias playing percussion. What a band! Jaco would go on to make music history with Weather Report. Mike Stern is now recognized as one of the world's great jazz guitarists. Larry Willis is a jazz giant. A young saxophone genius named Gregory Herbert had joined us from the Ellington band. He was a young Coltrane, a brilliant soloist. Tony Klatka

was a talented arranger and one of the best bebop trumpet soloists in the world. This was without a doubt our finest lineup ever.
It was awesome!

These were years of tremendous upheaval in the record business. Most of the big New York–based companies were moving
out to LA. There was a huge power shakeup at Columbia Records.
Clive Davis had left in 1972 amid accusations of financial mal-
feasance and we'd lost our champion at the record company.
There was a whole new regime at Columbia. Most of Clive's
people were gone. Many of them moved to LA to launch Clive's
new company, Arista Records. So with all their political clout
gone at Columbia, Fred Heller and Bobby Colomby negotiated a
new deal with ABC Records. Our first album for ABC was
recorded in 1976 in Los Angeles. *Brand New Day* was a great
record, produced by Bobby with arrangements by Tony Klatka
and featuring our new all-star lineup. I got to sing a beautiful
duet with Chaka Khan. Every song was a thing of beauty. A
month after it was released ABC Records also collapsed in a storm
of financial scandals, and the album went down with them. It was
a big disappointment. We had worked hard on that record, but
we had one of the best concert bands in the world, so we shook
it off and went back to life on the road.

There were many memorable concerts in those years, but our
concert for the athletes at the 1976 Montreal Olympics was a real
highlight. We were to play for the assembled athletes inside the
Olympic Village. After going through the intense security clear-
ances necessary to get inside the heavily guarded Village, we took
the stage in front of maybe five hundred athletes who weren't
competing that day. As luck would have it, during our show
Nadia Comaneci scored the only perfect ten in Olympic gymnas-

tics history. Every event in the Olympic stadium was halted as the news of this milestone was flashed on closed-circuit TV throughout the facility. It took some time to get everything up and running again and the satellite feed was left with perhaps thirty minutes of dead airtime, so the director said, "Cut to the concert in the Village," and there we were, singing "Hi De Ho" by satellite to the entire world. After the set our publicist rushed up to me and said, "Congratulations, you just sang to one-third of the planet." I was mystified. I asked him what he meant. He said, "That satellite feed was seen by approximately one billion people around the world." I'm glad he waited until after the show to tell me. I would have probably blown a lyric had I known.

Then there was our triumphant return to the Newport Jazz Festival. Following the debacle in 1969, when thousands of fans trampled down the fences and mobbed the festival, the city fathers of Newport had banned all rock acts. In 1976, faced with dwindling ticket sales, they relented and allowed Blood Sweat & Tears to perform at Newport again. It was a beautiful sold-out concert to a well-behaved crowd of around 5,000 people. The city fathers gave us the keys to the city.

We performed for the prime minister of Canada, Pierre Elliott Trudeau, and his wife, Margaret, at the National Arts Centre in Ottawa. I met them backstage after the show and was dumbfounded at how beautiful she was. Her photos never fully captured the radiance of this Canadian beauty. I tried to be cool, but when she entered the room and was introduced to me I stuttered and stammered, stood up and spilled my drink all over the floor. She pretended not to notice. Either she was the classiest lady ever or she was accustomed to big dumb Canucks choking in her presence.

I taped my own TV special for CBC in Toronto and Terry was in the audience. I sang "You're the One" for her, and when she stood up there was an audible gasp from the audience. Like I said, Terry Nusyna was a knockout. There were sold-out concerts and numerous TV appearances in the States—the *Mike Douglas Show*, the *Andy Williams Show*, the *Sonny & Cher Show*. Terry travelled everywhere with me: New York, Los Angeles, Las Vegas, Puerto Rico. We flew first-class. Five-star hotels and limos were a way of life. The band played exciting high-profile gigs. We were hot, the money was rolling in, Terry and I were in love and life was good. I asked Terry to marry me and she said yes.

Our wedding was the social event of the year in Toronto. There were over 500 guests at the Inn on the Park and Bobby Colomby was my best man. Following a blissfully happy honeymoon in the south of France, we bought and renovated a beautiful old three-storey townhouse in downtown Toronto in the shadow of Casa Loma, in one of the most exclusive neighbourhoods in town. Terry was a smart, charming hostess. We had lots of friends, and when we weren't travelling around the world we entertained frequently.

Doug Riley bought a house on the next block and we spent a lot of time together. Doc and I recorded a solo album in Toronto during this time, called *Clayton*. It was produced by Jack Richardson, one of Canada's finest producers, and we brought up the best players in New York for the sessions—the Brecker brothers, Dave Sanborn and Mike Stern, as well as musicians from the current BS&T lineup. Most of them stayed at our house during the recording. We emptied my wine rack in three weeks and partied all night between sessions. The house was always full of musicians, friends and neighbours. We had a ball recording that album and it comes through in the music. The *Clayton* album rocks from start to finish. I still love that recording.

Bobby Colomby was offered a vice-presidency at a major record company in LA and gave up actively performing with the band, but he still retained his ownership of the name. He was replaced first by Roy McCurdy from the Cannonball Adderley Quintet and later by a hot young drummer from Miami named Bobby Economou. We never missed a beat. Dave Bargeron had a growing family and just couldn't handle the year-round commitment required by BS&T, so he left to become one of the top session players in New York. Now I was the only one left from the original group. I was flying in and out of Toronto every week to gigs and commuting back and forth to New York, where Fred had his offices. It was an exciting time. The money and the wine were flowing, Terry and I were in love and it seemed like the good times would last forever. But life has a way of throwing a curveball just when you least expect it.

Fantasy Stage

Well here I am, in rainy Rio de Janeiro
Play it again, Sam, I really got nowhere to go
Puttin' in time till that early mornin' flight
The woman looks fine, dance the samba till daylight

And I know it's just a fantasy stage
And I know I should be actin' my age
But oh everybody wants to belong
And everybody needs a song

Say *habla español*, baby, have you been here long
I just don't know, everything I say is wrong
What can I do when you don't understand a word
I'll sing for you the sweetest song you ever heard

And I know it's just a fantasy stage
And I know I should be actin' my age
But oh everybody wants to belong

19

AMSTERDAM

It was 1978 and the psychedelics and the relatively harmless pot of the sixties had given way to a nasty intruder—cocaine, the party drug of the seventies. It had crept quietly into the band and into our lives, taking over everything without our really knowing it. It was everywhere, and with the money we were making it was all too readily available. Cocaine is a seductive drug. At first just a little toot at a party, and before long your life is revolving around it. We were spinning out of control but we were having so much fun that no one really noticed. Then disaster struck.

The band was touring Europe, playing prestigious concert halls like the Olympia in Paris, the Berlin Symphony, and Royal Albert Hall in London. On the last leg of the tour we were to play Amsterdam, the drug and party capital of Europe. Gregory Herbert had joined the band earlier that year, a thirty-one-year-old saxophone virtuoso who made his name with the Duke Ellington Band. He was a gifted young musician with a wife and child in Philadelphia and a baby on the way. I loved Greg, as did everyone else in the band. He was a great guy and one of the most eloquent sax players I've ever heard. On the road he and I and Tony Klatka, the trumpet player, were inseparable. We were only a couple of days from finishing the European tour when we arrived in Amsterdam with the night off.

Early that evening Tony, Greg and Larry Willis knocked on my hotel-room door. They said, "C'mon, man, we got the night off, let's party." I knew what that meant—they were going out into the city to score some coke. It wasn't hard. Drug dealers were everywhere in Amsterdam, and somehow word seems to travel when you're rich and famous and do coke. Sometimes the coke dealers would be waiting for us at the airport. Most nights I might have gone with them, but I was expecting a call from Terry, it had been an exhausting tour and there was a big concert coming up the next night, so I decided to pass and get a good night's sleep. To be honest, I had done my share of coke, but I was never into it the way some of the guys were. My main concern on the road was my voice, and that required some maintenance— proper sleep and voice rest. Coke was just too hard on the pipes. Larry Willis also decided not to go out that night, since I wasn't going—a decision that undoubtedly saved his life.

About 1:00 a.m. I was awakened by someone banging on my door. It was Tony. He was ashen and in shock. "Clayton," he cried, "it's Greg, in my room. I can't wake him up." Still half-asleep, I stumbled down the hall to Klatka's room and found Greg lying on his back on the bed. I frantically pounded on his chest and tried my best to clear his airways, but he wasn't breathing. I yelled at Tony, "Get a doctor, fast!" but it was too late. Gregory Herbert was dead. Tony Klatka was in a state of panic, but a strange calm came over me. I knew I couldn't lose it now. I'd cry for Greg later. Right now my priority was the band. We were a long way from home and this was a dangerous place. Someone had to take charge. I woke Larry Willis and told him to get everyone out of bed and to warn them, "If you have any drugs in your room, flush them, now! The police will be here any minute."

The Dutch police arrived with the paramedics and everybody was dragged out into the hall. Our bags were turned inside out and we were all taken in for questioning.

The next several hours were a nightmare. The entire band was held as material witnesses then released when no other drugs were found. When we got back to the hotel we discovered that everybody's suitcases had been looted. Cash, jewellery ... gone. The police had robbed us. Fred Heller had retained a Dutch lawyer, and when the guys started to complain about the missing money he told them to shut up or we might not be leaving Amsterdam for a long time. The lawyer advised us to pack up and get out of the country as quickly as possible.

We found out later what had happened. Greg, a diabetic, took insulin every day so he was no stranger to needles. He and Tony had scored a "cocktail," a heroin and cocaine mixture, and had come back to Tony's room to get high. Greg had shot up some of the mixture and Tony snorted it. That and the vodka he had been drinking that night probably saved Tony's life. He went into the bathroom and threw up, then passed out on the bathroom floor. When he came to, he tried to arouse Greg. When he couldn't, he stumbled next door to my room for help. The autopsy showed that the dope was laced with strychnine. It was no accident. Someone wanted to kill them. Greg and Larry Willis were both African Americans and I think they felt safe hanging out with the brothers in Amsterdam, but this wasn't Philadelphia. Many of the "brothers" in Holland were Moluccan terrorists, and they hated all Americans, black or white.

Gregory Herbert was loved and respected by everyone in the band. I'll never forget the sight of all the musicians sitting in the hotel lobby as the sun came up, sobbing quietly to themselves.

We were in no shape to perform, so we cancelled the remaining two concerts, Amsterdam and London. Larry Willis and Greg had been friends for years. Larry had brought Greg into the band and now had to call his wife in Philly and break the news to her. Fred Heller and the Dutch lawyer made arrangements to get Greg's body home. That night on the bus, as we made our way to the airport in Amsterdam, I finally lost it. I had been steely cold and totally in control for nearly twenty-four hours, and now that it was almost over I broke down and cried, big racking sobs that hurt deep in my chest. Larry Willis sat beside me, his arm across my shoulders, staring grimly into the night, tears rolling down his cheeks.

That night left an enduring mark on me. I would never do drugs again. It became my mission to keep the band clean. It was the hallmark of BS&T bands for the next twenty-five years. When we travelled overseas I was obsessed with bringing everybody home safe. The guys in the band knew that the boss wouldn't tolerate drugs on the road. Anyone who jeopardized the band's safety would be fired on the spot. I never again wanted to go through the agony of bringing a friend home in a body bag. It was the end of that edition of Blood Sweat & Tears. We returned to New York a broken band. Tony Klatka went to New Orleans and climbed into a bottle for the next ten years, blaming himself for Greg's death. It wasn't his fault, but the pain we all felt was almost unbearable. The rest of the guys went back to their home-towns to deal with it, each in his own way, but one thing we knew for sure—we would never make music together again.

I returned to Toronto and ran head-on into another calamity. Within days after I got home from Amsterdam I found out that the Toronto attorney I had trusted to keep the books had been robbing me blind. Now that there was no more Blood Sweat & Tears, I needed to know where I stood financially. I was shocked to find I was almost broke. The lawyer had been living the life of a rock star and, like the rest of us, had been sucked into the glitzy world of celebrity and cocaine. He had been travelling all over the world with Fred Heller, flying first-class and staying at the best hotels, all at my expense. The lawyer had taken to affecting capes, $2,000 suits and gold-headed canes. He drove a Mercedes and lived in the most exclusive part of town. Becoming my lawyer had made him a superstar in the Toronto legal community, and he represented many prominent Canadian artists. When I demanded an accounting, the floodgates opened and everyone wanted to know where their money was. The lawsuits flew for the next several years, but most of the money was gone—spent on his lavish lifestyle or blown up his nose. Everyone was grateful that I had exposed this crook, but that was no comfort to me. I had problems of my own. There was a lot of money missing, my taxes hadn't been paid in three years and the government wanted their money. It's easy to say "How could I have been so stupid?" but when you are on the road year-round generating millions of dollars, the cash flow is bewildering. When you're caught up in the pressures of travelling and performing every night, it's difficult to keep track of the money. Even the guys handling the money didn't know where it all was. Once when a tour manager was let go they found over $50,000 in unused airline tickets in his desk drawer. In the blur of constant travel arrangements, he had simply forgotten about them. The cash coming in and going out was impossible to monitor. You had to trust somebody to keep the books.

I felt cornered and betrayed by everyone. I blamed Fred Heller and the crooked lawyer, I blamed Terry and I cursed the government, but I knew in my heart that I had fucked up. Money and excess, booze and drugs and my own out-of-control ego had done what an abusive father, the brutality of prison and the years of struggle couldn't do. It broke me. Fuelled by years of drinking and drugs and high-powered living and still suffering from post-traumatic shock from the tragedy in Amsterdam, I hit the wall … hard. I had what I now recognize as a complete nervous breakdown. I withdrew from Terry and began sleeping on the sofa downstairs. I'd wake up in the middle of the night in a cold sweat with the image of Greg Herbert dead in that hotel room in Amsterdam still haunting my dreams. I would wake from one nightmare to face another, the stark reality of financial ruin. I was nearly broke, and except for my ongoing royalties I had no income. I had no bookings to fall back on. Blood Sweat & Tears was shattered and I didn't know if it would ever come back from the devastating blow it had suffered in Amsterdam. I just couldn't face anyone. My entire self-worth had been wrapped in the protective mantle of stardom, and now I was stripped naked. Bill offered to help me out financially but I had too much pride to accept his help. Terry tried to get me to see a psychiatrist but I never kept the appointment. Our marriage couldn't survive these multiple catastrophes. My entire world had collapsed and I was not fun to live with anymore. Terry left me and filed for divorce. I had no choice but to sell the house and file for bankruptcy.

Being famous is a double-edged sword. When you're on top, everyone knows about it, but when you fall, you fall hard and there's nowhere to hide—you fall on your ass in front of the whole world. The press, of course, delights in this kind of story, and my troubles were splashed across the newspapers in my hometown. My mother had to read about her son's fall from grace in the local papers. "Ex-convict David Clayton-Thomas, lead singer of Blood Sweat & Tears, whose saxophone player Gregory Herbert was found dead of a drug overdose in Amsterdam, today declared bankruptcy in Toronto. Mr. Clayton-Thomas's wife, Terry, has filed for divorce." That's what happens when you become fodder for the scandal sheets. Everything negative in your past becomes a part of the story and it snowballs. I had come to believe that fame and money could control everything, and now it hit me: the accomplishments of the last ten years meant nothing. The Grammy Awards and the gold records meant nothing. Now the story was all about drugs and divorce, my prison record and the financial scandal.

I put the house up for sale, put my furniture in storage and made arrangements with a musician friend of mine to care for Casey. He had a house up in the lake country with acres of fields and woods, and I knew the big high-spirited dog would have a good home. I tossed a bag in my '74 Porsche Carrera and started driving. I had no destination in mind. I just wanted to drive until the pain went away, until I could figure out how the hell this could have happened. I drove blindly all summer, checking in to a motel when I needed sleep, driving aimless and alone all over North America. I had a well-known face and name, but for that entire summer few people knew where I was. I grew a full beard and spent most of my time in the Porsche. I drove clear across Canada to Vancouver, down to San Francisco to stay for a few days with Forrest Buchtel, then to Los Angeles for no reason at all. There would be no answers or comfort in that pitiless town. I drove to Miami to visit Bobby Economou and to New Orleans to see how Tony Klatka was doing. It was as if I was reaching out to the guys who were there that terrible night in Amsterdam, as if someone might have some answers. They didn't.

I spent the summer of '79 driving alone in the little Porsche with only a CB radio for company. Four months of driving, trying to get my sanity back, trying to forget the memory of Greg Herbert in that hotel room in Amsterdam, trying to figure out how I could have fucked up so completely. I had been given a second chance and I'd blown it. It seemed like one day I had it all—money in the bank, a lovely home, a career, a beautiful wife—and the next day all I had was this battered old Porsche. Driving has always been therapeutic for me. There's just something reassuring about being out on the highway, winding through the countryside in a fine-handling piece of machinery. You can't be touched out there, and I guess after spending so much of my life in the public eye this was my way to escape, to re-examine, to just be alone and think. By the end of the summer, now straight and sober for the first time in years, I had begun to make some sense of it all. There was no one else to blame. Not Terry—she did the best she could with an out-of-control maniac for a husband. Not the crooked lawyer—I didn't take care of business, and there will always be sharks around if there's blood in the water. Not even the coke dealers—it was my choice to let those slimy bastards into my life. No, what I learned driving across America that summer was that there was no one to blame except that face I saw in the rear-view mirror every day for four months. I had abused the blessings I had been given, and it was up to me to make it right again. I still had my God-given talent and a lot of people out there who for some reason still believed in me. With a little luck and some serious self-discipline, I just might put my life back together again.

Redemption

Toil and labour on the ark, Noah, God meant it
Scorn and pity's all the world around, you'll ever know
Rain and thunder in the dark, Noah, God sent it
Sing redemption everywhere you go
Praise the Lord, he has led you ... Noah

Thirst and hunger on the rock, Moses, God gave you
Pain and sorrow's all the world around, you'll ever know
Fire and fury in your talk, Moses, God save you
Sing redemption everywhere you go
Praise the Lord, he has led you ... Moses

Cold and lonely in the dark, Joseph, God left you
Greed and hatred's all the world around, you'll ever know
Pull your coat of colours round, Joseph, God blessed you
Sing redemption everywhere you go
Praise the Lord, he has led you ... Joseph

Words and music by David Clayton-Thomas, Richard Halligan and Steven Katz. © 1971
(renewed 1999) EMI Blackwood Music Inc.

20

THE CANADIAN
BS&T

If I was going to reclaim my life, the only things I could build
upon were my voice, my songs and the great show that had
died that night in Amsterdam. Driving across the country that
summer, I had come to the conclusion that it was the musical
standards that defined Blood Sweat & Tears, not the personnel.
Any team of great musicians could be Blood Sweat & Tears.
There were no original guys in the last band, and no one seemed
to mind. There was a fine musical community in Toronto and I
knew everyone up there. I came up with a crazy idea: maybe I
could build a new BS&T made up of Canadian musicians.
Would anyone really care where they came from as long as it was
a great horn band and it had that Blood Sweat & Tears sound?
The sound was in the charts, not the players. Of course they had
to be great musicians to play those difficult arrangements, but
Toronto had a fine musical community and there were lots of
great players up there.

I headed back to Toronto, but on the way I stopped in New
York for a meeting with Fred Heller. He invited me to have
dinner with his family that evening, and for several hours we
talked it out. We talked about how the band had controlled
everything in the past and how ludicrous that was. Nobody gave
a damn who played second trumpet, and to give that guy an

equal say in the running of the band's business was crazy. A nine-man democracy just didn't work. When push came to shove everyone would vote according to his own interest. A great band needed leadership and direction. Heller and I had both come to the conclusion that the flower-power commune concepts of the sixties just didn't work in the big-money world of the music business. The truth is that it's easy for everybody to be equal when you've got nothing, but throw millions of dollars on the table and the alpha dogs come out. We had a chance to turn the tragedy in Amsterdam into something positive. The old BS&T had been totally destroyed and now we had the opportunity to build a new one from the ground up, to learn from the mistakes of the past and form a band with strong leadership. But Heller was emphatic about one thing: if I was to be the leader of this new Blood Sweat & Tears, I had to lead by example. There would be no drugs, no booze and no doubt about who was in charge. Heller did not want to deal with another out-of-control bunch of prima donnas who thought they were all superstars. We had already proven that the public didn't really care who was in the band as long as they were great players and I was the lead singer. I had a proposition for him: if I could put the BS&T show back together with Canadian musicians, could he book it? "No problem," he told me. "If Bobby will let us use the name, I'll handle the bookings." I said, "Okay, let's do it." It was the beginning of decades of renting the use of the BS&T name from Bobby Colomby.

We shook hands and I headed home to begin assembling a new band. I knew the Toronto music scene well: the best players in town were Doc Riley's people. Doc was the major contractor in Toronto for everything from jingles and film scores to serious jazz and rock recording sessions. All the top players in town worked for him in one way or another. As soon as I hit Toronto I called Doc and told him about my idea. He loved it. A Canadian Blood Sweat & Tears, eh? Doc knew just the people to pull it off. If you worked for Doc, you were a team player, and I knew we wouldn't have the ego problems that had plagued the New York band. He suggested I call Bruce Cassidy, a brilliant trumpet player/arranger who had played with Doc's band, Dr. Music. Cassidy would be musical director for the new band. Two talented brothers, Rob and Dave Piltch, played guitar and bass. Another Riley protégé, Lou Pomanti, handled the keyboard chores. The only musician from the previous band was Miami drummer Bobby Economou. He had married a Canadian girl and was living in Toronto now. Bobby had been with me that terrible night in Amsterdam and we would always share that bond. He and I had toured the world together for two years, and he gave me a rock-solid foundation to build the new band on. Two fine sax players, Earl Seymour and Vernon Dorge, completed this Canadian edition of the group, and Blood Sweat & Tears was back in business again.

Fred Heller now billed the show as "Blood Sweat & Tears featuring David Clayton-Thomas," and the bookings rolled in once again. We worked constantly. I was on the road so much I didn't even bother with a home. I lived in first-class hotels around the world, and whenever I was in Toronto my room at Bill Pugliese's house was always available. We landed a new record deal with Jerry Goldstein, the producer of War, the band from LA that had several big hits, like "Cisco Kid Was a Friend of Mine." Goldstein obviously knew how to record a funk band.

This new band with its Toronto-based players was much funkier than the earlier editions of BS&T. These Canadian boys were much more in tune with my blues roots than the New York guys, and the Toronto music scene had always had deep R&B roots, going back to the Bluenote days. Even my tunes like "Spinning Wheel" and "Lucretia MacEvil" were more soulful, with a bluesy fusion-jazz sound. There was also a new depth to my singing. The flash and theatrics of the glory years had given way to a more mature and sober David Clayton-Thomas. I was relaxed and comfortable with these guys and it showed onstage. Bruce Cassidy and Rob Piltch, both talented arrangers and composers, began working with me on new songs for the Goldstein album. We planned to record the tracks in Miami and mix them at Goldstein's studio in Hollywood. I drove the Porsche down to Florida to record the tracks. I had beaten the hell out of her driving all over North America the previous summer, so that winter I'd had the battered old sports car totally rebuilt from the frame up by a custom shop in Toronto. She was an absolute beauty!

The '74 Porsche Carrera 911S Targa had been punched out from the stock 2.7 litres to 3.3. It was now powered by a 500-horsepower turbocharged engine, 19½ PSI boost with titanium bearings and forged pistons, a tuned exhaust system and a high-performance suspension. It was wicked fast, 0 to 60 mph in under five seconds, top end around 175. The body had been flared and carried a diamond black paint job. It had BBS gold mag wheels, low-profile Pirellis, Recaro seats and a killer Alpine sound system. That car was very special to me. It had been my therapy, my companion on a very personal voyage of self-discovery, and I just couldn't part with it. I only carry on about the Porsche because it would take me on another adventure and would figure prominently in what was about to unfold.

We finished recording in Miami and then had some bookings that would take us across the southern States—New Orleans, Houston, Phoenix, winding up at an outdoor street festival in Los Angeles, where Goldstein planned to record the show for a "live in concert" album before we mixed the Miami tracks. I drove the Porsche out to LA, tailing the band's tour bus. The gigs were well spaced out so there was no pressure. It was a nice leisurely drive along Route 10 across the southwestern deserts with the Targa top off all the way. I had a chance to reflect on some of the lessons I had learned in that first aimless drive across America. I had been so busy running away from my past that I'd never stopped long enough to deal with it. Maybe I had to hit the wall to stop running.

I arrived in LA sunburned and fit. We recorded a kick-ass concert in downtown LA, then checked into a residency hotel in Burbank to begin mixing the Miami album, by now entitled *Nuclear Blues*. I was for all intents and purposes homeless. I had been living in five-star hotels and travelling all around the world with the Canadian edition of Blood Sweat & Tears. We had been playing concerts in South America, Australia, South Africa and all over the States. It was a fine band made up of guys I'd known most of my life. We were nearly all Canucks and shared a very Canadian mindset. We laughed at jokes that only a Canuck would get, despaired for the Leafs like a Bostonian despairs for the Sox, and travelled as a tight-knit group of friends.

A memorable experience for us all was our tour of South Africa. Bruce Cassidy was so deeply moved by the experience that he returned to live there for the next twenty years. The controversial tour, organized by the Quibell brothers from Jo'burg, was groundbreaking. This was pre-Mandela South Africa, and the

Afrikaner government in Pretoria ruled with an iron fist. Concert tours had previously been organized with black artists performing only for black audiences and white artists performing for exclusively white audiences. The popularity of local artists like Johnny Clegg, who performed with mixed-race bands, had already forced Pretoria's hand. For the first time blacks and whites were buying tickets for the same concerts. Pretoria's idea of a compromise was to paint a line down the middle of the theatre, whites on one side, blacks on the other. This was a last-ditch effort by the government to hold back the tide of freedom that was sweeping across the country, and it was a complete failure. Once people were inside the hall, the only way to stop them from mingling was by use of force, and that didn't look good on the evening news. The old system of apartheid was breaking down, and music was playing a large role in its destruction. South Africa was ready to take a giant step forward in its struggle for racial equality, and we had a chance to participate.

The Quibells offered us the first fully integrated tour of South Africa. Tickets would be sold on a first-come, first-served basis, without prejudice, and there would be no separation of people in the hall. Thelma Houston would be our opening act. This was a brave move in 1980. The promoters received hate mail and death threats and took a lot of heat from the all-white government, but they defied Pretoria and went ahead with the tour. It was a resounding success. The country was hungry for change, and when it came to showtime the controversy evaporated and it was all about the music. I'll never forget the sight of thousands of young people, white and black, standing and cheering for the same music, their hands linked in the air. Even the audience in conservative Pretoria responded to the show with flowers and beaming faces and standing ovations. We hung out with many South African musicians who had been on the cutting edge of the revolution sweeping their country. Mixed bands like Johnny Clegg's Savuka, and Soweto township groups like Ladysmith Black Mambazo had long carried the message of racial equality in their music. They welcomed us like family and took the band to clubs in the "township," where we jammed all night with the local players. We went on an unforgettable camera safari in the Kruger National Park, bouncing across the dusty Londoloza in an open Land Rover with lions and elephants so close you could almost touch them. We all fell in love with Africa, its incredible beauty, its warm and generous people and the tumultuous changes they were now experiencing. We felt a tremendous surge of pride and accomplishment in being able to participate in our own small way in such a historic effort, and returned to LA to finish mixing *Nuclear Blues* a happy and satisfied band.

While we were working on the album I began going out with Jennifer Goodson, a vivacious, good-looking girl from Madison, Wisconsin, who I met through Jerry Goldstein. She was recently divorced and had a great sense of humour, and we had fun together. We laughed a lot, and she was just what I needed. At the time I wasn't up for another heavy relationship and neither was she, but if there's one thing I've learned about affairs of the heart, the best-laid plans mean nothing.

After a few weeks, the *Nuclear Blues* album was completed and it was time to hit the road again. I realized I was really going to miss Jennifer and she felt the same way. We had been living together at the apartment in Burbank for several weeks. She came to the studio with me every day and we had grown very close. Neither of us really had anything permanent in LA. So one day out of the blue I asked her, "Hey, Jen, want to drive to Toronto with me?" She didn't hesitate. She said, "Sure, let's go!" Jennifer was always up for an adventure, one of the things I loved about her. I said, "Pack a bag, baby, we're outta here." And just like that, Jennifer Goodson and I ended up driving the Porsche cross-country from LA to Toronto. After surviving the ultimate train wreck, things were definitely looking up. I had a hot new girlfriend, a mean turbo Porsche, an ass-kickin' band and a new album in the can, and I was headed back home to Toronto.

Ashleigh's Song

You're my child little girl, you can be what you want to be
You're my life little girl, you mean all of the world to me
And may you grow up strong and true
And may the world be good to you
And when you're safely on your way
Remember how I used to say
From my heart into your dreams, flowered fields, golden sunbeams
Butterflies, unicorns too, golden dreams I give to you

I'll be here little girl, even when I'm away from you
I'll be near little girl, making all of your dreams come true
And in the mornin' when you rise
It's puppy dogs and sunny skies
But now it's time to close your eyes
Or you might see your daddy cry
From my heart into your dreams, starry skies, silver moonbeams
Charming prince, sand castles too, golden dreams I give to you
From my heart into your dreams, golden dreams I give to you

Lyrics by David Clayton-Thomas. Copyright © Clayton-Thomas Music Publishing Inc., 1986.

21

ASHLEIGH'S SONG

Jennifer and I rented a small apartment in downtown Toronto. It was only temporary, but I'd been living in hotels for the past year and we needed a place to get organized and figure out where we wanted to live. I got my furniture out of storage, stashed the Porsche in the underground garage and hit the road again almost immediately. We did a lot of international touring that year, so I spent the summer of '81 flying all over the world with the Canadian band. I wasn't home a lot in those first few months, but Jen made the downtown apartment a nice comfortable place to come home to. She quickly became a member of the BS&T wives' club. With their men on the road constantly, the girls all banded together in a support group and they made her feel right at home in Toronto.

By the end of the summer we found out that Jennifer was pregnant and it felt right for both of us. We loved each other, and Toronto's a good place to have a baby, with fine health care, my Canadian medical plan and lots of friends around to give advice and help out. Like most anxious young parents-to-be, we became very concerned with Jennifer's health and nutrition. We decided to move up to the country for the fresh air and healthy lifestyle. I bought a rustic old Canadiana farmhouse thirty miles north of Toronto and just a few miles from Bill Pugliese's place. Bill's wife,

Linda, had raised five kids, so she was a good companion for Jen and could keep an eye on her when I wasn't around. Touring became impossible during Jennifer's pregnancy. She really needed me while she was carrying the baby and I wanted to be there for this miraculous event. So at the end of the summer tour I disbanded the Canadian BS&T, shook hands with Fred Heller and we all came home. It was very amicable with the guys. We had been travelling the world for nearly three years and everyone needed a break. We were all friends, and we loved being back home in Toronto with our wives and families. It was time for us to get off the road for a while.

Jennifer and I settled into our rural farmhouse and awaited the arrival of our blessed event. It was a good time for us. Fine local produce and healthy home-cooked meals were a way of life. Bill and his family were close at hand and we spent a lot of time with them. In the fall there were corn roasts and family dinners at the Puglieses'. Doc and I went to hockey games that winter and hung out with our musician friends at the downtown jazz clubs. For the first time in years there was barely a mention of the music business. Jennifer and I got married in a small private ceremony attended only by a few of our closest friends. We were a family now, and all our attention was focused on Jennifer's health and nutrition, and having a healthy baby.

That winter I covered the Porsche and put her up on blocks in the barn on our property. A high-powered sports car wasn't much use in rural Ontario, where six-foot snowdrifts were not uncommon. I bought a four-wheel-drive Jeep Cherokee (much more useful in farm country), and by spring we were ready for the arrival of Ashleigh. We knew we were expecting a girl and she was already named. The tour manager for the Canadian band was a guy named Stuart Murray. He was a class act. He would later go on to become a member of parliament in Canada. We travelled the world together for three years. His fiancée was a girl named Ashleigh. Jen and I thought the world of Stu and Ashleigh. They were smart and classy people. We both loved the name and the traditional British spelling, so Ashleigh it was.

On the evening of March 9, Ashleigh Clayton-Thomas decided to announce her presence to the world right in the middle of a wicked blizzard. Jennifer thought her time might be getting near and we were hoping to get her to the hospital before the storm got worse. We made our way down Highway 400 in the Jeep Cherokee at 15 mph in a whiteout—zero visibility, six-foot drifts and Jen having contractions in the passenger seat. The snowplows weren't out in Toronto yet, and by this time it was coming down too fast to clear anyway. We made it as far as Doc Riley's house and banged on his door at 1:00 a.m. That's when you find out who your real friends are. For several hours that night we thought Ashleigh might be born right there on the Rileys' sofa, but by morning the streets were cleared and we made it to Toronto Western Hospital, where Ashleigh Victoria Clayton-Thomas was born on March 10, 1982.

She immediately set about changing my life. I fell completely under the spell of this little charmer. I had stopped smoking cigarettes during Jennifer's pregnancy, booze and drugs were a thing of the past and I would never go down that path again. I've heard it said that abused children often grow up to be abusers themselves, but in Ashleigh's case the opposite was true. The cycle of abuse that had been passed down from father to son in the Thomsett family was over. I was determined that she would never experience the kind of fear that I had grown up with.

I'll never forget the time when Ashleigh and I drove up from New York to spend Christmas with my family in Canada. She was about eight years old. I wasn't looking forward to dinner with my father, but my mother hadn't seen Ashleigh since she was a baby and I wanted Ash to know her grandmother. My father and I barely tolerated each other. We had never spoken about the brutality of my childhood, and there was never a word of pride or approval from him even now, when I was a successful and respected artist. We were halfway through dinner and Ash was pushing her food around her plate with her fork. She had always been a picky eater and maybe she sensed the tension between Fred and me. "Something wrong with your dinner?" my father asked her, his voice low and menacing. "I don't like peas," my daughter answered. BAM! My father slammed his fist down on the table, the dishes jumped and Ashleigh sat frozen, her eyes wide with shock. "You'll eat what's put in front of you in my house, young lady," my father barked. "I work hard to put food on the table." It was the same old tyrannical Fred Thomsett, and it made my blood run cold. Ashleigh's eyes welled up and my father glared over at me. I stood up abruptly, knocking my chair over, and glared right back at him, my fists clenched on the table. He saw something in my face that he'd never seen before, and I'm sure his life flashed before his eyes. In that moment, had he raised his hand to my daughter, I would surely have killed him. The blood drained from his face. He got up from the table without a word and went downstairs to his workshop. We didn't see him for nearly an hour. Ashleigh ran into a back bedroom and my mum and I went in to comfort her. She was sobbing and shaking. She'd never been spoken to like that. With hugs and kisses from her grandma she soon calmed down, and Mum and I went back to the kitchen. My mother was still shaken. She said to me, "David, I've never been afraid of you before, but there was a look in your eyes I hope I never see again." I hugged her close and told her, "Mum, it ends here. The Thomsett bullshit is over. Now you know why I changed my name. My daughter is a Clayton-Thomas, and she won't be raised the way I was." My mother nodded. She understood. She'd been living with the Thomsett temper for more than forty years, and while she loved Fred and would never leave him, she'd had enough too. I think she was secretly glad that someone had finally stood up to him.

An hour later I looked into the living room and Ashleigh was sitting in her grandfather's lap. He was holding her tight and there were tears in his eyes. Well, I'll be damned! Maybe after all these years Freda's faith that he would mellow someday had finally paid off. Maybe there was hope for the mean old bastard after all. My relationship with my father changed from that moment on. We would never be all warm and fuzzy, but at least I could visit them from time to time and we could actually be in the same room together. The thing my mother wanted most in life was to see some kind of reconciliation between my father and me. When she lay dying in the hospital, her happiest moments were when my dad and I would visit her. She was in hideous pain and heavily sedated, but a smile would light up her face when she saw Fred and me arrive together. When I was inducted into the Canadian Music Hall of Fame in 1996, my father finally told me he was proud of me. My mother had passed away a few years earlier, so she never lived to see the moment she'd always dreamed of. It had been a long time coming and it was way too late, but with a man like Fred Thomsett you take what you can get.

It's Only a Song

Seems like I'm always leavin' town
Seems like I always let somebody down
So here's a song just for you, for the girl I left behind
Here's one for the band and one for the man I might have been

It's only a song, just a candle in the night
But it keeps me movin' on, another town to maybe get it right
It's only a song, but it's the best thing that I do
Just remember when I'm gone, that I wrote this one for you
Just remember when I'm gone girl, that I wrote this one for you

Who's gonna comfort you tonight
Who's gonna tell you things will be all right
So here's a song just for you, for the girl I left behind
Here's one for the road and one for the load I'm carrying
Here's one for the road and one for the load I'm carrying

22

STADTHALLES AND SYMPHONIES

I stayed home for the first eighteen months of Ashleigh's life, but sooner or later I had to get back to work. There wasn't much work in Canada and Jen was probably going to kill me if I didn't get out of the house soon. We talked it over and decided to go back to New York, where Jennifer could be closer to her family in Newport, Rhode Island, and I could get back into the New York music scene. I'd been there for nearly fifteen years and I knew my way around. I'd have no trouble finding work in New York. Even though Ashleigh was born in Canada, she had dual citizenship and Jennifer was insistent that she be raised as an American. The Canadian band had drifted away during my hiatus. Some of the guys had new families to care for and weren't interested in going back on the road, and others had moved on to other gigs. Cassidy had returned to South Africa. Fred Heller was pretty much out of the music business by this time and was running his family's fleet of cabs in Manhattan. Besides, I really didn't want to start another Blood Sweat & Tears at this point in my life. I was forty-two years old and I figured if I didn't take a shot at a solo career now I never would. We sold the farmhouse, and the Porsche Carrera would help us out one last time. I got a nice price for her and she helped finance the Clayton-Thomases' move to the big city. Once again I had come full circle—I was back in New York.

Jennifer and I rented a house in Rockland County. I knew Rockland well from the days of recording at Bobby Colomby's studio in New City and it was a way to be close to Manhattan without having to raise Ashleigh on the mean streets of New York City. I contacted Sid Bernstein, the promoter who first brought the Beatles to New York. Sid was an old friend and had once booked BS&T into Madison Square Garden. He rounded up a few solo dates on the west coast and I put together a small band of session players in New York, rented a tour bus and took off for California.

The bus driver was a guy named Larry Dorr. Larry was a taciturn red-haired Bostonian. He and I had a lot of time to talk as we bused out to the west coast and back, with Larry driving and me riding shotgun. I explained my present situation and told him that Blood Sweat & Tears was over and I was looking to move on. He said he understood where I was coming from and told me that he wasn't just a bus driver. He was actually a tour manager with years of experience, and he'd like to get involved with my career. I was impressed with this guy. He handled himself well on the road and he knew the business inside and out. I liked him, and when the west-coast run was over I offered him a job as my manager. He would be my best friend and closest business associate for the next twenty years.

My favourite Larry Dorr story occurred at the House of Blues in LA. I overheard him talking to some slick Hollywood promoter type. I caught just a snippet of their conversation. Larry was saying, "Look, I don't play tennis, I don't do lunch, frankly I don't even like you—just sign the fuckin' contract. I got a show to put on." That was classic Larry Dorr, a tough, no-nonsense old-school road manager. He'd collect from a promoter with a baseball bat if necessary. He didn't have a lot of formal education; he'd learned his trade on the road just like I did. We were both street cats and we understood each other. He was one of the best road managers in the business. He began his career at fifteen as a roadie on the James Brown band and had worked his way up through the ranks. Bus driver, road manager, stagehand, he'd done it all. He had been a tour director for Broadway shows, so he knew how to move a large touring company around the world effortlessly. He was a seasoned pro and just the kind of guy I needed to get started in New York again.

There really was no Blood Sweat & Tears anymore. All the original guys were long gone, and there had been several editions of the band since. Heller was out of the business, Colomby was in LA and I felt it was time to stand on my own. So I put together a small five-piece band in New York, and Larry Dorr began booking David Clayton-Thomas dates. Larry didn't actually travel with the band much. We needed a home base, and Larry was much more effective booking the band from his office in Boston. He'd come out on the road every so often to see that everything was running smoothly, but most of the time he was home manning the phones. We were driving from gig to gig, the band in a fifteen-passenger van pulling their gear in a U-Haul trailer and me in my '84 BMW, playing as many as twenty-five club dates a month from coast to coast. We put over 150,000 miles on the vehicles in one year. We had a couple of roadies and soundmen taking care of business on the road. The gigs were mostly club dates and we didn't expect to get the same money that I got with BS&T, but what the hell—it was a start.

We immediately ran into an impossible situation. I started out with no intention of using the BS&T name. A promoter would book us into a club. Our contract specifically spelled out the billing, absolutely forbidding the use of the name Blood Sweat & Tears. But once out there on the road we were at the mercy of the local promoter. I would show up for the gig with my five-piece band and on the marquee there it was: "Tonight, Blood Sweat & Tears." These scumbags were paying a fraction of the price they would have had to pay for BS&T and had used the name anyway. I had no choice but to go ahead and play the show. Refusing to perform could be disastrous, especially in some of the redneck roadhouses we were playing.

Jennifer and Ashleigh were alone and somewhat isolated in suburban New York, and in spite of my best efforts I was seldom there. Jennifer and I went for weeks on end without seeing each other. The only had contact we had was by phone. We had a nice house in Suffern, New York, but Jennifer was miserable and I wasn't happy out there playing honky-tonks across America twenty-five days a month. She felt abandoned and alone in Suffern, and I felt she didn't appreciate what I was going through to pay the bills every month. We argued on the phone constantly. Finally Jennifer had had enough of raising our daughter by herself and took Ashleigh up to Newport to be closer to her family. It was heartbreaking for me, but I knew Jen was doing the right thing. Ashleigh was growing up quickly, and in Newport she would have her grandmother and aunts and uncles around her—a good support group for Jennifer and a solid family environment for Ashleigh—and no matter where they lived I'd still only see them for a couple of days a month anyway. I was having a difficult time touring without the BS&T name, the gigs weren't paying a lot of money and we had to do a lot of them to make ends meet. Jennifer knew that the music business had finally won out over the marriage. Maybe she had always known it would. Our daughter was our most important consideration, so we quietly dissolved the marriage with a minimum of legal hassles and agreed to joint custody of Ashleigh. Over the years Jennifer and I have remained friends and we were always supportive of each other in raising Ash. I dumped the rental house in Rockland County and went back to living on the road. Story of my life ... no home, nice luggage.

I found myself in joints that could never afford BS&T, playing for money that would have been a joke two years earlier. I fought with the club owners every night about the billing and eventually I just gave up. This solo-career idea wasn't working out too well. We may have been playing my songs and it may have been my voice on those records, but the name on the Grammy Awards was Blood Sweat & Tears. That's what the promoters wanted, and they were going to use it whether I liked it or not. I soon realized that the conspiracy went far beyond the local club owner. Everybody from Larry Dorr to the agents and the local promoter was winking at the terms of the contract. They needed to keep the act working to generate money and they weren't going to allow a technicality like the billing to stand in the way. There were constant threats of lawsuits from Bobby Colomby, but even he knew it was out of my hands. Everybody knew we couldn't file a lawsuit against every funky roadhouse that infringed on the BS&T name, so the club owners would simply ignore the contract. "Hey, David Clayton-Thomas is Blood Sweat & Tears ... Everybody knows that." These gigs were humiliating for me and damaging to BS&T's reputation. It soon became obvious that we would have to make a deal with Bobby Colomby for the use of the BS&T name.

Larry Dorr contacted Colomby, now living in Los Angeles, and made arrangements to once again rent the name. Bobby had distanced himself from the group after the tragedy in Amsterdam and my own personal train wreck, and I no longer had any direct contact with him. I can't blame him. He was a corporate vice-president now. He couldn't afford to be associated with any bad publicity, and it seemed like I had a talent for generating bad press. My name was well-known, but the joints we were playing weren't exactly prestigious and I could be a target for any small-town lawman who wanted to get his name in the paper. My prison record still followed me everywhere I went. Any contact with the law whatsoever and I was automatically a criminal. A simple traffic stop could mean being taken away in handcuffs while some redneck sheriff had me checked out. After Amsterdam, BS&T carried the taint of being a drug band and even though the band was now completely clean that reputation still followed us. Bobby Colomby wanted nothing more to do with me or Blood Sweat & Tears, but he was willing to rent the use of the name to Larry Dorr. This allowed him to still make money from our activities without appearing to be directly connected to me or the band. Larry and I agreed to rent the name for a year or two—just long enough to get us out of these low-life joints we'd been playing and back into the concert halls where we belonged.

Once we had the right to use the name, we signed the act to a major LA-based agency and I set about the task of putting together a horn band in New York that could play the BS&T repertoire. Overnight our price soared and the quality of the venues went right back to where it had always been. Inside of a month we went from bars and roadhouses to festivals and concert halls. Such is the power of a name in this business. Ironically, higher-priced gigs meant we weren't playing six nights a week anymore. The big concerts were mostly on weekends and we were flying to most of them, so my days of driving 150,000 miles a year were over. Had Jen and I stuck it out for a few more months we might have saved our marriage. But it was too late now—we had both moved on. The divorce was final, Jennifer had a new boyfriend and I had my career back on track.

I met a fine trumpet player and arranger in New York named Steve Guttman. Steve would be the musical director for the new Blood Sweat & Tears. He organized the charts and began recruiting musicians. There was no shortage of great musicians in New York. By now the music schools were spitting out young players who had grown up with the music of BS&T. Most of the major universities were teaching the music of Blood Sweat & Tears as part of their curriculum. This band was much different from the previous editions of BS&T. This wasn't a group, and it wasn't meant to be. It was a rotating team of top New York City session musicians. Each player in the band had a sub who could step in at a moment's notice. I didn't want personal friendships in this band. I got along well with these guys, maybe even more so now because I was "the boss" and everybody knew where they stood. Musicians came and went weekly and I had no interest in getting involved in band politics. That was Steve Guttman's job. Larry Dorr booked the dates and organized the road crew. He assembled a crack team of top soundmen and tour managers. Promoters were always blown away by the professionalism and efficiency of the BS&T operation.

There was a lucrative market opening up with the Indian-reservation casinos that were cropping up everywhere. They all paid good money. Some had decent showrooms, some didn't. They ranged from luxurious multi-million-dollar establishments like Foxwoods and Mohegan Sun to joints out in Middle America that had been truck stops before the local tribe got a gaming licence. Their clientele was mostly an older crowd, so they booked "oldies" acts, and BS&T now fit solidly into that category. I had guys in the band who weren't even born when BS&T had its first hits. The audience was getting older and the band was getting younger every year.

I once walked through a casino in Las Vegas with Larry Dorr and we saw a great singer who had several big hits in the sixties playing in the lounge to twenty people, vainly trying to be heard above the din of the slot machines and cash registers. It was sad. I remember saying to Larry, "If I ever get to this, just shoot me, okay?" Well, we hadn't quite "got to this" but some of these joints were close. Fortunately, we had maintained a level of musicianship that could play other venues. We played major international jazz festivals and first-rate concert halls with our lineup of top-notch New York City jazz musicians. The level of musicianship in the band was still superb. The music demanded it. Your everyday lounge musician couldn't really play this repertoire. The music created by the original band was just too challenging, and it required the best musicians in the business.

There were some wild and wonderful European tours in the eighties and nineties. My favourites were the *Stadthalle* tours, German for "standing hall." We would assemble a band of our A-team players in New York and fly them into Munich with a skeleton crew consisting of our sound tech and road manager. In

Germany we would take on a European crew of stagehands, roadies and even our own caterer. We'd charter a large double-decker luxury coach and take off across Europe—Germany, Austria, Italy and Switzerland, playing nearly every night in a different town. The *Stadthalles* would be packed with fans, up to 2,000 young people, shoulder to shoulder, jammed right up against the edge of the stage. The audiences were wild. They cheered and screamed and fired the band up every night. We stayed at beautiful four-star hotels in the big cities—Milan, Vienna, Berlin and Geneva—or in scenic chalet-style inns in the smaller towns. By day we were out on the Autobahns, cruising along at 120 kilometres an hour over the mountains of Bavaria, across the Alps and through the magnificent northern Italian countryside. The coaches had an upper deck with panoramic windows. The band would gather up there, playing back-gammon, reading or just watching the lovely European land-scape roll by. Ancient castles dotted the slopes of the Bavarian Alps, and fans would follow the bus, waving out the windows of their cars, stopping when we stopped for lunch at the Mövenpick rest areas. Beautiful Euro-babes would attach themselves to the tour, following us from city to city in their BMWs or riding in the tour coach with the band. It was a big rolling party, the bus loaded with beer and babes. We would play as many as twenty concerts in three weeks. Then we'd return to Munich for the final show, exhausted and happy, and the promoters would throw a big send-off party before we returned to New York. Through the late eighties and early nineties, we were in Europe several times a year.

We also began playing concerts with major symphony orchestras. This was Steve Guttman's brainchild. He expanded the BS&T charts to full symphony scores and we appeared with some of the top orchestras in the country. The symphony concerts presented an opportunity to congregate with other musicians. The orchestras were full of conservatory graduates who had studied the music of BS&T in college. Their brass sections were loaded with players who had gone to school with our horn players, and the BS&T name commanded respect wherever we went. "Pops" concerts are often tolerated by orchestras as a fundraising necessity, but when BS&T came to town they knew they were in for a treat. Our symphony book contained elements of Bartók, Prokofiev, Ellington, Basie, Aaron Copeland. Guttman's scores were beautifully written, and you would see smiles break out in the orchestra as soon as they opened the book. Our symphony scores didn't just use the orchestra as accompaniment, as many pop acts do, but fully included them in the program, with an ambitious overture and original movements written for the orchestra alone and featuring their soloists. Steve Guttman commanded immediate respect as a conductor, and the conservatory-trained musicians in our band could hold their own in any symphony orchestra. Performing with fine orchestras like the Buffalo Philharmonic and the San Antonio and the Long Beach symphonies was a special treat. Hearing a seventy-piece orchestra strike up the intro to "God Bless the Child" always gave me chills.

One of our first orchestra concerts was with the Baton Rouge Symphony, and it was a joy. A large orchestra can be somewhat ponderous compared to the snap and precision of a jazz combo. Doc Riley once described it as "like trying to steer an ocean liner." Classical musicians don't always understand the rhythmic feel of funk and jazz. In addition, symphony musicians have a reputation for being somewhat stuffy and formal. Not so for the wonderful BRSO. This orchestra rocked. Half the string bass players played jazz down in New Orleans, and the brass section was well versed in jazz and the blues. We played an absolutely delightful outdoor concert in the park with the sixty-piece orchestra. They were fun, they were lively and the band loved playing with them. Immediately after the concert the orchestra's resident conductor said to us, "Gentlemen, don't go away. We have a surprise for you." He led us to a large barnlike building behind the stage. Cajun music was booming from the speakers, and piled on a long table were tubs of steaming-hot peppered crawfish, vats of gumbo and kegs of ice-cold beer. The concert-master greeted us with a big smile and said, "Dig in, boys. Welcome to Loosiana." There was the entire Baton Rouge Symphony Orchestra, the men stripped down to their under-shirts, the ladies in T-shirts and jeans. On the dance floor they were dancing to Clifton Chenier and Dr. John. We partied late into the night, our faces greasy with "crawdad" juice. We had a ball, and all our preconceived notions about classical musicians were blown forever.

Larry Dorr and I had become close friends. We spoke several times a day and collaborated on every detail of our business operation. I was best man at his wedding and together we had built a multi-million-dollar business enterprise that was sup-ported entirely by touring. Larry handled the bookings from his home in Boston and I ran the day-to-day operation of the band from my offices in New York. My company was called Antoinette Music Productions. After the financial meltdown I had survived in Toronto, I was determined to handle the money myself. All the expenses of running the band were paid from my office and I signed every cheque. Everybody got workman's compensation, unemployment insurance, Social Security, et cetera. We were paying $100,000 a year in accounting fees alone. There were lawyers and agents and travel expenses, and Larry Dorr was well-paid to manage his end of the operation. Then, of course, Bobby Colomby was still taking his slice off the top. I was right back to where I had been in the seventies except that now we had hi-tech monitor systems and top-notch soundmen and I wasn't burning my voice out every night. That took a lot of pressure off me, but there was still a huge payroll to support and the band had to work constantly or it would fall apart. I'm not complaining—I personally made a lot of money. I lived well, built a healthy investment portfolio and eventually would put Ashleigh through college with the money I earned in those years, but it did take an enormous toll on my body. Wake-up calls at 3:00 a.m. to make 6:00 a.m. flights were a way of life for this band. After finishing a show at, say, 10:30, you didn't get to bed until midnight, and that 3:00 a.m. wake-up call came early. The chances of flight delays and cancellations increase as the day goes on, and a missed flight can be catastrophic for a band on tour. The promoter doesn't want to hear about your travel problems; he's sold tickets and the people want their money back, and of course the band must be paid whether we play the date or not. So most mornings we would be waiting at the airport when the doors opened so we could catch the first flight out of town. When a musician began to burn out from this relentless schedule, we would just send in a replacement and the show would go on. There were literally dozens of musicians who passed through the band in those years. Sometimes I would be introduced to guys at the airport who would be in Blood Sweat & Tears that night.

Musicians came and went, but the production team remained constant. They were with me for nearly twenty years. They were the heart and soul of this operation. Musical director Steve Guttman was a brilliant musician with an extensive musical education. He was also a practicing psychotherapist in New York, which enabled him to be a steadying influence in the crazy world of eccentric jazz musicians and their sometimes-volatile lead singer. Taking up the baton in front of a symphony orchestra is a daunting task. Classical musicians can be ruthless if the conductor doesn't have it together and Steve Guttman commanded respect wherever we went.

Tour manager B. Harold Smick III and production manager Frank DeGennaro had touring down to a science. Under their direction our shows ran like clockwork. Smick was from a well-to-do South Jersey family; his family owned a chain of lumberyards. He originally joined us as a soundman, but with his talent for business and organization he was soon promoted to tour manager. Smick was well-liked by the musicians and handled the band, the promoters and the business of touring with finesse and class. Frank DeGennaro was a US Marine, steady and dependable. He was a rock, a big guy with a busted nose that told you he'd been in a few scraps in his day. Frank had been a Marine Corps MP. He was one of those guys who never seemed to hurry and didn't talk much. He just got the job done. Sometimes you can't avoid contact with some real nutcases out on the road, but onstage or signing autographs I was never concerned. Frank and Smick always had my back.

My affection for these guys was largely the reason I stayed with the band for so many years. When you spend this much time with people they become an extended family. In fact, we probably spent more time together than we did with our own families. On tour you become a tight-knit group of friends moving through a constantly changing world of strangers. I stayed on the road years longer than I really wanted to and much longer than I probably should have, but these guys depended on me as much as I depended on them. Larry Dorr was a tough, hard-nosed negotiator and he worked tirelessly to keep the gigs rolling in. Steve Guttman was a good friend and confidant and he always provided an understanding ear when I was frazzled and frustrated and just needed to vent. Frank and Smick were both top-notch professionals who took a lot of pressure off me on the road. They shielded me from promoters and politics and kept the show running like a well-oiled machine. All I had to do was show up every night and sing.

Life on the road is surreal. One city becomes just like the next. It all blurs into an endless stream of airports, hotels, dressing rooms and stages. A full night's sleep is rare, so the performers sleepwalk through the day, catching naps in airports, on the plane or bus, wherever they can, following the tour manager's itinerary so that come showtime they can flip that switch and light up the stage for a couple of hours. After a few weeks on the road it doesn't matter where you are anymore, and answering too many questions from the band just takes up too much of the tour manager's valuable time. So everyone follows the crew from town to town and trusts that somebody knows where the hell we're going. I had to laugh when a fan would come up to us in an airport and ask, "Where did you guys play last night?" The band would all look at each other with a blank look and turn to the road manager. You have to look at the phone book beside your bed when you wake up just to figure out what town you're in, but the crew knows where you're going and how to get you there. They're up an hour before the band and don't get to bed until after the business of the show is taken care of and everyone is tucked in for the night. When the musicians are catching a nap in the afternoon, they're busy setting up the stage and preparing for sound check. They only time they get to sit back and relax a little is when the show hits the stage and all their hard work pays off. On the road the tour manager is king and the crew handles all the problems. All the musicians have to worry about is the show that night. A great crew makes the road livable, and I had one of the best.

Suzie's Got Her Big Hair on Tonight

Tantilizin' dress and high-heeled shoes
Suzie got a different attitude
Somethin' happened to the girl we knew
The woman's looking out for somebody new
You should have paid attention when she cried
You could have told the truth, but no, you lied
You should have paid attention, serve you right
Cause Suzie's got her big hair on tonight

Suzie's got her big hair on tonight
Suzie's gonna shake this town up right
The way she's lookin' just might start a fight
Cause Suzie's got her big hair on tonight

The woman's lookin' out for number one
The girl's just tryin' to have herself some fun
You should have paid attention, serve you right
Cause Suzie's got her big hair on tonight

23

POMONA

In 1986 I bought a house in a pretty little suburban New York town called Pomona, and that would be home for the next eighteen years. My life during those years revolved around touring and I really needed a home base, not only as a centre for my business operations but to provide a sense of stability for Ashleigh, a place to call home in the New York area. I was playing only two or three concerts a week but they were all over the map. I could be in Germany one week and California the next. A full-time limo driver handled my airport runs and drove me to local gigs. Albert DiFazio had been the desk sergeant at the notorious Fort Apache in the Bronx. Albert was a highly decorated retired police officer, a thirty-year NYPD veteran who now moonlighted as a bodyguard and limo driver. He still carried a badge and a gun, and he was experienced at security and crowd control. He was soft-spoken and polite but he was a cop in the South Bronx, and you just knew he wasn't a man to be trifled with. Albert was with me for fifteen years and became like part of our family. He picked up Ashleigh from school and watched over her at concerts like she was his own daughter. Albert was a handy guy to have around. I'd fly into New York on a Monday morning with a briefcase full of cash from the weekend's gigs. He would meet me at Newark Airport and take me directly to my office in Rockland County, where I'd do the banking and pay the bills. Once the money was safely tucked away in the bank and the paycheques had been signed, he'd take me home. I had maybe three days to relax, then Albert would pick me up at 3:00 a.m. on Friday and I'd do it all over again. This was my life for the eighteen years that I lived in Pomona. Hopefully, there would be time on my days off to drive up to Newport and see Ashleigh. If her school schedule permitted I could bring her down to New York for a few days, even take her on the road with me from time to time. By the time she was in high school she was an experienced road hand and Albert was like a fiercely protective uncle.

The house in Pomona was in the Ramapo Mountains forty-five minutes from Manhattan. It was a sprawling four-bedroom ranch-style bungalow on nearly two acres of heavily wooded land, set well back from the road on a quiet street with a long, winding driveway. I had the house completely renovated and built a forty-foot pool in the backyard. There was a billiard room with a turn-of-the-century pool table, a living room with a large stone fireplace, a super-modern kitchen. Ashleigh had her own room, and I converted one of the spare bedrooms into a small home recording studio. I built an extra garage on the property and was able to indulge my passion for high-performance cars. My friends tell me I have more fun detailing and tinkering with my cars than most people do driving theirs. We spent so much time in airports that being able to drive to a concert was a luxury. Anything within a six-hour radius of New York was an excuse for me to load the band on a tour bus and take one of my cars out on the road.

There were lots of local gigs to be had. BS&T had a loyal fan base in New York State, New Jersey and New England. Nearly every year we played the New York State Fair in Syracuse, and we had regular bookings at the Atlantic City and Connecticut casinos. Upstate New York was fertile territory for the band. We played often in Albany, Buffalo, Syracuse and Rochester. This was always a good reason to drive on up to Toronto and hang out with Bill and Doc. There was a great jazz club in Toronto called the Montreal Bistro, which featured world-class jazz and good food and was a meeting place for the Toronto music community. Doc played there regularly, and whenever he did I'd drive up to Toronto for a few days to catch his set, sit in with him and maybe take in a hockey game at Maple Leaf Gardens.

I drove to Aurora every year to spend Christmas with Bill and his ever-expanding family. I've always maintained that there's no Christmas like a Canadian Christmas. It's the biggest holiday of the year in Canada, and Christmas at the Puglieses' was always a joyous occasion with a huge, brightly lit tree, piled high underneath with presents. Their lavish home was a riot of festive decorations, with kids and toys everywhere. Bill and Linda had five children who grew up and married and had kids of their own. Twenty or more family members for Christmas dinner at the Puglieses' was not unusual.

I developed the habit of celebrating Christmas twice. I'd drive to Canada a few days before Christmas and spend the first part of the holiday with Bill and his family, visit my parents in Schomberg, then return to New York to have a second Christmas and ring in the New Year with Ashleigh. That way Ashleigh would have Christmas in Newport with her mum, then a second Christmas in New York with her dad. It meant a lot of driving for me over the holidays, but I never minded that. We may have been apart for much of the year, but Christmas was special—it was worth the extra effort to be a family for a few days.

I always loved seeing my mum at Christmas, and I know my visits were the high point of the year for her. I'd bring her up to date on Ashleigh's progress at school and she always wanted to hear about my travels around the world. Her face would light up when I told her stories about my trips to exotic countries like Japan and Australia and concerts in places like Las Vegas and Hollywood. She had given up her career in music to be a wife and a mother and had worked as a secretary for most of her life. Her travel was limited to a couple of weeks a year at their cottage in Muskoka. After they retired, Fred bought a huge forty-foot motorhome and they would make annual 2,000-mile drives to Nova Scotia and Newfoundland and back. I believed this was more Fred's fantasy than Freda's. I think he always wanted to be a long-distance trucker with a Cat diesel and a CB radio. Ten-four, good buddy! She went along with it because it made him happy, but my mum would rather have seen a Broadway show or travelled to London or Paris. Freda was a bright, artistic woman with an enormous curiosity about the world. I think she lived vicariously through the exploits of her wandering son.

Over the years I brought my parents to special events like the State Department send-off in Washington, DC, and our opening at Caesars Palace. Once I flew them to Los Angeles to see me perform at the Hollywood Bowl. Fred came along grumbling and pretending to be unimpressed. He was happier trudging through the woods with his guns and his dogs. My mother loved the excitement of show business and all the eccentric, creative characters who were my friends. My dad thought they were a bunch of "kooks and weirdos." I'm so glad I had the chance from time to time to let my mum experience what life was like outside of Fred's world. That glamorous week in Hollywood hobnobbing with movie stars and celebrities was the happiest week of her life.

Freda died in 1990 after a long painful battle with cancer. I visited her in the hospital often during her last months, driving from New York to Toronto almost weekly to be with her. I would hold her hand and sob quietly, and she knew I was all right now, that somehow her troubled son had come through it all and was now a respected artist and a good father to Ashleigh. I think that gave her some measure of peace. I was backstage before a concert in New England when the news of her passing was brought to me by Larry Dorr. I'd been expecting this day for months, but when it finally came I was devastated. Larry offered to cancel the concert. No one could have blamed me under the circumstances, but cancelling was out of the question. There were 5,000 people out there, and Freda would never have wanted me to disappoint them. My music was my mother's gift to me and she was so proud of my accomplishments. She would have been angry with me if I'd cancelled a show because of her. That's the kind of selfless woman she was. A few days later when I spoke at her memorial service I told the congregation, "This was a woman who never knowingly hurt anyone in her life. God, I wish we could all say that."

Even though I was on the road constantly, I still found ways to spend time with Ashleigh. Newport was only three hours away. It's a beautiful, historic old town and a great place for a kid to grow up. She had a loving family in Newport, her dad and his band in New York and an extended family in Toronto. She's a bright, inquisitive girl and was exposed to music, theatre and the arts from an early age. Most of my New York–based musicians played Broadway shows, so orchestra seats were readily available to us and we attended first-run Broadway shows together at every opportunity. *Annie, Les Miz, Phantom of the Opera,* all the top shows were a regular part of her upbringing. As she grew older her love of music, film and theatre intensified, and after graduating high school in Newport she enrolled at SUNY Purchase, a New York State college with a fine theatre arts program. Her interests were now focused on media production and creative writing. She moved to an apartment in Nyack, just a few minutes from my house in Pomona and convenient to her college just across the Tappan Zee Bridge. We spent a lot of time together during those years. I loved having my daughter close by, and a girl has to have a place to do her laundry.

There were a few women in my life in those years, but nothing really lasted. I had casual girlfriends, an occasional flight attendant who would pass through New York and spend the night before winging off to wherever flight attendants go. There were girls I would meet on the road and fly into town for a couple of days, but their tickets were always round trip and after a few days of dinners and shows in the city they would go back to their lives and I would return to mine. Actually, I preferred it that way. My life was all over the map, and in the few days I had at home I valued my privacy and the time I could spend with my daughter. But there were a couple of ladies who rocked my world during the years in Pomona, and I can't leave them out because each in her own way affected the person I am today.

There was Maggie, who I met on tour in Australia. She was a voluptuous red-haired Aussie beauty, a magazine model from Melbourne. She was a great girl. Maggie came to live with me at the house in Pomona. We got along well. I never had an argument with her in all the time we were together. She was beautiful, bright and looking to settle down. After a year the only way

Maggie could remain in the US was to become a resident. The best way to accomplish this was to get married, and even though I adored Maggie and was very happy with her, marriage scared me to death. I was already a three-time loser and I knew the futility of trying to maintain a marriage with my crazy lifestyle. So Maggie went back to Australia. I missed her when she left. She was easygoing and comfortable to be with, the kind of girl you can sit in front of the fireplace with all evening and not say anything or feel that you have to.

Then there was Suzanne … my mid-life crisis. A hot young lounge singer from Kentucky, Suzie was a born-again Southern Baptist and was one of the most sexual creatures on God's green earth—slim and petite with a tight perfectly formed body, beautiful, volatile and demanding, with a sexual appetite that was simply amazing. I met her after a show in Owensboro and an hour later we were tearing up the bed in my hotel room. She lived with me in Pomona off and on for the better part of a year. She would move in with me and a month later she would move out. She hated New York. It was Sodom and Gomorrah in her sexy little fundamentalist Southern Baptist mind. It was full of homosexuals, heretics and heathens, and, unfortunately, most of them were friends of mine. Suzanne was brought up in a small Southern town where all community life revolved around the Baptist church. She was raised in the church, and she couldn't function without it. But in the bedroom she was a total sexual animal, wild and uninhibited. The bouts of wanton lovemaking were followed by dark, moody periods inevitably followed by outbursts of anger and recrimination. It was an emotional roller coaster, but the sex was incredible and, God help me, I was becoming addicted to it. She could be incredibly loving when she wanted to and just as difficult when she didn't. Suzanne was a very conflicted girl. She desperately wanted to be a star, but living with me was about as close as she would ever get to that dream. Musically she just wasn't all that talented. Her evangelical side was racked with guilt about living in sin, and of course that was all my fault too.

One crazy weekend I took Suzanne with me to Nevada for a gig at Harrah's and we got married on the spur of the moment in one of those "Elvis" wedding chapels in Reno. I don't know, maybe I thought that would make her happy. The next day I called Ashleigh in Newport and told her we were married. She broke into tears and cried, "Oh no, Dad, you didn't." Yes, honey, I did ... What was I thinking? It lasted a hot three months. It was a volatile, sexually charged relationship and it burned out fast. The constant emotional turmoil was hard on Ashleigh. At the time she was an impressionable thirteen-year-old. It must have been difficult for her to watch her dad making a fool of himself over a manipulative little sexpot half his age. Young women were not uncommon in my life. I lived in a young rock & roll world. At concerts I was still hooking up with sexy twenty-five-year-olds even when I was in my fifties, but this wasn't out on the road. I had brought this foolishness home with me.

Finally, in the midst of one of Suzie's temper tantrums, I walked out without a word. I got in my car and drove eight hours to Bill's house in Toronto, called my lawyers and told them it was over. A price was agreed upon, nothing I couldn't handle. Suzie took the money, signed the divorce papers and went on to marry a Baptist church deacon in Indiana. She was way too young for me, and I was way too old for all the drama.

After Suzanne I finally realized that marriage was something I just wasn't good at. I once told Deering Howe, who was also a multiple-divorce survivor, "I just can't respect a woman who is dumb enough to put up with my shit." It was meant to be funny, but maybe there's more truth there than I like to admit. I have always had problems with intimate relationships. When other kids were learning about sex and dating and high school proms, I was getting my master's degree in the merciless ass-backward world of prison, where the only person who wanted to date me was a guy with twenty-two-inch biceps and jailhouse tattoos. From there I leaped headlong into the world of show business and suddenly people were calling me a "star." Beautiful women were everywhere and readily available, and I'll admit I didn't know how to handle all this attention. Emotionally I was still a horny sixteen-year-old, and I had to make up for lost time.

My love life consisted mainly of one-night stands on the road. It was all part of the game. I'd be gone in the morning and they'd probably never see me again. It's the way the game is played in the world of rock & roll, and they knew the rules. They just wanted to snuggle up to someone famous and I just wanted to get laid, to escape for a while the dark hours between the last encore and the 3:00 a.m. wake-up call. The loneliest time in a performer's life is the hours after the show, when you go from the incredible high of being adored by thousands of fans to the depths of loneliness in a hotel room. You feel like you've given everything to the crowd. They all go home smiling and happy, and you go back to watching late-night TV alone in your room. You're still pumped up from the show, the adrenaline is flowing and you can't sleep. This is the time when rock stars crash and burn. They turn to drinking and drugs and meaningless sex, anything to ease that crash landing.

I never really trusted those girls backstage who now suddenly found me so irresistible, but what the hell … They were gorgeous and I was lonely. It's hard to tell the girls who really care from the groupies just looking for a thrill, and it seems like you're never around long enough to learn the difference. In my younger days, when I fell in love, I fell hard, but it always came down to a conflict between love and career and I was addicted to my career. In my mind it was the only thing standing between me and where I came from, and I wasn't going back.

Doubletalk

Big tobacco wants to save my life, by tellin' me I never should smoke
Petro money wants to save the world from pollution, people ain't that a joke
Big brother wants to let me know that he cares about this family of mine
And big trouble's waitin' for the guy who gets himself a little bit outta line

So the river flows, runnin' down the mountain to the sea
So the story goes, I'm drownin' in the river and it's washin' over me

Misdirection makes the world go round
And nothin's ever what they said it would be
Mud splatters when it hits the ground
And makes the picture so much harder to see
Doubletalk turns me upside down
It's got me goin' back and forth in my mind
Bullshit follows me around
And nowadays I'm just so easy to find

Takes a talkin' head to figure out what a politician has on his mind
Takes a better man than me to know how to listen in between the lines
Takes a poll to tell me where I stand, I make my mind up instantaneously
If my opinion's what they really want
I'm sure there's someone who will give it to me

24

INTO THE
DIGITAL AGE

The little studio in the spare bedroom at the house in Pomona would now begin to dictate the course my life would take. I had pretty much stopped writing new music in the eighties. There was no time to write and no motivation, surrounded as I was by people who were earning their living by touring. I became fascinated with the emerging technology called "midi," using musical instruments interfaced with a computer as a composing tool. I used to write my songs by recording my guitar and vocals into a tape recorder. Every writer has his own process. Some begin with a drum groove and build on that. Others have notebooks full of lyrics looking for a melody. I tend to write a chord structure first, then find a groove that fits. Often I sketch in the melody using a scat vocal. This enables me to find a melodic structure that feels comfortable for my voice and my range. Then comes the lyric. This is the fun part for me. Once I've established the subject matter, the lyrics fall into place pretty quickly.

This new technology completely changed the way I looked at songwriting. Because everything was built on a digital time code, the drums always came first. They were the framework you could hang everything else on. Then came the chord structure. At first I'd write the chords on guitar, as I had always done, but soon I realized that the keyboard was a more efficient way to input data into a computer so I began to teach myself to play piano. It was a little late in life to master a complex instrument like the piano, but the technology was growing by leaps and bounds and before long, with the advent of digital audio, I was able to program my Mac with my guitar, my voice or virtually any instrument the composition demanded. Now there were no limits to what I could do in my little home studio in Pomona. Soon the spare bedroom was overflowing with electronics—keyboards, drum machines, midi gadgets, computers and mixing boards. Ashleigh used to say it looked like the deck of the starship *Enterprise*.

By the early nineties I was experimenting with digital audio programs, samplers and analog drum loops. I sensed that this was just the beginning of a massive explosion of digital technology that would revolutionize the music business, and I wanted to learn everything I could about it. This was exciting stuff and the possibilities were endless. I could record new compositions with real instruments directly into my computer, writing melodies and lyrics, editing, cutting and pasting. It was like fingerpainting with music. I could create new songs and arrangements right there at home, then take the demos into a professional studio and give them to live musicians. Most of the young guys in the band had grown up with this stuff, so it was important that the "old man" could communicate with them on their level and knew what he was talking about. Frank DeGennaro kept himself up on the latest developments and was enormously helpful in building my home studio. I realized early on that my programmed bass lines and drum tracks would never replace live musicians, but it was a way I could get my ideas across to the band. This process fascinated me, and I began writing again after several years of creative drought. I discovered something about myself in that little home studio in Pomona. I was still a pretty good songwriter, and this new technology had lit the fire again.

Being a songwriter and a performer is a somewhat schizophrenic existence. Finding a balance between these two sometimes conflicting lifestyles is the secret of survival in this game. As a performer you are out there surrounded by people. It's a high-energy contact sport, and I love it. Songwriting is a more reclusive exercise.

The long hours in my home studio were beginning to pay off. I had a large stash of new songs and more on the way. The joy of creating new music is indescribable. Each song is your child, and like any proud parent you want everyone to know how special your child is. I was writing new music and it had to be heard.

There lies the rub. New York studio time is expensive, and New York musicians don't come cheap either. Since the current band had no record deal, the sessions would have to be paid for by the BS&T road show, meaning we had to tour even more to meet the expenses of recording, leaving even less time to focus on the writing and recording of new music … Catch-22. For Larry Dorr and the band, this was a gold mine. I needed money to record my new songs, so I couldn't afford to turn down any dates, which meant more work for everyone. In addition, I was giving the guys a lot of work in the studio. My insistence on recording new music was a pain in the ass and a drain on the cash flow, but what the hell, I was the franchise and, bottom line, I was paying for it. From my point of view, if I had to drag my ass through a dozen airports and play a dozen oldies shows to pay for the recording of one new song, it was well worth it.

I recorded a blues album at Ornette Coleman's studio in Harlem. Frank DeGennaro had done some engineering work for

Ornette and we had a chance to get some cheap studio time. We didn't spend a lot of money on the album. It was mostly just for fun, and I was hungry to get back into the studio again. It had been a long time. Doc flew down from Toronto and we put together a small band made up of a few blues players I knew from around town and some of the guys from my road band. The record was called *Blue Plate Special*. It was a tribute to my blues idols. It contained some classic blues tunes that I had always wanted to record and a few of my new songs written at the house in Pomona. There were no charts—it was just a blues jam, but it turned out great. The tunes are funky and soulful and you can tell the players are having a great time. A year passed, and when Larry Dorr couldn't seem to find a distributor for the album, Doc stepped in and arranged to have it released on a Canadian blues label called Stony Plain Records. I wasn't upset that Larry couldn't find a deal for this record. I figured it was a pure blues album, and I didn't have much credibility as a blues singer after the pop success of BS&T. I was just happy to be in the studio again and to see the record released, even if it was on an obscure little roots blues label in Canada.

The *Blue Plate Special* experience got my creative juices flowing again, and I began to put together a new project at a studio in Rockland County called Beartracks. It was home base for the jazz fusion band Spyro Gyra. Just a few minutes from my house in Pomona, it had a beautiful, rustic 150-year-old farmhouse with a large stone barn that had been converted into a modern state-of-the-art recording studio. The new project was entitled *Bloodlines*. I was touring with Blood Sweat & Tears and I figured Larry would have a better chance of shopping a deal if we made an album that had something to do with what we were doing onstage. The fans were constantly asking about a new BS&T record, and I wanted to give them one. I knew I couldn't use the name Blood Sweat & Tears without Bobby's permission, but I figured this was a way to pay tribute to the rich musical history of the band and to record with some of the guys who played with me in concert every night. The project would be a collection of all-new, original songs featuring the current members of BS&T, along with some of the band's illustrious alumni. Most of the A-team musicians in New York had been in BS&T at one time or another. Soloff, Lipsius, Bargeron, Mike Stern, Don Alias, Randy Brecker—they were all BS&T alumni. In fact, it was hard to call the top players in New York without including ex-BS&T members. I had a world-class studio just a couple of miles from my house, with top-notch engineers and a great recording environment. I had access to the top musicians in New York City, and Doc would fly down from Toronto in a heartbeat any time I called. I started making calls, and when I explained the concept behind the *Bloodlines* album, everyone was enthusiastic. I had some great new tunes and three talented arrangers in Doc, Tony Klatka and Fred Lipsius. This would be the coda on my career with Blood Sweat & Tears. One last album with all the great players I had worked with over the years, and then I could move on.

We worked on *Bloodlines* for the better part of a year, with Doc flying in from Toronto, Klatka from Denver and Freddie from Boston. They would stay with me at the house in Pomona. We'd get to hang out for a few days of swimming, cooking out on the back deck and working on the charts in my little home studio. Then we'd take the tunes in to Beartracks, where we'd cut the tracks. We basically recorded two or three tunes at a time, squeezing recording dates into our busy tour schedules and arranging sessions around the availability of our all-star cast of guest musicians. Every session was different and fun because you never knew who might show up. As word spread around town about what we were up to, ex-BS&T members began to call me. "Hey, man, I hear you're doing a session with Freddie and Lew. Need a guitar player?" We had a great time recording that album. Every session was like old home week. Many of us hadn't been in the studio together for years, and it felt good to be making music with all these old friends again.

I paid for the album myself, close to $100,000, and when *Bloodlines* was completed I again turned to Larry Dorr. As my business manager, it was his job to find a record deal. I didn't figure there'd be a problem. The album was a killer, and some of the biggest names in jazz were playing on it. I had printed up a couple of thousand CDs and they were selling like hotcakes out on the road. The BS&T fans loved this record. A year passed, and when the album hadn't been released I began to wonder … Maybe Larry had no interest in getting record deals for my solo projects. His money came from booking BS&T on the oldies circuit, and my insistence on writing new music was a threat to his income. Maybe he didn't *want* a new record release by me. A new album might enable me to strike out on my own and, oops, there goes the franchise. He knew I'd never be content to just ride off into the sunset as an oldies act. I was too driven by my own creative demons to settle for that. He also knew that I was actively looking for a way to put my dependence on the Blood Sweat & Tears name behind me once and for all. I was terribly conflicted about that name. On the one hand I was so proud of what it represented in terms of its musical legacy, but on the other hand

I resented the control it exercised over my life. I knew I would never have ownership in the name, and Bobby Colomby could revoke the licence any time he wanted to. You can't run a business or ever feel secure with that sword hanging over your head. When we took on the name, Larry and I had agreed that it would just be for a couple of years until we could establish my name and launch my long-overdue solo career, but what I had feared was now a reality. Nearly ten years had passed, and the BS&T name was generating so much money that it was controlling everything. Any thought of a solo career was long forgotten.

Bobby Colomby wasn't interested in endorsing a new BS&T album and a David Clayton-Thomas album with the original BS&T members playing on it ... Never! It was the kiss of death for *Bloodlines*. I should have realized that Colomby would not allow Dorr to shop a deal for *Bloodlines*, but I had naïvely believed that Larry Dorr was his own man. I thought that he was my friend and my manager and that he had my best interests at heart. Now the truth finally hit me. Larry Dorr may have been working for me, but he rented the use of the name from Bobby Colomby and he was taking his orders from him. Once more the ownership of the BS&T name would jump up and bite me in the ass.

I confronted Larry about his failure to find a record deal for *Bloodlines*, but he told me that Colomby had killed the project and there was nothing he could do about it. Bobby had apparently threatened to revoke the use of the name if this record came out, and Larry wasn't going to risk that. I can't blame him for this decision. Had Bobby pulled the name it would have put twenty-five people out of work—good, loyal people, some who had given twenty years of their lives to our company and had families depending on us for their livelihood. Larry and I weren't willing to risk that, so I suggested a compromise. There were several record companies interested in a new BS&T album, so how about we call *Bloodlines* a Blood Sweat & Tears album and cut Bobby in for a share? It made sense. It was a damn fine recording, most of the original guys were playing on it, BS&T still had a huge fan following and Colomby was still making a ton of money from our concerts. It seemed to me that everybody's interests would be served by releasing this record. Colomby wouldn't even consider it. He still maintained that there was no legitimate Blood Sweat & Tears without him. Of course, he was still receiving cheques every week from this band that according to him didn't exist. I was disgusted with this hypocrisy and told Larry Dorr that I couldn't live this way. I had to put an end to my dependence on Colomby and the BS&T name once and for all. If he couldn't do it, I'd find a manager who could. I told Larry that he was fired, contacted our agency in LA and told them I was coming out there to shop for new management. This move blew the lid off everything and the truth came out. Since Colomby had leased the name directly to Larry Dorr and Larry had signed the name to the agency, it now became apparent that I couldn't fire him … He didn't work for me. He worked for Bobby Colomby. I signed his paycheques, but Bobby gave the orders. That god-damned name again.

Larry called Bobby and told him that I had fired him, and of course Bobby called the agency and told them they couldn't use the name unless Larry Dorr was the manager. Check and mate. This caused an immediate panic. The agency had a million dollars worth of concerts booked over the next year or so. Contracts had been signed, commitments had been made and without the name there were no gigs. Airline tickets had been purchased for months in advance, and they don't give refunds on group tickets. There would have been lawsuits, and of course it would mean unemployment for everybody in our organization. I was trapped. I couldn't get out of BS&T for at least another year, *Bloodlines* would never be released and Larry Dorr was still my manager, like it or not.

Things were very tense between Larry and me that summer. The truth was out and I felt betrayed by my best friend. But Larry was a damn good salesman and he pleaded his case. He told me that he was just as much a victim in this as I was. He said he despised Colomby and hated being controlled by him, and he promised to dedicate himself to getting us out of this mess. He came up with another brilliant idea. He suggested that I make a Christmas album. Larry said he could easily find a distributor for such a project, and Colomby wasn't threatened by a Christmas album so he wouldn't stand in our way. Dorr said it would help him promote my name as a solo artist and would open the doors for my own record deal. He urged me to forget about *Bloodlines* and get back into the studio right away.

I was reluctant to throw away twenty years of friendship with Larry Dorr. I really wanted to believe him and I understood all too well what he was up against, so I decided to give it one more shot. I figured maybe if the Christmas album was successful it would save Larry and me both from a lifetime of being controlled by Colomby. Steve Guttman and I booked a studio in downtown Manhattan and we went to work on the Christmas album. It's a beautiful piece of work, consisting of funky jazz renditions of traditional songs like "Little Drummer Boy" and "We Three Kings." The recording featured some of the best musicians in New York City. Steve and I were extremely proud of this record.

But Christmas came and went, and then another Christmas, and that album wasn't released either. This one cost me $75,000 and six months of work. It was the last straw. A Christmas album is the easiest thing in the world to sell. Everyone from Pat Boone to Alvin and the Chipmunks had a Christmas album out, and this was a beautiful recording by an artist who was still playing for thousands of fans every night.

It was the end of my relationship with Larry Dorr and ultimately with Blood Sweat & Tears. Larry had been faced with a clear choice. It was either loyalty to his best friend or control over the name. He chose the name. He once said to me, "The BS&T name is a licence to print money." Our friendship had given him control over that licence and now it controlled him. Larry Dorr had a sure thing with Blood Sweat & Tears, and staking his future on the solo career of a sixty-year-old rock singer was a risky venture at best. Larry Dorr wasn't a risk taker.

Doc Riley, who played on every one of those albums that would never be released, was pushing me relentlessly. He told me, "It breaks my heart to see you writing these great songs that no one will ever hear. What a waste." My closest friends were all advising me to get away from Blood Sweat & Tears once and for all. It was a dead-end street, and they knew me well enough to know that I was still a fiercely creative individual who would wither and die if I couldn't write new music. They were worried about me. The constant touring was taking its toll on my health, and with no possibility of recording new music I was suffocating creatively. The failure of Larry Dorr to give me an outlet for my new music was becoming intolerable. Having a manager who lived in constant fear that I would say or do something to offend Colomby, resulting in his revoking the use of the BS&T name, was a Damocles' sword I could no longer live under. The idea of still being controlled by Bobby Colomby, a guy who hadn't played in the band for thirty years, was becoming more repugnant to me all the time. I loved the guys in BS&T and I loved what it stood for musically, but I hated what that name was doing to us all. Once more, the war for control of that name had poisoned everything it touched. That name was born of a power struggle between some massive egos and now, thirty years later, it was still controlling my life. I'd had enough of Blood Sweat & Tears. I wanted out. I wasn't getting any younger and the road wasn't getting any easier. Robbie Robertson observed in the movie *The Last Waltz,* "The road is a goddamned impossible way of life." It was becoming more goddamned impossible for me every year.

The Lights of Broadway

I remember the day, I remember the sound
I remember one day in September
When the world came thunderin' down
This is my hometown, the lady's lookin' down
Clouds of dust, ashes in her eyes, cinders on her gown

But the lights up on Broadway still shine
And the bells of St. Patrick's still chime
Go tell the world we're singin' songs of freedom
And the lights up on Broadway still shine

So we never forget, so we always remain
So that heroes never are forgotten
And their lives were not given in vain
This is my hometown, the lady's lookin' down
Clouds of dust, ashes in her eyes, cinders on her gown

You know the lights up on Broadway still shine
And the bells of St. Patrick's still chime
Go tell the world we're singin' songs of freedom
And the lights up on Broadway still shine

25
9/11

The late nineties were a mixed blessing. The house in Pomona was comfortable and it was great to have my daughter nearby, but it was a family community—a great place to live if your life revolved around Little League and PTA meetings. I was only there a few days a week, mostly weekdays, and on those days the little town emptied out by 9:00 a.m., as my neighbours commuted to work in the city and Ashleigh left for school. I was very much alone all day. After Suzanne, I was reluctant to subject myself or my daughter to another live-in girlfriend. I was getting a little old for such foolishness. I worked long hours in my studio writing new songs, but by now it was obvious that as long as I was in Blood Sweat & Tears no one would ever hear them. Quitting was not as simple as it might seem. We were booked for nearly a year in advance and my name was on those contracts. It would take time to wind down this money-making machine, so I trudged through airports week after week and dreamed of the day when I'd be out of BS&T. But we still had some of the best players in the business and the music of the band kept me going. When on occasion we played a class venue, the old spirit would come back and I would prove to myself that we could still knock it out of the park. But for every class concert we played there were a dozen oldies shows at third-rate casinos, Woodstock revivals and rib festivals. ("Hey, can we hold the show until after the pig races?") It was heartbreaking to see this once-great concert band playing under the roller coaster at county fairs as the subtleties of the music were drowned out by the clang of the midway. But Larry Dorr had a payroll to meet every week and he couldn't afford to be too picky about the venues, and Bobby Colomby didn't care where we played as long as those cheques kept coming in. Neither of them gave a damn about the show. They weren't out there. The repertoire hadn't changed in years either. There was barely enough time to rehearse new players for the show that night, let alone introduce new tunes. The oldies crowd wanted to hear the hits from the sixties. That's what Larry Dorr was selling, and that's what we delivered. I found myself singing the same songs night after night. There was nothing to challenge me musically anymore. I could do the BS&T show in my sleep.

As for the musicians, they may have been carrying the name of a group called Blood Sweat & Tears, but they weren't really a group anymore. These guys were hired guns. They were in it for the money, and they made no secret of it. There is a certain mercenary honesty to New York City musicians. If you want the best, you'll have to pay serious money, and you will get what you pay for. You can buy the best players in the world in New York City, but make no mistake—they're not your buddies, they're money players. Somebody offers them fifty bucks a night more, and they're gone in a big-city minute. Most of the band didn't even have my home phone number. The only reason they would have to call me was if they wanted a raise, and I steered clear of band politics. If they had problems they could call Larry Dorr or Steve Guttman. It was their job to handle the business of the band.

The magic of the early band was that initially we weren't in it for the money. Playing little clubs in Greenwich Village with a nine-piece band is not exactly the way to get rich. We were driven by the music we were creating, and as complex and contentious as the relationships may have been, there was love in that early band. We argued like family and we fought like brothers, but when we hit the stage the personal differences were forgotten and the band came together with a common purpose—the love of the music. It was all for one and one for all when we were a struggling band on Bleecker Street. Then twenty million dollars was thrown into the mix and it became every man for himself. The spirit of that early band was long gone, and I was tired of working to support a payroll for guys who cared nothing about the creative legacy of Blood Sweat & Tears. This was not what I wanted for my life, and I knew that for my own self-respect and physical well-being I had to put an end to it. The only way to get out of Blood Sweat & Tears was to get out of New York. As long as I was there I was tied to the band and the million-dollar-a-year business operation that was BS&T. I talked it over with Doc and Bill and told them I was coming home. They offered to help me in any way they could. Ashleigh was graduating from SUNY that year and there would be nothing holding me in New York anymore. I began making plans to leave BS&T and move back to Canada. It was no secret that I was leaving. A for-sale sign stood on the front lawn of the house in Pomona.

There were numerous recording opportunities for me in my home country, where I had become somewhat of a musical icon. I had been inducted into the Canadian Music Hall of Fame in 1996 and a few years later into the Canadian Songwriters Hall of Fame. Doug Riley was by now one of the most respected musicians in Canada. In 2004 Doc was awarded the Order of Canada, the highest civilian honour our country can bestow. Bruce Cassidy had returned to Toronto after several years in South

Africa and was now a highly successful musician and composer. He and Doc would make sure that I was surrounded by the finest musical talent in Canada.

Then, two days before my sixtieth birthday, on September 11, 2001, everything changed. I had been in Manhattan nearly every day that summer, working on the Christmas album with Steve Guttman. We'd been recording at a studio on 47th Street just off Broadway, right in the middle of Manhattan. I have a lifelong love affair with New York City. Sometimes it has been a love-hate relationship, but thirty years of my life have been lived there, so my feelings for the city run deep. New York City had been such a force in my life for so long that I considered myself a New Yorker. It was 9:30 in the morning and I was at the house in Pomona sipping a last cup of coffee before I left for the city when the horrific pictures from the World Trade Center disaster flashed across the morning news.

I took 9/11 very personally. This was *my* city that was under attack. Pomona was a bedroom community, and some of my friends and neighbours who worked on Wall Street didn't come home that night. Kids that my daughter had grown up with lost parents on that terrible day. The airports were closed, all concerts were cancelled and there was no going into Manhattan for several days. So I stayed up in Pomona and watched the tragedy unfold on television with the rest of America. As I watched the incredible heroics of everyday New Yorkers, I felt the need to contribute something myself, so I did what I have always done in times of trouble. I holed up in my studio for several days and wrote a song. It was called "The Lights of Broadway," and it was my gift to the city I loved. A month or so later, with a chorus of NYPD officers, we recorded the song at the studio on 47th Street and donated it to the victims' families so that all money generated by the song will forever go directly to the widows and orphans of the people who died on that tragic day.

In the weeks and months that followed, it became apparent that America would never be the same again. For a band like ours, which travelled several days a week, it was exhausting. Long delays, increased airport security and cancelled flights crippled our touring schedule. Our problems were a minor inconvenience compared to the agony the whole country was feeling, but they cut the heart out of the band. Touring became even more difficult. The gigs were fewer and farther apart. We spent long hours in airports waiting on delayed flights and would come home from the road exhausted and demoralized. But now I couldn't leave. I drove up to Toronto and had dinner with Doc and Bill. I explained to them that my plans to return to Toronto had been put on hold—9/11 had changed everything. I just couldn't run away to Canada when my friends and neighbours in New York needed me.

Over the next three years New York slowly returned to normal. And as the memory of 9/11 faded into history I began to refocus on my plans to move back to Canada. I put the house in Pomona back up for sale and told Larry that this would be my last year with Blood Sweat & Tears. He was to accept no new contracts. The gruelling tour schedule that had been a way of life for the past thirty years became even harder in the post-9/11 years, and I couldn't keep it up any longer. The trust between me and Larry had been broken and there was no way to fix it. Since apparently I couldn't fire him, I had to leave. It was long overdue anyway. BS&T hadn't recorded in twenty-five years and my attempts to release new music had hit a brick wall. Colomby had no intention of recording BS&T and Larry Dorr had no intention of making a record deal for me. For a songwriter, this is intolerable. I was writing better than ever, and I had things to say. I needed to make records that would actually be heard.

Mercy Lord Above

I'm movin' in a new direction, can you deal with that
Clear up a little misconception, show where it's at
Stop tellin' me to make my mind up, can't you let me be
Stop tellin' me how much you gave up just to be with me

Oh yeah, now there's no more me and you … understand
Oh yeah, there's not a damn thing I can do
It's the same old story, same old plans
Same old somethin' just keeps slippin' through your hands

I believe you just go round one time, I believe in true love
I believe it's all gone in no time, mercy, Lord above

Lord knows I did the best I could do, wasn't good enough
I bet you called all your girlfriends, talkin' all kinds of stuff
I need a little inspiration, need to catch my breath
Some devil in the way you do things scares me half to death

Oh yeah, now there's no more me and you … understand
Oh yeah, there's not a damn thing I can do
I must have been crazy, I must have been blind
Now you can tell all your friends I must have lost my mind

26

I AM GOLD

My old friend Bill Pugliese was now a multi-millionaire with powerful business connections in Canada. Bill is a unique character. A high school dropout who became an international entrepreneur, he has been called by financial journals "Bullion Bill the Billionaire Biker." Even today this corporate CEO still rides his Harley.

In 1989 Bill and a team of Canadian geologists investigated reports of an enormous gold deposit in Mali, West Africa. In a remote villge called Sadiola they discovered a virtual mountain of gold. Bill called me in New York at the time and told me, "Hey, David, I've just found King Solomon's mines." I laughed. "Yeah, right. So how's the golf game?" He wasn't kidding. Local folklore believes that this was indeed the source of the legend of King Solomon's mines. Over the next few years, teaming with a South African mining conglomerate, they invested millions in Mali. They rebuilt the town of Sadiola. They piped in water, and built schools and hospitals and housing for the thousands of local families employed by the mine. The Mali operation yielded close to fifty billion dollars in gold in the first five years. Bill is the chairman of IAMGOLD, one of the most successful gold-mining operations in the world. The company he founded in 1990 now operates mines in Africa, South America and Canada. It produces about a million ounces of gold per year and is listed on the New York and Toronto stock exchanges. In 2007 my friend Bill

Pugliese received the Ernst & Young Entrepreneur of the Year award. Not bad for a working-class kid from Willowdale, eh?

Bill is a tough, hard-nosed businessman, but beneath his gruff exterior lies a keen and inquisitive mind. Even in our teens our conversations were not the usual teenage banter of our friends. They talked about hockey, cars and girls. Bill and I read sci-fi novels and grappled with abstract concepts in comparative religion and with the meaning of life ... and of course we talked about hockey, cars and girls. We got into some heavy topics for a couple of working-class kids from the suburbs of Toronto, but it was the foundation of our friendship. We were reading science-fiction writers like Asimov and Bradbury when the other kids were reading the sports pages. To this day, Sunday dinners with the Puglieses are a regular part of my life. Bill's wife, Linda, is a wonderful cook and the dinners are usually attended by several members of the family. The food is delicious and the talk around the table is always lively. Conversation at dinner is usually about the latest movies and TV shows, the Leafs, the kids and the grandkids. But when the dishes are cleared away, Bill and I find a quiet corner, and over a glass of fine cognac we turn our imaginations loose. Our talks are always interesting. The topics range from new technology and the latest scientific breakthroughs to world financial trends, the origins of the universe, the big bang and quantum theory. We are very different people and we live in very different worlds. Bill's world is one of acquisitions and stock trades and boardrooms. Mine is a world of art and music and theatre. But in those Sunday get-togethers, the old Willowdale friendship kicks in and we know why we've been friends for so many years. Each of us in our own way is driven by creativity and an insatiable curiosity, and we understand each other.

Bill offered to help me move my financial and business affairs from New York to Toronto. It was 2005 and the US was still enjoying the fruits of the Clinton surplus. The dollar was strong, real estate was at an all-time high and the stock market was booming. The financial wizards were euphoric. They thought the US dollar was bulletproof. Bill strongly felt that the US economy was about to hit the wall. He'd been telling me for years that the US was printing too much money, they'd been living on credit and their banking system was about to collapse. He advised me to get out of the stock market, sell the house in Pomona and dump all my real estate holdings while the market was on the bubble. Sell everything and bring those high-value US dollars into Canada and buy gold—gold bullion, gold certificates, stock in Bill's gold-mining company. I followed his advice and, sure enough, three years after I moved to Canada the US dollar tanked. In 2008 the real-estate bubble burst, banks failed, the sub-prime crisis hit the country like a sledgehammer and gold went through the roof. I took the profits and diversified into a broad-based investment portfolio, again with Bill's guidance. Thanks to his shrewd advice I was no longer dependent on the music industry for my livelihood. I was financially secure for the first time in my life.

Ashleigh had worked hard at SUNY Purchase. She was passionate about her studies and made the dean's list every semester. I was so proud of her. Once she graduated from SUNY, she wanted to go on to postgraduate studies, and Toronto has some of the finest colleges in the world for what she is interested in— writing for film and television. There was nothing holding me in New York anymore and I began driving back and forth to Toronto several times a month, looking for a place to live, checking out schools for Ashleigh and moving Antoinette Music Productions to Canada.

Back in 2004 I played out my last concerts with BS&T. Larry and the boys weren't happy about me leaving, but they knew I'd had enough. My life would never again consist of 250 days a year on the road, and that's really all they wanted from me. Larry Dorr had made his choice and I was no longer of any use to him. My days of touring year-round were over and I had nothing to offer to a guy like Larry who made his living by booking road acts. In all fairness to Larry, he had a family to support and bills to pay and people who depended on him to generate dates. He was a capable businessman, but there wasn't an artistic bone in his body. He'd listen to one of my new tunes and tell me, "People aren't buying that kind of music anymore, David, it's all about rap today. Why don't you write some hip-hop tunes?" He just didn't get it. It wasn't about cashing in on trends. My songs were my life, and I didn't give a damn if they were in fashion or not.

Larry wasn't long on imagination, but he had his good points. I've trusted him to walk around backstage with twenty grand in cash in his jeans and never gave it a second thought. He was always straight up with the money—a rare thing in this business.

Larry Dorr was an interesting paradox. This was a guy who made his living selling music, but the truth was he didn't listen to music and he didn't like musicians and he was the first to admit it. Music was an easy way to make money and musicians were just annoying problems that had to be dealt with. In a strange way this made him very good at what he did. He was detached and dispassionate about the band and their problems, and the guys lived in fear of him. He'd help a guy out if he was a good soldier, but cross him and you were gone. Ironically, this made my job easier. Dorr was the hatchet man, and nobody crossed me for fear of bringing down the wrath of Larry Dorr. Musicians are bright, clever people, but they can be spoiled and manipulative. With Larry Dorr in charge, this band wasn't going to tear itself apart the way some earlier editions did. When you have a nine-piece band with new guys coming and going all the time, this kind of discipline helps to keep things running smoothly. Larry Dorr ran a tight ship, and I have to admire him for that.

The production guys were fine people and good friends. They had been with me for nearly twenty years and I cared about them. I knew their families and their kids and I was sorry that I had to be the one to end it, but I couldn't trust Larry Dorr anymore, and without trust the artist–manager relationship is meaningless. But that's not the only reason I had to call it quits. I was now in my sixties, with arthritic knees and all the aches and pains that come with forty years of rock & roll, and I simply couldn't keep up that pace. Even if Dorr had continued as my manager, he would have had to change his focus from the road to more creative endeavours, and "creative" wasn't in his vocabulary. He was a booker and that's all he knew.

I love performing and I have no intention of ever quitting, but it's the relentless year-round travel that kills you. The only thing that makes it worthwhile is that brief time onstage every night. When that's not fun anymore it's time to quit. I hated most of the gigs we were playing. The quality of the bookings had been spiralling downward as, more and more, the demands of the payroll dictated the quality of the gigs. Life on Larry Dorr's tour schedule was exhausting for guys half my age, and I wasn't prepared to spend the rest of my life on this endless treadmill of airports and oldies shows.

Even without me the name Blood Sweat & Tears was still worth money on the nostalgia circuit and Larry Dorr went with the cash flow. After I left, Bobby Colomby once again rented the name to Larry, who hired some new guys and called them Blood Sweat & Tears. Now they're out there playing the oldies shows. That's fine with me. They're taking gigs that I don't want anyway. The use of that name locks them forever in 1969 and I'm finally free to move on. At first I was angry that Larry was going to continue to book the name with no original members, but what the hell—except for me there hadn't been an original Blood Sweat & Tears member since the mid-seventies, and I had certainly profited from the use of the name. But then again I wrote most of those songs, it was my voice on those records and I had given half a lifetime to that name. I had earned the right to use it. I couldn't help resenting the fact that they were calling these new guys Blood Sweat & Tears. That name once meant something. For God's sake, let it die with dignity. But that's not going to happen. As long as Dorr and Colomby can squeeze a few more bucks out of it, they'll continue to flog it. I don't blame the musicians. It's not their fault, it's just another gig to them. I know a couple of the guys in the new band. They're nice guys and fine players. One of them called me in Toronto. He wanted to know if I'd be upset if he took the BS&T gig. He said, "Hey, man, it's really tough out there right now and I can't afford to turn down the work." I told him, "It's all right, man, take the gig. I'd never ask a guy to turn down work. We've all had to play weddings and bar mitzvahs. At least in BS&T you'll get to play some really good music."

Early in 2008 new legislation was passed that requires an original member in order to use a name. It was called the Mary Wilson Act, for the Supremes singer who lobbied for a law to prevent exploitation of a name without the founding members. Before the Mary Wilson Act there were a dozen "Supremes" and "Drifters" and "Platters" out there. Whoever owned the name could sell it, and they flogged these classic names shamelessly. There might be a "Drifters" playing in five different cities all on the same night. It was a rip-off. The folks buying tickets didn't know it wasn't the original Drifters and for the most part they didn't care as long as they heard those great songs that took them back to their youth. Blood Sweat & Tears was perilously close to falling into that category. The Mary Wilson Act put an end to all that.

Deering Howe called me from Florida and told me the law had gone into effect down there. He said, "Well, I guess that's the end of BS&T." I laughed. I'd been around the track too many times to believe that. Larry Dorr wasn't going down that easy—not as long as there was still money to be made from that name. I told Deering, "Just watch, Dorr will find an original BS&T member who's been out of the band for thirty-five years and needs the money. He'll bring that guy out of retirement just to keep the name alive." I was right. A few weeks later Steve Katz was back in the band after a thirty-five-year "hiatus." Strange bedfellows, but Larry Dorr had his original member and BS&T was still in business.

Oh well, so it goes ... I've been around long enough to know that as long as there is a buck to be made, someone will find a way to make it, and I can't begrudge anyone the right to earn a living. I know how tough that can be. But if they are going to drain the last drop of blood from Blood Sweat & Tears, they'll have to do it without me.

I've always been driven by the need to write new music. It's what took me from the bars of Yonge Street to the clubs of

Yorkville. It's the reason I starved in New York for two years when I had hit records in Canada. It's what made Blood Sweat & Tears the creative force that rocked the music world in 1969. It's that drive to create new music that gave them the hits they are selling on the nostalgia circuit today. If, God willing, I have another decade or so to spend in the music business, I choose to spend it writing new music and playing concerts that I enjoy, not grinding it out on the road somewhere, living in hotel rooms, playing tunes that I wrote thirty years ago. I choose to do business with promoters who present original artists, and to perform for audiences who know the difference. Call me crazy, but it's the right choice for me.

Wild Women and Po' Boys

Take me out dancin', my sweet Marie
Let me be the one you're with tonight
Take me out dancin' my *belle cherie*
You know I will always treat you right
By golly I guarantee, come along with me, we'll do it right
Down in Bay St. Louis that's the only place to be on a Saturday night
Wild women and po' boys just go hand in hand
A shot of blackjack whisky, you'll be dancing with the band
Well the music is funky, the food is just fine
And you can get crazy all night long

Take me out dancin', my Marie Claire
Let me be the one right by your side
Take me out dancin', *mon dieu, ma chère*
Sure do love my Loosiana bride

Lyrics by David Clayton-Thomas. Copyright © Clayton-Thomas Music Publishing Inc., 2005.

27

JUSTIN TIME

I had long dreamed of a lakefront penthouse in Toronto. Every time Doc and I went to a hockey game together I would point to the soaring luxury apartment buildings along the lakeshore and say, "Someday, Doc, someday." In January 2005 I sold the house in Pomona and bought a rooftop penthouse in Toronto overlooking Lake Ontario. It's a large two-bedroom condo with a rooftop terrace in a luxury building with all the amenities—a doorman, a concierge and a fully equipped health club. The open-concept apartment has a modern kitchen, a dining room, an entertainment area and my studio all in one large high-ceilinged room. I moved my furniture and my digital recording gear up from New York and settled in to enjoy life in Toronto. The waterfront condo is perfect for my lifestyle, right downtown, a few blocks from the theatre district and the jazz clubs of Queen Street, close by the Air Canada Centre for Leafs and Raptors games and a couple of blocks from the Rogers Centre and the Blue Jays. The CN Tower rises into the sky right behind me. In the summer the harbour is full of sailboats, cruise ships and water taxis. The boardwalk outside my front door is teeming with life … tourists, rollerbladers, young lovers walking hand in hand along the waterfront.

Within a year after I moved back to Canada, Ashleigh enrolled at Humber College in Toronto to begin postgrad studies. One look at my new multipurpose crib and she joked, "Well,

Dad, you got your wish, you're finally living in a recording studio." I began writing almost immediately. The large, airy condo with its spectacular views and magnificent sunrises was inspiring, and in Toronto I was surrounded by a vibrant creative community. I was among people who were encouraging me to write. This was a breath of fresh air after so many years of being manipulated by people whose very livelihood was threatened by my creativity.

I signed a contract for three albums with a fine independent record company from Montreal called Justin Time Records, the top jazz label in Canada, a nice family-owned company whose president, Jim West, was well respected in the Canadian music industry. I took an immediate liking to Jim. He ran a company that really cared about its artists and seriously loved their music. My immediate rep at Justin Time was Jadro Subic, a bright and beautiful Croatian lady who spoke five languages and had a PhD in musicology. Jadro had seen BS&T in Yugoslavia when we toured Eastern Europe in 1970. It was this experience that inspired her to study music in Rome. Now, thirty-five years later, married with two kids, she was my project manager at Justin Time Records in Montreal. It's amazing how music can shape the lives of people halfway around the world. Jadro and I spoke almost daily during my years at Justin Time. We became great friends and still are today.

Doc Riley and I co-produced the first album, *Aurora*. Doc assembled an all-star quintet of musicians: legendary jazz drummer Terry Clarke; an absolute genius of a stand-up bass player, George Koller; Rob Piltch, my old friend and collaborator from the *Nuclear Blues* days; and a brilliant young guitarist named Jake Langley, the 2004 National Jazz Awards winner. I was eager to get some new product in the can to kick-start my relationship with Justin Time, so there wasn't really time to write much new material. My life was in transition at the time. We chose a couple of jazz standards and some classic blues, and I managed to contribute a few new original tunes, some written for the abortive *Bloodlines* album and some literally written in the studio for the *Aurora* sessions. Doc handled most of the production, with me flying in and out of Toronto every few days (I was still closing down the house and business in New York and playing out the last few BS&T dates). The whole album took less than a month to complete. The sessions were a joy. BS&T in the last few months wasn't much fun, given the tension between Larry Dorr and me and the uncertainty of the band's future. The relief of being out of that BS&T pressure cooker came across in the studio. Doc, of course, was sensational, and the recording atmosphere was relaxed, just a bunch of old friends jamming live in the studio. Shortly after my furniture arrived in Toronto, I had a new CD out on a respected Canadian jazz label.

I took a full year off the road and devoted myself entirely to writing new music and enjoying the company of my friends. I was finally able to do things that most people take for granted. For years I'd always been on the road somewhere on weekends. Now I had time to enjoy life. During the week there were evenings at jazz clubs with Doc and our musician friends. Actually sitting in the audience and enjoying the music of other artists was something I hadn't done for years.

I spent nearly every weekend that summer with Bill and his family, cruising along the rocky Georgian Bay shoreline on their fifty-five-foot cabin cruiser, the engines thrumming softly under our feet, Bill and I playing backgammon and carrying on our never-ending conversation about the meaning of life. We'd anchor for the night in the shelter of one of the rugged little pine-covered islands scattered throughout the northern lakes. Out on the water, the boat gently rocking me to sleep, the silence of the cool Canadian evening broken only by the lonely cry of the loons. Fishing for bass and perch, pan-fried for breakfast on the boat, the morning mist slowly lifting on the mirror-smooth lake. Afternoons spent skimming across the choppy water on Sea-Doos, laughing like kids as we bounced across each other's wake. Docking for dinner at little home-style country inns. Simple pleasures that had been missing from my life in the constant grind of touring. I found a deep well of inspiration in the beauty and solitude of the Muskoka lakes, and new songs began to take shape. The song "The Evergreens" speaks of the peace I found on those weekends in Muskoka.

My body slowly recovered from the battering it had taken over the past three decades, and I was ready to begin performing again. Bruce Cassidy and Doc Riley assembled a big band, ten pieces, the *crème de la crème* of Canadian jazz, an all-star band with Doc on keyboards and a six-piece horn section. There was a different spirit in this band. I was tired of performing with people who had no commitment to the music and to each other. These guys were all old friends and had played together for years. Some of them were with me in the *Nuclear Blues* band. The hired-gun mentality was gone. These were the guys I used to jam with in Toronto just for fun. Bruce and Doc would attract the best musicians in the business. Doc kept the music rooted, and Cassidy brought a progressive edge to the sound of the band. These guys talked straight with me. Cassidy made his opinions known right away. He told me that he wasn't interested in putting together a scaled-down low-budget version of the New York band to "play the hits." This wouldn't be "BS&T light." This would be a high-octane big band with a sound and a personality all its own. He expanded the old BS&T charts, adding baritone sax and bass trombone, putting some bottom on those brassy BS&T arrangements. This new band immediately sounded bigger and more powerful than the traditional BS&T lineup. We began to collaborate almost immediately on new material for the band. The musicians Doc and Bruce assembled were exceptional. This new band not only sounded bigger and better than the New York band, but they also played with a fire and enthusiasm that had been missing for years. This was an elite group of musicians and each concert was an event. New songs were included in the repertoire right from the first rehearsal, and the first shows were explosive. There was a fresh new sound to the music of this band and I loved it.

I had no intention of becoming a slave to a payroll again, so I told the new band right from the start, "Boys, this is not a road band. We are not going on the road two hundred days a year to put gas in the bus." This was a fine arrangement for these guys. They all had families and busy careers of their own in Toronto. Each musician is a bandleader, an educator or a recording artist in his own right. They have no more interest in being on the road year-round than I do—we've all paid those dues. The hit songs from the BS&T era sounded better than ever. Now, with the opportunity to introduce new music into the show and a band that brought new energy to the old songs, I was enjoying playing the classic hits again. I can't imagine doing a show without "Spinning Wheel" or "God Bless the Child." Those songs are the story of my life … my musical biography.

Jadro Subic suggested that *A Musical Biography* was a perfect title for a live-in-concert album. It was a way for me to put all my songs on record under my own name for the first time. So with Jadro's help we took the big band into the old Opera House theatre in Toronto, where Jim West and I co-produced a live-in-concert album.

I wrote several new tunes. Cassidy's expanded charts sounded incredible and the band was burnin'. It was a great night with a wildly enthusiastic audience of hometown fans driving me and the band to an inspired performance. The concert was amazing and the recording was even better. This is quite simply a great live recording. The show was brilliantly captured by recording engineer Ian Terry. There's no overdubbing, no studio fixes. What you hear is exactly what happened that night—a kick-ass big-band concert with a fabulous audience. It was released on Justin Time Records in 2006, entitled *David Clayton-Thomas in Concert: A Musical Biography*.

Next we performed at the prestigious Montreal Jazz Festival, where the show was filmed and recorded in 5.1 surround sound for a Bravo TV special and a DVD entitled *You're the One*, which was released a few months later. These were the kind of creative endeavours I'd had in mind when I left BS&T. At my age your legacy becomes very important, and I needed to do something more permanent than playing Indian-reservation casinos night after night. In two years we had put out more new music than BS&T had managed in the last twenty-five. Thanks to Justin Time I had the new show on CD and on DVD and we had the promotional tools to secure some really fine bookings for 2007. Now I needed an agent.

I set up a meeting with a local Toronto agency that was interested in booking the new show. We were all gathered around a conference table at their offices, the agents with their yellow legal pads, all armed with gigs to entice me to their agency. The president of the company began the meeting by telling me, "Look, David, the reality of the situation is this: BS&T is still out there. They're undercutting any offers we get. What we need to know is how much latitude are you giving us to lower your price enough to be competitive with them." He lost me right then and there, but I decided to give them my pitch anyway. I smiled and spoke to the room full of eager young agents. "Gentlemen," I said, "if I come with your agency, here's what we're going to do. We're not going to compete with BS&T. That'll turn into a mud-wrestling match. They'll undercut us, then we'll undercut them, and in a year both acts will be trashed. We'll both be working for peanuts. We're going to take the high road. We'll raise our price well above theirs and keep our standards high. If necessary we'll turn down every gig for the next year but trust me, eventually we'll get the shows we want on our own terms."

Turn down gigs? Did he say "Turn down gigs?" The faces fell around the room and the agents began packing up their yellow legal pads. I could tell they were disappointed, and so was I. This meeting was going nowhere. I was about to leave when down at the end of the table I noticed one fresh-faced young agent. He looked about eighteen, and he was grinning from ear to ear. After the meeting he followed me outside and introduced himself. He told me his name was Nick Meinema and he said he'd like to represent me. I asked him if he understood that my days of touring year-round were over. I didn't need the money and I could afford to be selective about my dates. One high-profile prestige concert was worth more to me than a hundred third-rate casino dates. He smiled even wider and said, "Oh yeah, boss, I understand all right, that's why I'd like to represent you." Right then and there I told him, "Okay, Nick, you're my guy."

One lesson I learned from Larry Dorr: "It's not the agency, it's the guy." Find an agent you can work with and he'll make the agency work for you. An artist's agent is probably the closest and most important person in his professional life. Most artists have managers who deal with the agents, but after surviving the Larry Dorr tour schedule I didn't need another manager. It's just one more guy who makes his living by putting my ass back on the road. Booking agencies generally aren't too concerned with the quality of gigs. It's the profit column at the end of the year that counts. They get their commission whether the act plays two hundred sleazy dates a year for chump-change or one class date for serious money. It's not their responsibility to guide the artist's career or shape his image. That's the manager's job. Their job is to book dates. An agent's success is measured by how many offers he submits. It's the manager's responsibility to determine which ones are good for his artist's career. Now that I'm managing myself, those decisions are mine and I needed an agent who shared my point of view.

A few weeks later Nick Meinema tendered his resignation at the local agency and he and I went together to the Agency Group, a major international booking agency with offices in London, Toronto, New York and LA. Nick was true to his word. If a promoter told him he could get BS&T at a lower price, Nick would immediately end the negotiation and give him Larry Dorr's phone number. Holding out against pressure to generate dates, he turned down dozens of offers in the next year and slowly things started turning our way. Finally the offers started to trickle in with the kind of money and the quality of venues we demanded. I had at long last turned another corner in my career: I could get the kind of bookings I wanted without having to use the BS&T name. In fact, the constant demands of their payroll meant that Larry Dorr had to take gigs that we wouldn't even consider. This had driven their price down and the quality of their venues down even further. It was hard to watch them trash this once-proud name. The name that had headlined at Lincoln Center was now playing county fairs and cruise ships. But at least I was out of it and Nick and I were ready to start taking on a few carefully selected high-profile dates.

The Canadian band travelled to Russia, where the fan loyalty from the BS&T years was still very much alive. We sold out two wonderful concerts in Moscow and Saint Petersburg. The Saint Petersburg concert was to 1,800 people in a grand old symphony hall, and in Moscow we played in a large jam-packed rock club to 1,000 screaming young people. Both concerts were outstanding, and the band received standing ovations, encores and great reviews.

There was also an unforgettable trip to Norway to play the Haugesund International Jazz Festival. Haugesund is a small fishing village on the fjords of Norway an hour's flight from Oslo. Every year the little town welcomes thousands of music lovers to its jazz festival. The streets are packed with fans from all over Europe. It's a twenty-four-hour-a-day party for one week, featuring the biggest names in jazz. Jam sessions are everywhere and go round the clock. The Canadian boys had a great time. The band was loose and happy and they played their asses off. We received the only six-star review in the twenty-year history of the festival, from the National Press of Norway.

We played only twelve concerts in 2007, but each one of them was a gem—beautiful first-class theatres and festivals. No cheesy oldies shows, no third-rate casinos. BS&T was grabbing all those dates. Better them than me. I was enjoying performing again, travelling and making music with this band of old friends, at a sensible pace. No more 3:00 a.m. wake-up calls, no gruelling bus trips and, most important, I had plenty of time to write new songs and a great group of musicians to perform them. Everything was working out even better than I had planned. I had a beautiful condo on the waterfront, Ashleigh had moved to Toronto and was enrolled in a fine college, financially I was set for life and I was happier than I'd been in years.

The High Road

I didn't get wise by bein' smart and I know
Many times I got it wrong and wishin', baby, don't make it so

But when it's time to stand up, win or lose, you take the high road every time
And when the path is dark ahead and the future's hard to see
Remember what the wise man said, the simple choice is the right one
And when your love has hurt you, chalk it up and take the high road, you'll
   be fine

And when you're countin' up the plus and minuses of life
You'll know you always took the high road
Even when you walked it alone
And when the book is written and the story has been told
You'll know you always took the high road
And the high road's gonna carry you

And when the stage is empty, what a show, you took the high road every time
And now the path is straight ahead and the future's clear to see
Remember what the wise man said
The simple choice is the right one ... for me

28

FRED'S MEMORIAL

My father died in 2007. He had suffered several major strokes and for the last few years of his life he couldn't communicate at all. I never did get to ask him the question that had plagued me all my life: "What did I do to make you hate me so much?" I wanted to scream at him, "This is not how a normal family behaves! Don't you get it?" But it was too late. He was locked somewhere inside his crippled mind and those questions would remain unanswered. Here I was a grown man and I was still asking myself what I had done to deserve those beatings, still blaming myself. I guess the answer isn't all that complicated. The truth is Fred was a bully, a controlling tyrant, just like his father before him, and nothing I could've done would have changed that.

Within a year of my mother's death in 1990, Fred had remarried. His new wife was a matronly woman named Dorothy he'd met at a cancer survivors' support group. She had recently lost her husband and I'm sure they were a great comfort to each other. Fred really fell apart after Freda's death. I realized then that my father was all bluster and bad temper, but it was my mother who was the real strength in the family. Fred was helpless without her. He was incapable of living alone after fifty-one years of marriage, and Dorothy came along just in time. My father wouldn't have lasted a year on his own. He told me at the time, "She'll never replace your mother, David, but I need someone to take care of me." Dorothy seemed perfect. She was caring and Christian, and I believed she really loved him. It couldn't have been easy caring for him in those helpless final years. Dorothy was devout, what my father used to call "a Bible thumper." He was an avowed atheist and had nothing but contempt for organized religion his entire life. He liked to say, "When you're dead you're dead … Period!" I guess that about sums up his religious philosophy. Dorothy attended church several times a week and her life revolved around her congregation, but I doubt if she ever managed to drag Fred Thomsett into a church.

Shortly after they were married I drove up from New York and visited them at my dad's house in Schomberg. Dorothy had removed every trace of Freda from the house. She had boxed up everything and asked me to take it away. That was hard for me. This had always been my mother's house, and it was difficult to see her whole life packed into boxes and removed from the home she had loved. I thought at the time that this was rather mean-spirited. After all, Freda was no threat to Dorothy—it wouldn't hurt to keep a picture of this beautiful woman who had lived in this house and shared my father's life for fifty-one years. I was surprised that Fred allowed my mother's memory to be erased so easily, but I figured they had a right to get on with their lives, and if Fred could live with this then so could I. So I loaded up the car and took everything of Freda's back to New York. Over the next few years I only visited Schomberg a few times. I lived in the States, and between my hectic tour schedule and the time I spent with Ashleigh, I got up to Canada only a couple of times a year and then it was mostly to see Bill and Doc. My relationship with

Dorothy was always polite and cordial but my visits were brief. I never did have much to talk about with my father and even less with Dorothy, and now, with my mother gone, I wasn't comfortable at the house in Schomberg.

Fred's memorial was interesting. It was at Dorothy's church and was attended by most of her congregation. I thought about not going. Ashleigh was in San Francisco at the time and I would know almost no one at the service. Besides, there was something hypocritical about this lifelong atheist being laid to rest in a church. I finally decided to attend. For my own peace of mind I had to do the right thing. This was my last chance to make peace with the father I had hated for so many years, one last chance to put those poisonous feelings behind me once and for all. Unfortunately, it didn't work out that way.

Only a handful of Fred's relatives were present. Most of the people at the service were Dorothy's friends. The first thing I noticed was a photo display depicting Fred's life. Snapshots of Fred in uniform as a young war hero, dozens of photos of Fred and Dorothy, his prized hunting dogs, even shots of their mobile home. But I couldn't find a picture of my mother anywhere. Fifty-one years of his life erased like they never happened. I finally located a small snapshot of Freda in the bottom corner of the display. It had been taken in the hospital shortly before she died. It wasn't a flattering picture. She looked terrible, in a housecoat, no makeup, her hair patchy from the chemotherapy, obviously suffering from the ravages of cancer. Of all the photographs taken of this beautiful woman during her life, why use this one? My mother would have been mortified. Freda was always meticulous about her appearance. She never went out in public without looking her best. It was vicious and petty and it hurt. Oh, but the best was yet to come.

The Anglican minister, in his white robes, announced that he would now read the eulogy but that the writer wished to remain anonymous. An anonymous eulogy? I'd never heard of such a thing. The whole point of a eulogy is to pay your respects to the departed. Why would anyone want to do that anonymously? Uh-oh, I thought, this can't be good. I began to sense a trap. The minister began reading in a sombre monotone: "Fred Thomsett wasn't famous, but God doesn't judge a man by his fame here on earth." He went on. "It's not fame that will allow a man to enter the kingdom of heaven." He looked out over the congregation and continued. "There is a special place in heaven for men like Fred. He wasn't famous, he was just a simple working man." His voice rose in pitch and picked up tempo. "Fame will not make you a good man. Fame is fleeting." He looked right at me. "God is not impressed by fame," he thundered. I jumped. Apparently God was not pleased with *me*. I could feel all eyes on my back. This was a small rural community and I was probably one of the few "famous" people who had ever visited there. But this was supposed to be Fred Thomsett's memorial. It wasn't about me. Something was very wrong here. I sat through most of the tedious eulogy. My cheeks were burning and I was furious. Finally I couldn't take it anymore. After the umpteenth reference to fame I stalked out of the funeral chapel, embarrassed and angry.

I was suspicious of the motives behind this uncalled-for attack and immediately called an estate attorney. A brief investigation and the facts were revealed. Fred wasn't a wealthy man, but he had accumulated several tracts of land, hunting camps in northern Ontario—over eight hundred acres. Then there was the house Fred had built for Freda in Schomberg. It stood on ten acres of land thirty miles from Toronto. They had bought the land cheap in the sixties when it was "country," but the city of Toronto had exploded outward and it was fairly valuable real estate by the time he died.

In his final years Fred was totally immobilized, unable to leave his chair, unable to speak. A health-care provider came by twice a week to bathe and change him. When I visited him on birthdays and holidays, Dorothy always hovered close by. I never did get to speak to him directly. Any conversation was always with Dorothy as an intermediary. His speech was incoherent and disjointed and Dorothy claimed to be the only one who could understand him. The visits were brief and uncomfortable. It was hard to see my big strapping father reduced to this mumbling, helpless shell of a man. He was totally dependent on Dorothy, and at some time in his final years he had changed his will and given her complete power of attorney. A token amount was left to Fred's side of the family but the bulk of his estate went to Dorothy, and most of it had already been disposed of. Now I understood the attack at the funeral.

The lawyers advised me to contest the will but I couldn't do it. Dragging an old lady into court over a few acres of land was something I just wasn't capable of. I had found out all I needed to know. I truly didn't give a damn about Fred's real estate, and God knows Dorothy earned it in those difficult final years. I called off the lawyers—it just wasn't worth it. In fact there was a certain poetic justice to it all. Everything the old man had scrimped and saved for his entire life was gone. It was a final slap in the face from a man who had given me nothing but the back of his hand my entire life. When I looked down into the casket that day I really wanted to feel something, but nothing happened. All feeling for him had been beaten out of me years ago. I just kept thinking, "This is what I've been so afraid of all these years?" He looked so frail and small and peaceful, maybe for the first time in his angry, tormented life. I didn't hate him anymore, but as much as I wanted to I just couldn't cry.

When I think of my father, I think of licorice allsorts. Strange that this memory has lasted down through the years, but it sums up everything I remember about the man. When I was a kid Fred kept a jar of licorice allsorts by his chair in the living room. We were absolutely forbidden to touch them. These were Fred's licorice allsorts. That made them even more enticing ... forbidden fruit. Sometimes I'd try to steal a few just to see if I could get away with it. Of course I never did. Fred always knew exactly how many candies were in that jar, and if even one was missing it would drive him crazy. Sometimes I think I took them just to piss him off. I took some of my worst beatings over Fred's precious licorice allsorts. In a strange way this has shaped my relationship with my daughter. Ashleigh has always known that what's mine is hers. My home is her home and anything in it belongs to her. She'll never be made to feel like a thief in her own home and she'll never live in terror of her father.

To this day I can't stand licorice allsorts.

The Evergreens

It took a while to get to Canada, forty years of life on the run
I must have run a million miles or more, gettin' back where I started from
And the need drivin' me was beyond my control
But every time I see the evergreens, it brings peace to my soul
Muskoka stars shine so bright, and the lake's black as coal
And every time I see the evergreens, it brings peace to my soul

It took a while to get to Canada, but this wanderin' boy has come home
Cause when the show becomes a way of life, it takes on a life of its own
And it can all burn you down, and it all takes its toll
But every time I see the evergreens, it brings peace to my soul
Muskoka stars shine so bright, and the lake's black as coal
And every time I see the evergreens, it brings peace to my soul

Lyrics by David Clayton-Thomas. Copyright © Clayton-Thomas Music Publishing Inc., 2007.

29

THE
EVERGREENS

In 2007 I spent much of the summer recording a new CD with Doc entitled *The Evergreens*. The album is drenched in Canadiana, from its songwriting to its Group of Seven artwork. The songs speak of the idealism of young love in Willowdale, the peaceful beauty of the Muskoka lakes, the donnybrooks in the bars of Yonge Street and the bohemian existence that was Yorkville. The record is a beauty. I'm very proud of this work. The music doesn't stray far from the blues. Doc insisted that we keep it simple and stick close to my roots. The album was beautifully recorded by engineering genius Ian Terry. Ian was the recording engineer on our live-in-concert album *A Musical Biography*. The superb audio quality of that recording speaks for itself. The lyrics on *The Evergreens* are honest and very personal and the musician-ship is superb. Doc is his usual amazing self and I loved making this record. In the final analysis that's all that really counts.

Over lunch one day a record-company guy was bemoaning his declining sales due to downloads and the Internet. I told him how excited I was about the new *Evergreens* album. He looked at me cynically and said, "That's all well and good, but what if it doesn't sell?" I smiled at him. "Then I'll make another one," I said. "What's your point?" That's why the record industry is in trouble. The lawyers and accountants and marketing guys who've been running the music business for decades just don't get it: it's all about the music. People will always find good music, whether it's at a record store or on their laptops. Without the music those guys are just peddling cheap little plastic discs.

The industry has gone through enormous changes. We are in the Internet age, and the old bricks-and-mortar retail record business just ain't what it used to be. There was a time when shelf space in the stores determined a record's success or failure and the record companies courted the retailers extravagantly with gifts and payoffs. That time is over. Here in Canada, Sam the Record Man, the largest record chain in the country, closed 140 retail outlets in one year. In the States the mighty Tower Records went the way of the dodo. It was the end of an era.

By 2007 my three-album commitment to Justin Time Records had been fulfilled and I decided not to re-sign with them. I produced *The Evergreens* for my own company, Antoinette Music Productions (Canada) and made a simple distribution deal with Fontana North/Universal. I'd enjoyed recording for Justin Time, they'd been good to me, but I saw the writing on the wall. I really liked Jim West and I tried to warn him. I told him, "Jim, there's a train coming down the tracks and you'd better get on board or it will run you over." But they were so entrenched in the old ways of doing business that they never saw it coming. Jadro Subic told the company that digital downloads and Internet sales were the wave of the future, but they didn't listen to her either. She resigned.

Record companies were falling like dominoes. When the retail record industry went down, it went down fast. Overnight, websites and downloads replaced the retail outlets. The big chains like Walmart and Best Buy still sold CDs, but the neighbourhood record store became a thing of the past. The laptop became the record store for the twenty-first century. The small independent record companies got hit the hardest. They were completely dependent on their retail-store network, and when that collapsed they went down with it. Shortly after I left Justin Time, their distribution company declared bankruptcy.

Justin Time continues as a label and it still has a fine catalogue, but it took a heavy blow. I was sad to see this. The industry needs independent record companies like Justin Time. They were honest and really cared about their artists, but they were caught in the retail trap too. They may have been devoted to their artists, but they never could pay them what they were worth. The profits were being chewed up by a bloated retail network and a system where the artist was the last one in line to be paid. I hope Justin Time survives. I owe them a lot. Jim West gave me the opportunity to finally break free from Blood Sweat & Tears. He gave me a chance to record with Doc and move back to Canada with a first-class record company behind me. Justin Time fostered some fine talent and always made great records, but they were slow to adapt and the business today is moving at lightspeed. I wish them well. I'll never count Jim West out. He's a good guy. He is well respected in the industry, and he's in it for the right reasons. He truly loves the music.

This is an exciting new world for recording artists. They can now play a concert and the next day watch their websites light up with Internet orders for their music. It's a far cry from the days when we had to wait years for a royalty statement from a record company that took its cut off the top before the artist ever saw a penny. Here's the reality of that game: a CD sells for around $18; about $2 goes to the artist as a royalty. But the artist will never see that two bucks. Everything from production costs to promotion is recoupable from the artist's end. The game is rigged. They make you famous and you make them rich. The more records the artist sells, the more is spent on promotion and the more he owes to the company. The musician still makes his money on the road. The record company buys him exposure, which helps him sell tickets, which in turn sells more records. The company makes millions while the artist digs himself even deeper in debt to them. A few artists may get big enough to renegotiate their contracts, but they are in the minority. Most are just hanging on from album to album and they'll never get out of the hole. Still, it's the only way young bands can get exposure. They mortgage their lives and drive in their battered vans from small towns all over the country to the big city with the dream of being signed, and they're so broke and desperate they'll sign anything.

While we were recording *The Evergreens*, a young band was recording in the next studio. They'd just been signed by a major label. Nice kids, somewhat in awe of the heavyweight musicians recording next door—Doc Riley, Bernie LaBarge, Paul DeLong, heroes to these young musicians. Their studio was always full of people, a constant flow of managers and publicists, groupies and girlfriends, record-company types. By contrast, our sessions were lean and economical. We were old pros, and we weren't there to party while the clock was ticking at $500 an hour. We were there to take care of business.

One day we arrived at the studio and there must have been twenty people hanging out in the lounge. They had just ordered lunch and everyone was enjoying a feast of catered Mexican food. "Must be nice," I joked. "We're running on coffee and doughnuts next door." "Hey, help yourself," their young guitar player said.

"The record company's paying for it." My team of grizzled veterans looked at each other and smiled. We'd all been around the block and we knew the reality of that situation. The record company's paying for it, huh? No they're not, kid ... You are. My guys took their cups of funky recording-studio coffee and went back to work. We didn't have the heart to tell them. They were on top of the world, and no one wanted to bust their bubble.

Their record was released a few months later along with the obligatory video and it went nowhere. Who knows why? Internal politics, Neilsen numbers or maybe the company just needed a tax writeoff. It doesn't matter. They were expendable. The band went back to their dreams and their day gigs, and the record company signed some other starry-eyed young band. For every superstar who owes his success to a record company, there is a trail of broken artists who made the mistake of believing the bullshit and were just too fragile to deal with it. In defence of the record companies, for every artist that makes money for them, there are a dozen who don't, and the successful ones have to carry the load for the failures. Who wins in this record-company lottery is too often determined by politics and payoffs. There are many who believe that the Internet-driven demise of the corrupt old record industry was long overdue and richly deserved.

Let's face it: the record companies have been screwing artists for decades. Rock musicians in the fifties signed lifetime contracts for a new Cadillac. In the sixties they gave up their publishing rights and songwriter royalties in exchange for a recording contract. Into the seventies and eighties, record-company presidents still shamelessly listed themselves as co-writers on songs. Hell, they were lawyers and accountants, not songwriters, but this was the price the writer paid for being signed, and you didn't exist in this business without a recording contract. We all knew we were being screwed, but we needed the promotion and distribution that only a record company could provide. They could take you out of that funky bar and make you a star—just don't expect to see royalties. The companies that were so uncreative in the making of the music were remarkably creative in their accounting.

It's been said that the music business is in trouble. Wrong! The *record* business is in trouble. The music business is doing just fine. In the late nineties the explosion of the Internet and new digital recording technology broke the stranglehold the record industry held on the music business. Six-figure budgets were no longer necessary to make a record. Musicians didn't need a million-dollar studio anymore. State-of-the-art recordings could be made in your basement. The Internet allowed artists to reach fans around the world without signing their lives away to a multi-national corporation, and they began to take charge of their own careers. They can sell their CDs at concerts and on their websites and keep 90 per cent of the profits. Many artists today are turning down record deals. They can do the math. They've figured out that 90 per cent of a few thousand records nets them more than 0 per cent of a million.

The marketing power of a major record company is still essential to the young unknown artist who needs the exposure, but established artists have other options today. They are forming their own record companies and making their own distribution deals with the majors. Digital downloads and Internet fulfillment are an important part of these deals. A large percentage of artists' sales are from their own websites—that puts a powerful marketing tool in the hands of the guy making the music. Musicians today are smarter and better educated in the intricacies of the business. We have learned from those who went before. The days when songwriters like Robert Johnson and Woody Guthrie sold their songs for a bottle of whisky are long gone. Artists own their own music today, and this is fine with me.

A Blues for Doc

There was music in his hands
But his hands were just a window to his soul
And he never lost the wonder of a child
And he never lost his love for rock & roll

Oh, there's a big hole in my life
I feel the loss of something fine
How can I solve the problems of this world
Without the Doctor and a midnight glass of wine

If I could be with him again
To wonder at the wisdom in those hands
He'd say playin' music is a gift from God
And complete devotion's all that it demands

I'm so glad at least I knew
A man this special for a while
He had more than most to overcome
But he found his heaven on the gentle isle

30
A BLUES FOR DOC

Two thousand seven was a tumultuous year. It was the best of times and the worst. The year began on a high note. In January my song "Spinning Wheel" was inducted into the Canadian Songwriters Hall of Fame along with several songs by Joni Mitchell. The event was broadcast nationally by CBC TV. It was a great evening, attended by the who's who of the Canadian music industry. I opened the show with my Toronto big band playing "Spinning Wheel." Then there were memorable performances by James Taylor and Chaka Khan singing the songs of Joni Mitchell. It was an honour to be inducted alongside Joni. She is as beautiful as ever and one of the most gifted songwriters I have ever known. I guess I still have a bit of a crush on her.

A few months later I was asked to co-host the National Jazz Awards in Toronto with my friend Dione Taylor—another warm and wonderful evening, filled with old friends and the finest jazz musicians in the country. Doug Riley was the musical director for the event, and two of the guys in my band, George Koller and Russ Little, received their own National Jazz Awards. It was a great way to come back home.

In July of that year I played the Charlottetown Jazz Festival with Doc and stayed at his lovely oceanside home on Prince Edward Island for two days following the concert. It was like old times. We walked along the waterfront early in the morning and bought lobster fresh off the boats. We shopped the local farmers' market for sweet corn and he gave me a guided tour of his beloved "Gentle Island." After a wonderful dinner filled with laughter and memories of the good times we had shared, his wife, Jan, went up to bed and Doc and I sat in front of the fireplace until after midnight, sipping wine and talking about life, music, our kids and the Leafs, as we had done so many times before.

Two weeks later I drove my brand-new Audi A8 down to New York for dinner with some of my old neighbours in Rockland County, then continued on up to Boston, where I met with the band for a Saturday-night concert in Lowell, Massachusetts. Deering Howe and his wife, Barbara, joined me for the show. It was a lovely concert outdoors in the park on a warm summer evening with an enthusiastic crowd of around 3,000 people. The Canadian boys had a great time and right after the show they piled onto the tour bus and headed back to Toronto. We stayed overnight in Lowell, and the next day Deering, Barbara and I drove up to their remote mountaintop cabin in Maine to hang out and relax. Their log-and-stone cabin looks out over fifty miles of rolling mountains. They have their own fully stocked private lake for fishing and ATVs to get around the heavily wooded property. There are no utilities, no phones. The whole place is powered by solar panels and a 10K generator. The closest town is maybe ten miles away, and it's basically a service station and a general store. We spent the evening by a crackling fire, listening to Deering's extensive record collection and reminiscing about old friends and good times.

I left the Howes' place right after breakfast on Monday morning and headed for Montreal. I planned to have dinner with Jadro Subic and then return to Toronto the next day to meet Doc and the boys for the final recording sessions of the *Evergreens* project. The rolling mountains of northern Maine were shrouded in mist and I had the road all to myself, cruising along the winding two-lane highway in the high-tech Audi. It was unbelievably beautiful and peaceful. I had the *Evergreens* tracks on the stereo and I was smiling to myself at just how good Doc Riley was. He played on every tune and wrote all the horn charts.

Then my car phone rang. It was bad news … as bad as it gets. Two weeks after Charlottetown, flying home from a concert in Calgary, Doug Riley had suffered a massive heart attack on the plane and died. It was an enormous blow. I pulled the Audi over to the side of the road and I cried, alone in my car in the beautiful misty mountains of upstate Maine. I pounded my fist on the steering wheel and I cried. I cried all the way to Montreal. Several times I had to pull over and get myself together before continuing. I checked in to my hotel and there were calls from journalists all over Canada who wanted to talk to me about Doc. He was a national treasure, and word of his passing had already reached clear across the country. I choked up on the phone and couldn't really say much. There were no words to describe the loss I felt. It was like someone had just blown the centre out of my life. I had dinner with Jadro that evening, and I'm glad she was there. I really needed to be with someone who understood how much Doc meant to me. The next day I drove back to Toronto. My first impulse was to cancel the recording sessions. How could I possibly do it without Doc? But by the time I reached Toronto I knew what I had to do. I did what he would have wanted me to do. I wrote a song for him, called the musicians and we finished the *Evergreens* album. We all felt his presence in the studio during those final sessions. Nobody spoke about it but we all knew … Doc was watching over us.

A memorial concert for Doug Riley was held in October 2007 at the University of Toronto. I sang the song I had written for him, called "A Blues for Doc." It was probably the easiest song I have ever written. The lyrics were written in one pass and I never changed a word. My love for the man just poured onto the page. But it was the most difficult song I have ever had to perform. With Doc's wife, Jan, and his two sons, Ben and Jesse, seated in the front row, I sang my tribute to him with a huge lump in my throat. It was all I could do to hold it together and finish the song. Sixteen hundred people packed Convocation Hall that night, and we all cried together for the loss we felt. Musicians Doc had influenced and people he had touched came from all over Canada, the US and Europe to pay tribute to this enormously gifted and humble man. The world of music has lost a giant, and I miss him terribly. He was my confidant, my brother and my best friend. He left a vast body of work—jazz compositions, symphonies, ballets, film scores and recordings with everyone from Bob Seger and Plácido Domingo to Anne Murray and Ray Charles. He played on every solo album I've ever recorded, but he left me with more than his music. His integrity was absolute and his advice was always sound. There's a big hole in my life, but I'm a better person for having known Doc.

The Evergreens is a lasting tribute to the genius of Doug Riley. The songs are real and honest and Doc's influence is all over the record. He had a unique feel for my songwriting style. His R&B-influenced arrangements and his soulful keyboard work created a perfect setting for my down-home lyrics and bluesy melodies. I'll never replace the musical rapport that I shared with Doc, and I won't even try. That understanding was built on forty years of friendship and happens once in a lifetime. I'm just lucky to have had him in my life for as long as I did.

Doug Riley was a very patriotic Canadian. When he was awarded the Order of Canada, he was so proud I thought he would burst. When I lived in New York I would occasionally become frustrated that people south of the border weren't aware of this musical giant. I'd urge him to travel more and share his talent with the world, but Doc would just smile and tell me that he didn't need to be known in the States, he was completely happy with his life in Canada. It took many years for me to understand Doc's point of view. I had something to prove, he didn't. Now that I'm back in Canada, I understand why he didn't want to travel. This is a wonderful place to live, and at this point in my life I don't have anything left to prove either. Doc and I always shared a love for this country. Even after thirty-five years in the States I still kept my Canadian passport. I always knew that someday I'd come home, and now that I'm here I'll never leave again. I love the ruggedly beautiful lake country, the booming multicultural cities, the absurdly polite and fiercely nationalistic people. I love their support for the arts and education, the laid-back lifestyle and the peaceful world view of the Canadian. Canada is where I belong.

Spinning Wheel

What goes up, must come down
Spinnin' wheel, got to go round
Talkin' 'bout your troubles, it's a cryin' sin
Ride a painted pony, let the spinnin' wheel spin

Got no money and ya got no home
Spinnin' wheel, all alone
Talkin' 'bout your troubles and you never learn
Ride a painted pony, let the spinnin' wheel turn

Did you find a directing sign on the straight and narrow highway
Would you mind a reflecting sign, just let it shine within your mind
And show you the colors that are real

Someone's waitin' just for you
Spinnin' wheel, spinnin' true
Drop all your troubles by the riverside
Catch a painted pony on the spinnin' wheel ride

Words and music by David Clayton-Thomas. © 1968 (renewed 1996) EMI Blackwood Music Inc. and Bay Music Ltd.

31

SPINNING WHEEL

I feel good about life today, and I'm optimistic about the future. I'm taking on only top-quality concerts and we're still being very selective about the venues. In 2008 we headlined the Grandstand Show at the Canadian National Exhibition in Toronto. "The Ex" is one of the largest and longest-running annual exhibitions in the world, a Toronto tradition since 1879. The biggest names in show business have graced the CNE stage over the years. I first saw Ray Charles at the Ex. For a local boy, playing the Grandstand Show was a childhood dream come true.

In February 2010 we played two nights at Toronto's venerable old concert theatre Massey Hall with the Toronto Symphony Orchestra—another dream come true. When I was a young musician playing five shows a night in the bars and strip joints on Yonge Street, I would walk by Massey Hall and dare to dream that someday I'd grace that stage. It was the holy cathedral of music, the place where Ella and Oscar played. It was the concert theatre where in 1953 Bird and Diz, along with Max Roach, Bud Powell and Charlie Mingus, gave what is considered to be the greatest jazz concert of all time. The acoustics of the hall are phenomenal and the place is drenched in history and tradition. The 2,300-seat venue was completely sold out, the band was on fire and the orchestra was magnificent. People came from as far away as Montreal and New York for the Massey Hall concerts, two memorable shows with my ten-piece band and the sixty-piece TSO. Who would ever have believed that a reformatory graduate would someday take the stage at Massey Hall with the TSO!

Ashleigh has completed postgrad studies in writing for film and television at Humber College and is currently working on projects in Toronto and San Francisco. She has dual citizenship and can travel freely between the US and Canada, a huge advantage for someone in her field. She'll never have to battle the immigration issues that plagued me. Ash convinced me that I should write this book. With her background in creative writing, her input was invaluable, but her guidance went far beyond that. Sometimes she had to get in my face, pushing me to open up and let my feelings show—"There's been more to your life than just names, dates and places, Dad." Opening up isn't easy for a guy with my defence mechanisms, but Ashleigh's not impressed by my tough-guy reputation. She was relentless. She has no problem speaking her mind to her dad. I like that.

It's a daunting experience to write your life story and subject it to your daughter's scrutiny. You want to be perfect in your child's eyes, but Ashleigh would hear everything—the good, the bad and the ugly. She's idealistic and opinionated, and she made sure I kept it real. After all, she was there for much of it, and she wouldn't stand for any self-serving bullshit. It speaks volumes about my trust in her judgment and intelligence. She's at an age now where she's not only my daughter, she's my friend. Ashleigh inherited her mother's looks and her father's drive to succeed. She's a lovely independent young lady, and I'm so proud of her.

Now that I'm living in Canada again, I've rekindled my relationship with my eldest daughter, Christine. She lives in a small town a hundred miles north of Toronto and has children and grandchildren of her own. My God, that makes me a great-grandfather! She was raised in a family I've never met and doesn't carry my name, but now that we're both grown up and I'm not on the road year-round anymore, there's finally been time to get to know her. I haven't been a part of her life for so long that it's hard to just show up at this late date and expect to be a normal family, but we get together from time to time and I know she's happy to be at last acknowledged by a father who's just been a voice on the radio for most of her life. Christine has paid a heavy price for being fathered by a man who left her when she was just a baby, and I carry an enormous burden of guilt for having abandoned her. I tell myself that she was probably better off being raised in a stable family environment rather than being dragged through the craziness that has been my life. Maybe the guilt I carry about not being there for Christine has contributed to my dedication to Ashleigh. The fact that I was never there for Chris has made me even more determined to be there for Ash. In any event, I've been a good father to Ashleigh and no father at all to Christine. Christine has been amazingly forgiving and loving, considering my shortcomings. There are no do-overs in this life, and I can't undo the damage I've inflicted on her, but I'm trying to make up for lost time.

I love dropping in to little clubs to catch the up-and-coming musicians on the Toronto scene. I'm knocked out by the talent of some of the young artists around town. I always give them my number and tell them to call me if they want to talk. My fifty-plus years in the music industry have given me some insights that may help them negotiate their way through the rocks and shoals of this crazy business. I tell them that it's a wonderful way of life, but I also warn them about some of the pitfalls they will be facing. I believe that artists are special people blessed with a unique ability to make a difference in this world. But they are dreamers and all too willing to believe the best of people. The vulnerability that makes them great artists can make them targets for exploitation. It can be a tremendously rewarding business, but it's also a highly delusional one, and it takes a strong spirit to survive.

It's a confusing new world the young artist is facing today. The music business has moved to Hollywood and there's no putting that genie back in the bottle. Personally, I liked the music a lot more when it lived in New York. It was gritty and real and it had its own identity. Hollywood turned popular music into a soundtrack for dance videos. It's a repetitious parade of menacing gangbangers posing with their Lamborghinis. It's drum machines and processed vocals and sequenced music tracks. It's video directors creating fake energy with jittery fast-cut editing. It's scantily clad divas bumping and grinding their way through overproduced songs with the bored sexuality of a nightclub stripper. Even the down-home folks of Nashville have gone Hollywood, turning country music into a glitzy spectacle of red-carpet awards shows and impossibly beautiful people. The music video, which originally was intended to be a promotional tool for the music, became an art form in itself and the music became incidental. The old record business is dying and the new systems for delivering music are still a chaotic and unregulated free-for-all. It's a bewildering, constantly shifting scenario, and the guys in the boardrooms of Hollywood just can't keep up. They're too busy trying to catch a ride on the latest trend, clinging to formulas and narrowly defined formats. Most of all they're concerned with keeping their jobs in the rapidly changing business of music. The record executives are scared and they're playing it safe. They don't have a clue where the music is headed, but it's safe to say the new direction won't come from Hollywood. The music industry today is soft and conservative and it's ripe for something outrageous. It's primed for the next Elvis. It's ready for another Beatles, another Dylan. Someone will come out of nowhere and blow the lid off this business. Personally, I can't wait to see it.

I think the most satisfying part of my life today is that Blood Sweat & Tears is finally over for me. Never was a rock band so aptly named. The organization I joined in 1968 was already racked by political infighting. It was a twisted mess of massive egos that somehow managed to turn out some really memorable music but took a toll on everyone who became involved with it.

The music of BS&T is timeless. The songs and performances stand up today. Those hits from 1969 are still being played all around the world, but only a few of the early members ever made any significant money. Bobby Colomby did well for himself in the corporate world of Hollywood. It's a perfect place for someone with his charm and political talents. Lew Soloff remains one of the world's great jazz trumpeters, performing with everybody from Barbra Streisand to Tony Bennett. Jim Fielder played bass for thirty years with Neil Sedaka. Most of the other guys returned to lives as working musicians or simply disappeared into obscurity after their tenure with the band. Some were never meant to be rock stars; they were embarrassed by the hype. Musical geniuses like Dick Halligan and Fred Lipsius never again sought the limelight. Dick went on to become a serious composer of film scores, and Freddie retreated into the academic world, becoming a professor of music at Berklee.

Steve Katz has rejoined Blood Sweat & Tears. Now he's the key to the use of the name, so he's Larry Dorr's best friend. It's all come full circle. All it needs is Al Kooper to make the circle complete, and if there's any money in it, that might well happen too. Nothing surprises me anymore. It's sad to see these people still vying for control of a name after all these years. That's how it all began, and that's how it's ending. I tried to advise Larry Dorr to walk away from it while he still could. It might have been tough for a while, but in the long run he'd be better off and today he'd be his own man. Now it's too late. He traded our friendship for a name, and that name owns him.

As for me, now that I'm no longer financially dependent on the music business I have the luxury of taking on projects for the pure joy of it. I'm currently working on an album called *Soul Ballads*, to be released at the same time as this book. As the title suggests, it's a collection of soul ballads by Ray Charles, Otis Redding, Sam Cooke—songs that I sang on Yonge Street forty years ago, the great soul tunes that shaped my life and I'm finally able to record. The album is being produced by my old friend Lou Pomanti, from the *Nuclear Blues* days. We didn't go looking for obscure tunes that no one has previously recorded; rather, we selected those great iconic soul ballads that everyone knows and loves. This is an album I have long wanted to make—a collection of the songs that inspired me to be a singer, songs that hit me in the heart when I was a struggling young artist and inspired me to keep on trying. Meanwhile, I'm still writing new songs, and an album of original material is in the works for 2011.

I've spent the last two years putting my life story down on paper and I've found it to be incredibly rewarding. I've always loved writing. Even as a songwriter the lyrics were my favourite part of the process. Maybe some youngster will read this book and benefit from my half-century in the music business. The joy of my life today is mentoring young artists. Perhaps one of these kids I'm advising will be the one to turn the music business upside down.

In these uncertain times the struggling young artist is willing to sign anything to get exposure. I tell them to forget about exposure and concentrate on performance. The only thing that matters is the music. Make it honest and completely your own and the world will come to you. Fame is overrated. It's just a puff of smoke, gone in an instant. It's your music that will change the world and make geniuses out of record-company presidents. Fame won't purge your inner demons, it won't solve your problems, and never forget, my young friends, being famous won't make you a better person, no matter how many times you reinvent yourself.

Like every other hungry young artist, I allowed myself to get sucked into the hype-driven world of rock & roll, where your worth is measured by your chart position. It was a great ride. I loved every minute of it and got out before it killed me. Some people think that rock stars who die young are the lucky ones. We'll always remember them as they were. There's nothing sadder than an aging rocker trying to recapture his past glories. I'd like to go out with some measure of dignity. I know I'll never again reach the heights I hit in the sixties, and I'm not sure I want to. A young record executive, after hearing *The Evergreens*, said to me, "This stuff is really good, David. I see a whole new career for you." I'd heard that line before. I laughed and replied, "Oh no … You mean I have to do it all again?"

Acknowledgments

To the people who made this story possible …

Freda May Thomsett

Fredrick Sydney Thomsett

Ashleigh Clayton-Thomas

Jennifer Clayton-Thomas

Christine Graham

Nancy Hewitt

Bill Pugliese and the entire
Pugliese family

Deering and Barbara Howe

Ronnie Hawkins

Duff Roman

Sylvia Tyson

Scott Richards

Tony Collacott

Bobby Colomby

Larry Goldblatt

Fred Heller

Bobby Economou

Larry Willis

Mike Stern

Terry Nusyna

Lew Soloff

Fred Lipsius

Jim Fielder

Larry Dorr

B. Harold Smick III

Frank DeGennaro

Steve Guttman

Bruce Cassidy

William "Smitty" Smith

Ken Marco

Jadro Subic

Index

Riverboat, 51, 64, 67
Robertson, Robbie, 38, 39, 251
Rolling Stone magazine, 119, 142–43
Rolling Stones, 49, 76, 141
Roman, Duff, 47, 49, 56, 66
Roman Records, 56, 66
Romania, Ceauşescu's, 126–30
Royal Canadian Signal corps, 2
Royal Conservatory, 46

Sadiola, Mali, 261
"St. James Infirmary Blues," 29
Sam the Record Man, 292
San Antonio Symphony, 222
Sanborn, Dave, 184
Sault Ste Marie brawl, 58–60
Savuka, 203
Scribner, Ron, 57, 61
Sedaka, Neil, 309
Seger, Bob, 302
Seymour, Earl, 199
Shakespeare, William, 53
Shays, 43, 45, 47–48, 49, 52
Silhouettes, 45
Sill, Joel, 169
Simon, Paul, 141
Simone, Nina, 108–10
Sinatra, Frank, 145, 147, 149, 150
Smick, B. Harold, III, 225
"Smiling Phases," 94, 126
Smith, Jimmy, 46
Smith, William "Smitty," 170, 177
Solitary confinement, 25–26, 28–29
Soloff, Lew, 83–84, 96–97, 98, 128, 129, 169, 245, 309
Solomon, Howie, 68
South African tour, 201–3
Spann, Otis, 37
Spyro Gyra, 244
Steinbeck, John, 53
Stern, Mike, 142, 181, 184, 245

Steve Paul's Scene, 75–79
Stills, Stephen, 63, 105
Stony Plain Records, 244
Streisand, Barbra, 309
Strip, the. *See* Yonge Street Strip
Subic, Jadro, 272, 276, 292, 300, 301
Super Session album, 69
Supremes, 266
Suzanne (DCT's fourth wife), 235–36
"Symphony for the Devil," 94

Taylor, Dione, 299
Taylor, Elizabeth, 147
Taylor, James, 94, 299
Temptations, 37
Terry, Ian, 276, 291
Terry, Sonny, 51
Thomsett, David Henry. *See* Clayton-Thomas, David (DCT)
Thomsett, Fred (DCT's father), 1–10, 19, 22–23, 48–49, 112, 113, 210–11, 232, 283–88
Thomsett, Freda (née Smith) (DCT's mother), 1–2, 3, 4, 49, 112, 113, 210–11, 231–32, 284, 285
Thomsett, John (DCT's brother), 4–5
Tillman, Bill, 178, 179, 180
Tin Angel café, 82
Tormé, Mel, 149
"Toronto sound," 52
Toronto Symphony Orchestra (TSO), 305–6
Tower Records, 292
Trudeau, Margaret, 183
Trudeau, Pierre, 183
Tutt, Ronnie, 158–59